Fundamentals of Technology

FIRST EDITION

By Chenxu Yu and Thomas Brumm

cognella® | ACADEMIC PUBLISHING

Bassim Hamadeh, CEO and Publisher
Michael Simpson, Vice President of Acquisitions
Jamie Giganti, Senior Managing Editor
Miguel Macias, Senior Graphic Designer
Sean Adams, Project Editor
Luiz Ferreira, Licensing Specialist

Cover image copyright © 2012 by Depositphotos/casaalmare; © 2017 iStockphoto LP/Bernie_
photo.

Printed in the United States of America

ISBN: 978-1-5165-2216-3 (pbk) / 978-1-5165-2217-0 (br) / 978-1-5165-4709-8 (al)

CONTENTS

CHAPTER 4: FUNDAMENTALS OF ELECTRICAL SYSTEMS

CHAPTER 5: FUNDAMENTALS OF THERMAL SYSTEMS

CHAPTER 6: DATA ANALYSIS

CHAPTER 7: FUNDAMENTALS OF ECONOMIC DECISION MAKING

FOREWORD

Generally, professors don't sit around thinking about the books they can write—textbook writing is not very lucrative. Often, there are adequate textbooks available for the classes they teach. Certainly that is the case for many subjects in engineering and technology. Yet for a fundamentals class in general technology, there was no appropriate textbook to be found. Clearly there was a need for us to create something—for teachers, as a repository of our teaching material, and for students, as reference material for the topics covered in such a class. Left with no other option, this textbook is the result of our desire to have education materials that are a bit more lasting and formal than a bunch of pdf files of our class notes from the 10+ years we have been teaching this course.

Originally intended to be comprehensive and complete, we realize that this first edition is just a start and expect revisions and improvements in later editions, especially with feedback from students. No first effort is perfect. Every effort, however, creates something that didn't previously exist, such as this textbook for teaching the fundamentals of technology. Similarly, we hope you find such satisfaction in your careers – creating something of value that didn't previously exist.

Chenxu Yu
Tom Brumm
June, 2015

SCIENTIFIC MEASUREMENTS AND SIGNIFICANT FIGURES

OBJECTIVES

When you complete your study of this chapter, you will be able to:

1. Define the nature of two types of numbers, and determine the number of significant figures in a scientific measurement
2. Define accuracy, precision and uncertainty in measurements
3. Define systematic and random errors, and explain how they occur in measurements
4. Perform proper rounding technique, and use scientific notation to represent numerical values
5. Perform numerical calculation with measured quantities, and express the results with the appropriate number of significant figures

1.1 Introduction

No knowledge or understanding of a given technological problem will be of much value unless it can be expressed in a quantitative manner. Quantitative description of anything requires the use of numbers. In this chapter, we will discuss several features of numbers, and computational techniques to use with numbers. We will also discuss how to properly express numerical information obtained through measurements.

1.2 Numbers and Significant Figures

Jobs in technology use two types of numbers: exact and approximate. There are only two ways to obtain an exact number, either by counting or by definition. The first is easy to understand, as counting will yield an integer, which tells the counter the exact numerical value of a quantity. For example, if a worker counted 102 parts that were manufactured in a workshop in one day, he would have exactly 102 parts. An extension to counting is ratio. Ratios are exact numbers because 2/5 of a circle is exactly 2/5 of a circle. However, ratios expressed as a decimal, say, 2/3 = 0.6666667, are approximate numbers because some ratios expressed as a decimal contain repeating digits, and rounding was used to cut off the digits at a certain point. The second way to yield an exact number, by definition, needs some explanation. Here it usually refers to unit conversion factors, or some physical and mathematical constants. For example, in converting inches to centimeters, we use a unit conversion factor of 1 in = 2.54 cm, or 2.54 cm/in. Here the number 2.54 is not an integer, but it can be considered as an exact number because it arises from the definition of a unit conversion. Another example is gravitational acceleration, g. A typical standard value for g is 9.80665 m/s². Although this value is obtained through scientific measurement, in most practical applications it could be treated as a physical constant, hence as an exact number. Another example is π, which is an infinite irrational number, 3.14159265... In all practical purposes, we usually use 3.14 for the value of π. Although this is an approximate value, we may treat it as an exact number since it comes from a mathematical constant.

Any number obtained by a measurement is an approximate number. The actual value of an approximate number is uncertain, because all measuring devices have a limit to their precision, and errors of measurement are likely to be present regardless of the precautions used when making the measurement. The approximate nature of a measurement is well represented in Figure 1.1, showing a measurement being conducted to determine the length of a metal bar, with a scale graduated in 1/8 of an inch, or 0.125 inch. The scale hence is only accurate to the nearest 1/8 inch. At the first glance it is obvious that the bar is over 2 inches in length. With a closer look, it is revealed that the length of the bar is not aligned with any of the marks on the scale. It is between 2 1/4 inches and 2 3/8 inches in length. You may record the length of the bar as a value between 2¼ and 2 and 3/8 inches. Here

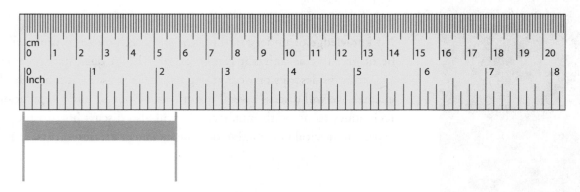

Figure 1.1: Example of an Approximate Measurement Yielding an Approximate Number

you need to use your best judgment to come up with the best estimation. Hence, our measurement must be considered approximate, and the result is an approximate number, for example, 2.32 inches.

For approximate numbers, we need a method to convey how "good" these numbers are in terms of determining how "good" the measurements are. The use of significant figures hence is introduced into science and technology to give us this capability. The significant figures are the digits in an approximate number that accurately reflect the result of a measurement. As a rule of thumb, for any measured number, as illustrated in the above example, the last digit of it is NOT accurate, as it is produced through an estimation. The number reported above, 2.32 inches, is accurate at the first digit after the decimal (i.e., 3), and the last digit, 2, is an estimation only. In an approximate number, the last significant digit is always an estimation. In the above example, the number 2.32 inches has three significant figures, or digits, and the last one of them, 2, is an estimation.

Digits can be introduced into a calculation that is not accurate (i.e., significant), and negatively impact the accuracy of the answer. This is particularly problematic when a calculator is used. Most calculators show eight or nine digits automatically, regardless of their significance. It is up to the calculator operator to determine how many digits are significant and to round accordingly.

The principle of significant figures is used to determine the number of digits that should be kept in a number after mathematical calculation. The rules for determining significant figures are different for exact numbers and for approximate numbers.

Because there is no uncertainty with exact numbers, all digits in an exact number are accurate. Besides, they do not convey or transmit any error. Hence, practically we can treat all exact numbers as having infinite significant figures. In other words, when determining significant figures for a calculation involving both exact numbers and approximate numbers, exact numbers need not be considered, because they will always have the most significant figures, and hence are not the limiting factor.

For approximate numbers, a significant figure, or significant digit, is defined as any digit used in writing a number, except those zeros that are used only for indicating location of the decimal point, or those zeros that do not have any nonzero digit on their left. For example, the number 0.0024 has only two significant figures, 2 and 4, because the three zeros do not have any nonzeros to the left, and they are location holders for the decimal point. If the number is written as 0.002400 instead, the number of significant figures will jump to 4, because now the two zeros to the right of 4 are also significant. Similarly, if the number is 1.0024, there are now five significant figures, the two zeros have a nonzero to their left, and they are significant.

Scientific notation, also called standard form, is used to express large or small numbers in a more convenient form. Scientific notation uses powers of ten to replace the nonsignificant digits of a large or small number. Scientific notation uses a whole digit, then a decimal point, and then the rest of the significant figures. For example, if the number 1,000,000 has one significant figure, it is expressed as $1. \times 10^6$; if it has two significant figures, it is expressed as 1.0×10^6. To use the scientific notation effectively, you must understand the powers of numbers, and how they can be manipulated during mathematical computations.

Table 1.1 shows the power of tens, for both positive and negative powers.

Another convenient way of representing powers of tens is with prefix names. Table 1.2 illustrates powers of tens (as multipliers) and their corresponding prefixes and symbols. The use of prefixes

Table 1.1: A Review of the Powers of Tens

$10^0 = 1$	
$10^1 = 10$	$10^{-1} = 0.1 = 1/10$
$10^2 = 100$	$10^{-2} = 0.01 = 1/100$
$10^3 = 1000$	$10^{-3} = 0.001 = 1/1000$
$10^4 = 10000$	$10^{-4} = 0.0001 = 1/10000$
$10^5 = 100000$	$10^{-5} = 0.00001 = 1/100000$

Table 1.2: Decimal Multipliers and Prefixes

MULTIPLIERS	PREFIX NAME	SYMBOL
10^{18}	Exa	E
10^{15}	Peta	P
10^{12}	Tera	T
10^9	Giga	G
10^6	Mega	M
10^3	Kilo	k
10^2	Hecto	h
10^1	Deka	da
10^{-1}	Deci	d
10^{-2}	Centi	c
10^{-3}	Milli	m
10^{-6}	Micro	μ
10^{-9}	Nano	n
10^{-12}	Pico	p
10^{-15}	Femto	f
10^{-18}	Atto	a

Source: Engineering Fundamentals and Problem Solving, 5th edition, McGraw Hill, New York, 2006

enables us to express any measurement as a number between 0.1 and 1000, with a corresponding prefix applied to the unit. For example, it is clearer for a reader if the distance to the next exit on a highway is expressed as 12 kilometers (12 km), rather than 12,000 meters (12,000 m).

When an instrument such as a scale, an analog thermometer, or a fuel gauge is read, the last digit will normally be an estimate, because the instrument is usually read by estimating between the smallest graduations on the scale to get the final digit. It is standard practice to count the one doubtful digit as significant. Hence, it should be remembered that the last digit in an approximate number obtained by measurement is always an educated guess; it is not accurate, even if it is zero, because zero here means that your best estimate is that the reading matches with a marked graduation perfectly. Of course, there is still room for some small deviation, and that makes the zero an estimate, not an accurate measurement.

Example 1.1: How to determine the number of significant figures

3.10: 3 significant figures, the 0 is the last one

0.001010: 4 significant figures, first three 0s are not significant, they are location holders only

320: 2 significant figures, the 0 here is a location holder to tell us where the decimal point is

320.: 3 significant figures, since the decimal point is shown, the "0" becomes significant

320 tickets: the unit (i.e., ticket) implies that the number 320 is obtained through counting, hence it is an exact number, and has an infinite number of significant figures!

2.54 cm/in: a unit conversion factor is considered as an exact number, hence it has infinite number of significant figures.

Calculators and computers maintain countable numbers (integers) in exact form up to the capacity of the machine. Real numbers are kept at the precision level of the particular device, regardless of how many significant figures an input value or calculated value should have. Therefore, it is the operator's duty to exercise care when reporting values from a calculator display, or from a computer output.

As you perform arithmetical operations, it is important that you do not lose the significance of your measurements, or, conversely, imply precision that does not exists by artificially increasing the number of significant figures in your final results beyond the justifiable limit. The following rules usually apply when determining the proper number of significant figures.

1. **Rounding**: Rounding is used to eliminate figures that are not significant. If the digits to be rounded are to the left of the decimal point, the digits are replaced by zeros. If the digits are to the right of the decimal point, just drop them. For example, if you need to round 41,580 ft^2 to two significant figures, the answer is 42,000 ft^2. If the digit being dropped is greater than 5, add one to the next digit remaining, as we did in our example. If the digit being dropped is less than 5, the first remaining digit is unchanged. If the digit being dropped is exactly 5, leave the remaining digit even. If the remaining digit is odd, add one; if it is even, leave it as is. For example, the number 41,580 ft^2, if rounded to one significant figure, the answer is 40,000 ft^2; rounded to two it is 42,000 ft^2; and rounded to three, it is 41,600 ft^2.

2. **Multiplication and Division**: The product or quotient should contain the same number of significant figures as are contained in the number with the fewest significant figures.

Example 1.2

a. $2.23 \times 14.324 = 31.94252$

If each number in the product is exact, the answer should be reported as 31.94252. If the numbers are not exact, as is normally the case, 2.23 has three significant figures, and it is less than 14.324 (which has five). Hence, the product cannot have more than three significant figures, and it can be reported as 32.0, or using scientific notation, as 3.2×10^1.

b. $1.279 \text{ in} \times 2.54 \text{ cm/in} = 3.24866 \text{ cm}$

In this case, the conversion factor is an exact number (a definition), and has infinite significant figures. Hence, the number 1.279 in has fewer significant figures (four), and the answer should be reported as 3.249 cm.

c. $786.23/52.1 = 15.0907869$

The answer, with three significant figures, is 15.1.

3. **Addition and Subtraction**: The answer should show significant figures only, as far to the right as in the least precise number in the calculation. This is because the last digit recorded is doubtful.

Example 1.3

a. 12.6543
  3.12
+ 100.1001
  115.8743

The least precise number in this group is 3.12, because the 2 is an estimate. According to our rule, the answer should be reported as 115.87.

b. 87.0
 −1.654
  85.346

Using our rule, the answer should be reported as 85.3.

As we look at these answers, suppose the numbers are all obtained by measurements. Therefore, the last digit in each number is doubtful. The addition or subtraction involving a doubtful digit will only yield a doubtful digit as a result. Therefore, in the first example, after adding the three numbers, since the second digit after the decimal point in 3.12 is doubtful, all digits in the final answer, 115.8743, beyond 7, are all doubtful. We can only keep one doubtful digit in an approximate number. Hence, the answer should be just 115.87. The same argument can be made for the second example, too.

4. **Combined Operations**: In combined operations, when conducted manually, rounding following proper rules should usually be conducted in the intermediate steps. However, when a calculator or computer is used, usually it is not practical to perform intermediate rounding. It is normal practice to perform the entire calculation and then report a reasonable number of significant figures, which usually matches the number with the least significant figures.

    Subtraction that occurs in the denominator of a quotient can be particularly problematic when the numbers to be subtracted are very nearly the same. For example, $42.3/(22.12−22.1)$ gives 2115 if intermediate rounding is not done. However, if rounding is used in the intermediate step for the subtraction, the denominator becomes zero, and the result becomes undefined. Common sense must prevail in cases like this to avoid problems.

1.3 Accuracy, Precision and Uncertainty

It is important to understand that accuracy, precision, and uncertainty have different meanings in measurements, and hence they represent different characteristics of numbers obtained through measurements. Accuracy refers to the nearness of a value to the correct or true value;

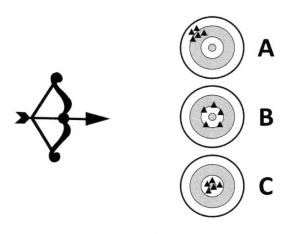

Figure 1.2: Illustration of Difference Between Accuracy and Precision in Measurements

in measurements the accuracy usually is determined by the decimal places of the number obtained. The greater the number of decimal places, the greater the accuracy. A measurement of 12.23 pounds is more accurate than a measurement of 12.2 pounds. It could be derived that an answer that has more significant figures is usually more accurate than an answer that has less.

Precision refers to the repeatability of a measurement—that is, how close successive measurements are to each other. The precision of a measurement is usually determined by the smallest size of unit of the measuring instruments, assuming the measurements are done consistently; hence artificial errors are minimized between repeated experiments. For example, if a metal piece is being measured for its mass, and two choices of instruments are available: one is a digital scale that has the smallest unit at 0.1 g, and the other is an analytical balance that has the smallest unit at 0.0001 g. The numbers obtained using the later will be more precise than the numbers obtained using the former.

Figure 1.2 illustrates the difference between accuracy and precision. The results in panel A are precise, because if individual results are close to each other, but they are not accurate, they are all far away from the true value (i.e., the center). The results in panel B are accurate, because each individual result is close to the true value, but they are not precise, because they are far away from each other. The results in panel C are both accurate and precise, and that is what we would want to achieve in any measurement.

Uncertainty refers to the variations in the obtained numbers through measurements. It is closely related to the precision of a measurement. If the uncertainty is not clearly stated after the number, say, 12.6 in ± 0.1, then you may assume the uncertainty is ± half of the smallest unit, as shown in Table 1.3.

It can be said that accuracy is dependent on the "correctness" of the instruments, and precision is dependent on the "refinement" of the instruments. Uncertainty is a measure of the precision of numbers obtained through measurements.

1.4 Errors

In any measurement, errors are inevitable no matter how good the instruments are, or how careful you conduct the measurement. There are two types of errors: systematic errors and random errors. Systematic errors can be eliminated and corrected. In contrast, random errors cannot be completely

Table 1.3: Levels of Uncertainty

NUMBER	UNCERTAINTY
25	±0.5
15.7	±0.05
2.567	±0.0005

Source: Theory and Problems of Technical Mathematics. Schaum's Outline Series, McGraw Hill, New York, 1979

eliminated, but they can be minimized, and their impact on the results of measurements can be characterized.

1.4.1 Systematic Errors

Panel A in figure 1.2 displays a good example of systematic errors. All results are biased, and differ significantly from the true value of the measured attribute represented by the center. Sources of systematic error may be imperfect calibration of measurement instruments (i.e., zero error), changes in the environment that interfere with the measurement process, and flawed methods of observation to obtain the results.

For example, consider a worker measuring distance between two locations using a steel tape that is 15 m long. If the steel tape, after being compared to the standard at the U.S. Bureau of Standards in Washington D.C., is found to not be exactly 15.000 m long; rather it is 14.900 m, then there will be a systematic error (−0.100 m) each time the tape is used. Suppose the tape is used 10 times, then the distance reported to be 150 m is actually only 149 m, and that −1.00 m (−0.100 m × 10 times) is an accumulated systematic error due to the imperfect tape.

Systematic errors may also be present in the result of an estimate based on a mathematical model or physical law. For instance, the estimated oscillation frequency of a pendulum will be systematically in error if slight movement of the support is not accounted for.

Systematic errors usually can be eliminated by applying a correction. In the previous example, if we know that a −0.100 m deviation exists between the tape's value and the true value, we can easily account for that in our measurements. After using the tape 10 times, instead of reporting a 150 m length between the two locations, we can apply the correction of −0.100 m × 10 = 1.00 m, and hence report a final result of 149 m.

The sources of systematic errors can be many, and they occur in all types of measurements: mechanical quantities, electrical quantities, mass, sound, odors, light intensity, and so on. We must be aware of their existence, eliminate as much as we can, and quantify and correct for those that remain.

1.4.2 Random Errors

Panel B and C in figure 1.2 also showcase random errors. Random errors are errors in measurement that lead to measurable values being inconsistent when repeated measures of an attribute or quantity are taken. The word "random" indicates that they are inherently unpredictable, namely, they are scattered about the true value. As shown in Panel B and C, the repeated measurements yield values that are different from each other, and different from the true value. The signs of these differences are also random; some of them will be larger than the true value, and some of them will be smaller than the true value. One good thing about random errors is that they tend to cancel each other out when a measurement is repeated several times with the same instrument. All measurements are prone to random error.

Random error is caused by unpredictable fluctuations in the readings of a measurement instrument, or in the experimenter's interpretation of the instrumental reading. Random errors are closely related to the concept of precision. The higher the precision of a measurement instrument, the smaller the variability of the fluctuations in its readings, which will lead to smaller random errors being generated. Random errors cannot be totally eliminated, but they can be significantly reduced by taking multiple measurements using the same instrument and then reporting the average (i.e., mathematical mean) as the measured value.

EXERCISES

1. How many significant figures are contained in each of the following quantities?

QUANTITY	SIG FIGS	QUANTITY	SIG FIGS	QUANTITY	SIG FIGS
4,930 feet		5.220×10^2		0.0030	
4.930		9.009		3,600 seconds/hr	
0.0493 seconds		0.0003		3.2203×10^5	
206.0		50,620 meters		0.00051	
5,280 ft/mile		0.09050		3.22	

2. Perform the following computations and report the answers with the proper number of significant figures.

COMPUTATION	SIG FIGS	RESULT	COMPUTATION	SIG FIGS	RESULT
(2.05)(360)			185.323 + 12.3 + 99.37		
(26.35)/(12.03)			163/(0.02168 – 0.02166)		
[(4.91)(32.2)]/12.03			436.2 miles / 1.06 hrs		

$$
\begin{array}{ll}
(4.5976 \times 10^2) & (4.01 \times 10^3 \text{ sec})/ \\
(7.3 \times 10^{-1}) & (3600 \text{ sec/hr}) \\
\\
0.009024 + & (\$36/\text{ticket}) \\
\underline{0.0653201} & \underline{(23,850 \text{ tickets})}
\end{array}
$$

3. Solve the following problems and give the answers rounded to the proper number of significant figures.

    a. $v = 2.14t2 + 35.35t + 2.25$ for $t = 3.2$
    b. $24.56 \text{ ft} \times 12 \text{ in/ft} = ?$ inches
    c. $\$400$ a plate $\times 20$ guests $= \$?$
    d. $V = [\pi(4.62 \text{ cm}^2)(7.53 \text{ cm}))]/3 = ? \text{ cm}^3$ (volume of a cone)
    e. $325.03 - 527.897 + 615 = ?$
    f. 32¢ per part $\times 45\,250$ parts $= \$?$

4. Estimate the volume of water used to take showers by the members of this class (67 students) in one academic year. Clearly state your assumptions.

5. Estimate the amount of water used in a one-year period by a family of four who live in a detached house. Determine the cost from local utility rates.

6. A major concern relative to global warming is the amount of carbon dioxide released into the air by transportation vehicles. Is there any truth to the statement that each car in the US emits its own weight in carbon dioxide each year?

Assumptions: The average car in the US gets 20 miles per gallon of gasoline, is driven 12,000 miles per year, and weighs 3,500 pounds. Gasoline weighs 5.9 pounds per gallon and contains 85% carbon by weight. Every 12 lbs of carbon emission is equal to 44 lbs of carbon dioxide emission.

Table and Figure Sources

1. Tbl. 1.2: Arvid Eide, Roland Jenison, Larry Northup, and Steven Mickelson, Engineering Fundamentals and Problem Solving. Copyright © 2006 by McGraw-Hill Education.
2. Fig. 1.2: Source: https://pixabay.com/en/bow-arrow-drawn-archery-target-311747.
3. Tbl. 1.3: Paul Calter, Theory and Problems of Technical Mathematics. Copyright © 1979 by McGraw-Hill Education.

2

UNIT CONVERSIONS

OBJECTIVES

When you complete study of this chapter, you will be able to:

1. Identify physical quantities and their dimensions
2. Understand the difference between fundamental and derived dimensions
3. Perform basic dimensional analysis to solve problems
4. Convert units between SI, US customary, and engineering systems using the Unit Factor Method

2.1 Introduction

Most countries have adopted the International Unit (SI) system, which is an international metric standard developed and maintained by the General Conference on Weights and Measures (Conférence Générale des Poids et Mesures, CGPM). However, In the US, other unit systems (for example, the US customary system and the US engineering system) are still widely used. Hence, it is critical for technologists, engineers, and scientists to understand the differences between these unit systems, and to know how to convert quantities measured in one unit system to another. This chapter discusses the dimensions of physical quantities, examines the SI, US customary and US engineering units, and demonstrates the conversion between different units using the unit factor method.

2.2 Physical Quantities and Their Dimensions

Technologists, engineers, and scientists are constantly asked to measure fundamental physical quantities such as length, time, mass, temperature, and force. To quantify a physical quantity, it is not enough to just provide a numerical value. The magnitude of physical quantities can only be understood when proper units describe them. A unit is a predetermined reference amount to which a measured quantity can be compared. The comparison will determine how many (a numerical value) units are contained within a physical quantity. For example, when a length is being measured, with 1.0 ft as the unit, and 20 unit length of 1.0 ft are contained in the measured length, it is expressed as length = 20.0 ft.

Dimensions are used to describe physical quantities. They are independent of units. For example, length, as a dimension, is represented by a symbol L. Its dimension hence is L, regardless in which unit it is being used. You may choose meters, feet, yards, etc., to measure it, but all results will have the same dimension of L. Usually, a dimension is denoted by a set of brackets. For example, the dimension for length is denoted by [L].

There is a dimension for each type of physical quantity. However, dimensions are categorized into two areas—fundamental and derived. Keep in mind the assignment of a dimension as a fundamental category is actually arbitrary. It is based on convenience or preference. It does not mean that the physical quantities represented by fundamental dimensions are more "fundamental" than others. Derived dimensions are combinations of two or more fundamental dimensions.

For example, in a typical mechanical dimension system, length ([L]) and time ([T]) are fundamental dimensions, while velocity (V) is a derived dimension, defined as length divided by time ($V = [LT^{-1}]$). One could choose velocity (V) as a fundamental dimension. In this case, with time [T] as another fundamental dimension, length [L] becomes a derived dimension ($[L] = [VT]$).

A dimensional system can be defined as the smallest number of fundamental dimensions that will form a consistent and complete set for a field of science. For example, for a mechanical dimensional system, three fundamental dimensions are needed. Depending on the selections, we have either the absolute system, where length [L], time [T], and mass [M] are the fundamental dimensions, or a gravitational system, where length [L], time [T], and force [F] are the fundamental dimensions, as illustrated in Table 2.1. Once a set of fundamental dimensions is set, a base unit must be specified for each of the fundamental dimensions.

2.3 Dimensional Analysis

Since all physical entities (for example, length, mass, velocity, and force) have dimensions, we can use dimensional analysis to find mathematical relationships existing between physical entities without knowing the exact underlining mechanisms or physics. Dimensional analysis can be a powerful tool to use to analyze technical problems and to find useful mathematical equations to relate different physical entities to each other.

Table 2.1: Two Basic Mechanical Dimensional Systems

QUANTITY	ABSOLUTE	GRAVITATIONAL
Length	[L]	[L]
Time	[T]	[T]
Mass	[M]	[FL^{-1}T^2]
Force	[MLT^{-2}]	[F]
Velocity	[LT^{-1}]	[LT^{-1}]
Pressure	[ML^{-1}T^{-2}]	[FL^{-2}]
Momentum	[MLT^{-1}]	[FT]
Energy	[ML^{2}T^{-2}]	[FL]
Power	[ML^{2}T^{-3}]	[FLT^{-1}]
Torque	[ML^{2}T^{-2}]	[FL]

Source: Engineering Fundamentals and Problem Solving, 5th edition, McGraw Hill, New York, 2006

The basic principle of dimensional analysis lies in the fact that any mathematical equation that describes a physical law must have the same dimensions at the two sides of the equation.

Example 2.1

Newton's law of gravity describes the force of gravity using the following equation:

$$f = K \frac{m_1 m_2}{r^2}$$

Eq. 2.1

where: f = the force of gravity between two objects
m_1 and m_2 = the masses of the two objects
r = the distance between the two objects
K = the gravitational constant

What are the proper units for K? To answer this question, dimensional analysis is used. First determine the dimensions of the physical entities in the equation.

On the left-hand side, f is force. Force has a derived dimension of $[M][LT^{-2}]$ from Newton's 2nd Law ($f = ma$). On the right-hand side, m_1, m_2 and r all have fundamental dimensions of $[M]$, $[M]$, and $[L]$, respectively. Substituting these dimensions into Equation 2-1 results in:

$[MLT^{-2}] = [K][M^2L^{-2}]$, where $[K]$ is the dimension for the constant K.

Algebraically canceling out dimensions from both sides and re-arranging terms results in:

$[K] = [M^{-1}][L^3][T^{-2}]$

Hence, K should have a unit of m³/kg·s² in the SI unit system.

Sometimes there is a dimensionless constant in an equation (for example, the number p). These dimensionless constants will have a dimension of 1.

Example 2.2

Dimensional analysis can be used to find mathematical correlations between physical entities. Consider the motion of a pendulum. As shown in Figure 2.1, a ball with a mass of m is tied to the end of a string of negligible mass, with length l to make a pendulum. An equation is desired that correlates the period of the pendulum motion to the known parameters, m, l, and the gravitational acceleration constant, g. The period is the time (t) for one complete cycle, a left swing and a right swing.

Assuming that the period t is a function of the three parameters m, l and g, the relationship between these parameters it can be expressed as:

$t = \lambda l^a m^b g^c$ Eq. 2.2

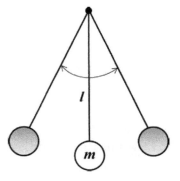

Figure 2.1: A Pendulum.

where: t = the period with dimension [T]
λ = a dimensionless coefficient to be determined, dimension [1]
l = length of the string with dimension [L]
m = mass of the pendulum with dimension [M]
g = gravitational acceleration constant with dimension [LT^{-2}]
a, b, c = constants to be determined

Substituting the dimensions for t, λ, l, m, and g into equation 2.2 results in:

$$[T] = [1][L]^a[M]^b[LT^{-2}]^c \text{ OR } [T]^1[L]^0[M]^0[T]^0 = [1][L]^a[M]^b[LT^{-2}]^c \qquad \text{Eq. 2.3}$$

Since the dimensions on both sides of the equation need to match each other:

L: $a + c = 0$ |
M: $b = 0$ | Eqs. 2.4
T: $-2c = 0$ |

Solving these equations yields:

$$a = \tfrac{1}{2}, b = 0, \text{ and } c = -\tfrac{1}{2}$$

Substituting these values into equation 2.2 yields:

$$t = \lambda \sqrt{\frac{l}{g}} \qquad \text{Eq. 2.5}$$

Therefore, just by looking at the dimensions, a working equation for pendulum motion can be developed.

2.4 Conversion of Units

Once a consistent dimension system is established, a specific unit for each fundamental dimension can be selected. There are a large number of unit systems that could be chosen for any given dimensional system and many have been used over the centuries. The three most widely used in the US will be discussed here.

2.4.1 Systems of Units

Over the years, most countries have adopted the SystèmSystème International d'Unitès (SI) unit system as a worldwide standard. This is a decimal-based system (units are multiples of 10) system based on the meter (m), kilogram (kg), and second (s) as the units of length, mass and time, respectively.

In the US, two other systems of units are commonly used. The first, called the US customary system (formerly known as the British Gravitational System), has the base units of foot (ft) for length, pound (lb) for force, and second (s) for time. The second system of units, known as the Engineering System, has the base units of foot (ft) for length, pound-force (lb_f) for force, and second (s) for time.

Although the SI system is the preferred system (by law) of weights and measures for US trade and commerce, conversion to this system is voluntary and has not been uniformly adopted. The other two systems are widely used, especially the US customary system. Technologists, engineers, and scientists need to be familiar with all three systems and need to understand how to convert quantities measured with one system to other systems. Table 2.2 gives a comparison of the three systems.

Table 2.2: Units Used in SI, US Customary and Engineering Unit Systems.

QUALITY	ABSOLUTE SYSTEM	GRAVITATIONAL SYSTEM	
	SI	US CUSTOMARY	ENGINEERING
Length	m (meter)	ft (foot)	ft
Mass	kg (kilogram)	slug	lb_m (pound mass)
Time	s (second)	s	s
Force	N (Newton)	lb_f (pound force)	lb_f
Velocity	$m \cdot s^{-1}$	$ft \cdot s^{-1}$	$ft \cdot s^{-1}$
Acceleration	$m \cdot s^{-2}$	$ft \cdot s^{-2}$	$ft \cdot s^{-2}$
Torque	$N \cdot m$	$lb_f \cdot ft$	$lb_f \cdot ft$
Moment of Inertia	$kg \cdot m^2$	$slug \cdot ft^2$	$slug \cdot ft^2$
Pressure	$N \cdot m^{-2}$ or Pa (Pascal)	$lb_f \cdot ft^{-2}$	$lb_f \cdot ft^{-2}$
Energy or Work	$N \cdot m$ or J (Joule)	$ft \cdot lb_f$	$ft \cdot lb_f$
Power	$J \cdot s^{-1}$ or W (watt)	$ft \cdot lb_f \cdot s^{-1}$	$ft \cdot lb_f \cdot s^{-1}$
Momentum	$kg \cdot m \cdot s^{-1}$	$slug \cdot ft \cdot s^{-1}$	$slug \cdot ft \cdot s^{-1}$
Impulse	$N \cdot s$	$lb_f \cdot s$	$lb_f \cdot s$
Temperature	°K (degrees Kelvin)	°R (degrees Rankine)	°R (degrees Rankine)

The main difference between the US customary system and engineering system is the mass unit. Both systems are gravitational systems, where force is considered a fundamental dimension and mass is a derived dimension. In the US Customary System, mass has a new derived unit (the slug), which is defined as a specific amount of mass that would be accelerated at one foot per second squared, given a force of one pound. This is an application of Newton's 2nd Law ($F = ma$). For the US Customary System, substituting the proper amounts into the 2nd Law gives 1.0 lb_f = 1.0 slug·ft/s^{-2}.

This is not the case for the US engineering system. In the US engineering system, force and mass were not established independently. Sometime in the fourteenth century, a quantity of matter was selected to be one pound-mass (lb_m). It was then decided that one pound-force (lb_f) would be the effort required to hold a one pound-mass in a gravitational field where the local acceleration of gravity was 32.1740 ft·s^{-2}. In other words, when one pound-force is applied to one pound-mass, it will be accelerated to 32.1740 ft·s^{-2}, not just 1.0 ft·s^{-2}. Therefore, when converting between the US customary system and the engineering system, 1.0 slug = 32.1740 lb_m.

2.4.2 The Unit Factor Method

A good way to conduct unit conversion is to utilize the Unit Factor Method. In this method, a series of individual quantities connected with unit conversion factors is constructed, and the units to be eliminated cancel each other out algebraically, leaving the desired results. A final answer is always checked to be sure it is reasonable. Table 2.3 lists unit conversion factors for a variety of quantities of length, area, volume, mass, force, energy and power.

Example 2.3

Consider the conversion of 140 psi (lb_f/in², lb_f·in^{-2} or pound-force per inch squared) to Pa (Pascal or N/m², N·m^{-2} or Newton per meter squared).

The desired unit is written on the left-hand side of the equation, and the existing unit is written on the right-hand side. A series of conversion factors are added to the right side which will eliminate the unwanted units:

$$X\,Pa = 140\ psi\ \times\ \frac{1\,lb_f \cdot in^{-2}}{1\,psi}\ \times\ \frac{a\,N}{lb_f}\ \times\ \frac{b\,in}{ft}\ \times\ \frac{b\,in}{ft}\ \times\ \frac{c\,ft}{m}\ \times\ \frac{c\,ft}{m}\ \times\ \frac{1\,Pa}{1\,N \cdot m^{-2}} \qquad \text{Eq. 2.6}$$

Where: X = the desired value in Pa
           a, b, c = numerical conversion factors

In equation 2.6, it is observed that the series of units on the right side cancel out algebraically, leaving $N \cdot m^{-2}$. Thus psi (lb_f in^{-2}) is converted to Pa (N m^{-2}). The next thing to do is to add in the proper numerical unit conversion factors (from Table 2.3):

$$a = 4.44822 \ (1.0 \ lb_f = 4.44822 \ N)$$
$$b = 12.0 \ (1.0 \ ft = 12.0 \ in)$$
$$c = 3.28084 \ (1.0 \ m = 3.28084 \ ft)$$

Table 2.3: Unit Conversion Factors.

U.S. Length
12 in (inch) = 1 ft (foot)
36 in = 1 yd (yard)
3 ft = 1 yd
5280 ft = 1 mi (land mile)
6,076.12 ft = 1 nmi (nautical mile)
5-½ yd = 1 rod
198 in = 1 rod
66 ft = 1 chain
16.5 ft = 1 rod
660 ft = 1furlong
40 rods = 1 furlong
8 furlongs = 1 mi
6 ft = 1 fathom
3 mi = 1 league

US Area
144 in^2 = 1 ft^2
9 ft^2 = 1 yd^2
30-¼ yd^2 = 1 rod^2
160 rod^2 = 1 ac (acre)
43,560 ft^2 = 1 ac
640 ac = 1 mi^2
1 mi^2 = 1 section
36 sections = 1 township

US Volume
Liquid volume (liquid = fluid)
8 fluid oz (ounces) = 1 C (cup)
128 fluid oz = 1 liquid gal (gallon)
1 fluid oz = 1.80469 in^3
2 C = 1 liquid pt (pint)
2 liquid pt = 1 liquid qt (quart)
1 liquid qt = 4 C
4 qt = 1 liquid gal

1 gal = 0.13367 ft^3
1 pt = 16 fluid oz
1 C =14.4375 in^3
Dry volume
1 C = 48 tsp (teaspoon)
1 C = 14.4375 in^3
1 dry pt = 2.32729 C
1 liquid pt = 0.85937 dry pt
1 liquid qt = 0.85937 dry qt
1 liquid gal = 0.85937 dry gal
1 tbs (tablespoon) = 3 tsp
2 tbs = 1 fluid oz
1 C = 16 tbs
1 peck = 0.31111 ft^3
1 bu (bushel) = 4 peck
1 peck = 16 dry pt
1 bu = 1.24446 ft^3

Grain Weight (bushels)
1 bu corn = 56 lb
1 bu soybeans = 60 lb
1 bu wheat = 60 lb
1 bu oats = 32 lb

SI/metric length
1,000 μm (micrometer) = 1 mm (millimeter)
10 mm = 1 cm (centimeter)
10 cm = 1 dm (decimeter)
100 cm =1 m
10 dm = 1m
10 m = 1 dam (decameter)
10 dam = 1 km
100 hm (hectometer) = 1 km (kilometer)
1,000 m = 1 km

SI/metric Area
100 mm^2 = 1 cm^2
10,000 cm^2 = 1 m^2
1,000,000 mm^2 = 1 m^2
100 m^2 = 1 are
100 are = 1 ha (hectare)
10,000 m^2 = 1 ha
100 ha = 1 km^2
1,000,000 m^2 = 1 km^2

SI/metric Volume
1 L (liter) = 0.001 m^3
10 mL (milliliters) = 1 cL (centiliter)
10 cL = 1 dL (deciliter)
10 dL = 1 L
1 m^3 = 1,000,000 cm^3
1 cm^3 = 1 mL
1 m^3 = 1,000 L

U.S. Mass
16 oz = 1 lb (pound)
1 lb = 1 stone
1 slug = 32.2 lb
100 weight = 100 lb
1 ton (short ton) = 2000 lb
1 ton (long ton) = 2240 lb
1 quarter = 25 lb
1 dram = 0.0625 oz
7,000 gr (grains) = 1 lb

SI/Metric Mass
1 kg = 1,000 g (gram)
1,000 kg = 1 MT (metric ton)

cont.

Between US and SI/metric Mass	**Temperature Conversions**	1 therm = 100,000 BTU

Between US and SI/metric Mass
1 lb = 0.45359 kg
1 kg = 2.2046 lb
1 g = 0.03527 oz
1 MT = 2,205 lb

Between US to SI/metric length
1 in = 2.54 cm
1 in = 0.254 m
1 km = 0.62137 mi
1 ft = 0.3048 m
39.37 in = 1 m
1 m = 1.093 yard

Between U.S. and SI/metric Area
1 in² = 6.45163 cm²
1 ft² = 0.0929 m²
1 acre = 0.4047 ha
1 mi² = 2.58999 km²
1 ac (acre) = 4,046.873 m²

Between U.S. and SI/metric Volume
1 fluid gal = 3.7854 L
1 ft³ = 0.02832 m³
1 mL = 0.03381 fluid oz

Temperature Conversions
°C = (°F − 32) / (1.8)
°F = (1.8)(°C) + 32
°K = 273.15 + °C
°R = 459.67 + °F

Degrees to Radians
(π/180) × (degrees) = radians

Prefixes
Micro (μ) = 1 × 10⁻⁶ (0.000001)
milli (m) = 1 × 10⁻³ (0.001)
centi (c) = 1 × 10⁻² (0.01)
deci (d) = 1 × 10⁻¹ (0.1)
deca or deka (da) = 1 × 10¹ (10)
hect or hecto (h) = 1 × 10² (100)
kilo (k) = 1 × 10³ (1000)
mega (M) = 1 × 10⁶ (1,000,000)
giga (G) = 1 × 10⁹
   (1,000,000,000)
tera (T) 1 × 10¹²
   (1,000,000,000,000)
peta (P) = 1 × 10¹⁵

Energy and Power
1 BTU =1,055.056 J (Joules)
1 BTU = 252 Calories
1 BTU = 778.169 ft·lb

1 therm = 100,000 BTU
1 N·m (Newton·meter) = 1 J
1 W (watt) = 1 J/s = 1 N·m/s
1 kW (kilowatt) = 1000 W
1 kWh (kilowatt-hour) =
   3,412.14 BTU
1 hp (horsepower) = 550
   ft·lb_f/s
1 W = 0.73756 ft·lb_f/s
1 hp = 746 W
1 hp = 33,000 ft·lb_f/min
1 hp = 550 ft·lb_f/s
1 Bp (brummpower) = 1,000
   ft·lb_f/s

Force and Pressure
Acceleration of gravity = 9.8
   m/s²
Acceleration of gravity = 32.2
   ft/s²
1 N/m² = 1 Pa (Pascal)
1 lb_f/in² = 6894.7 Pa
1 N (Newton) = 1 kg·m/s²
1 lb_f = 4.44822 N

Substituting these values into equation 2.6:

$$140 \, psi \times \frac{1 \, lb_f \cdot in^{-2}}{1 \, psi} \times \frac{4.44822 \, N}{lb_f} \times \frac{12.0 \, in}{ft} \times \frac{12.0 \, in}{ft} \times \frac{3.28084 \, ft}{m} \times \frac{3.28084 \, ft}{m} \times \frac{1 \, Pa}{1 \, N \cdot m^{-2}}$$

$$= 9.7 \times 10^5 \, Pa = \underline{\textbf{970 kPa}}$$

Keep in mind when it comes to significant figures, all unit conversion factors are considered as exact numbers. Hence, the significant figures of the final result are only determined by the initial value. In this example, 140 psi has two significant figures, so the end result (9.7×10^5 Pa) has two significant figures.

The fundamental principle of the Unit Factor Method is that units cancel algebraically, as in the example, ft/ft = 1. This fact can be used to guide future calculations—if the resulting units are what is desired, then the result has a better chance of being correct. All numerical calculations should include an assessment of the resulting units.

2.4.3 Temperature

For temperature, the SI unit system uses the Kelvin scale (K), or the absolute thermodynamic scale, which has the same increment as the Celsius scale. However, the zero point on the Celsius scale is 273.15°K above absolute zero.

$$T_C = T_K - 273.15 \qquad\qquad \text{Eq. 2.7}$$

where: T_C = temperature, °C

         T_K = temperature, °K

As listed in Table 2.2, the common units used for temperature in the US customary and engineering systems are degrees Fahrenheit (°F) and Rankine (°R). A unit degree on the Fahrenheit scale is precisely the same as a unit degree in the Rankine scale. However, the zero point on the Fahrenheit scale is 459.67°R, above the absolute zero on the Rankine scale.

$$T_F = T_R - 459.67 \qquad\qquad \text{Eq. 2.8}$$

where: T_F = temperature, °F

         T_R = temperature, °R

By definition, the Rankine scale is proportional to the Kelvin scale by the following relationship:

$$T_R = 1.8 \times T_K = \frac{9}{5} \times T_K \qquad\qquad \text{Eq. 2.9}$$

where: T_R = temperature, °R

         T_K = temperature, °K

The Fahrenheit scale can be converted to Celsius scale as:

$$T_F = 1.8 \times T_C = \frac{9}{5} \times T_C \qquad\qquad \text{Eq. 2.10}$$

where: T_F = temperature, °F

         T_C = temperature, °C.

2.4.4 Energy and Power

There are other units that are commonly used that are not listed in Table 2.2. For example, the British Thermal Unit (BTU) is a unit of energy. The BTU is defined as the amount of energy needed to raise the temperature of one pound of water by one degree Fahrenheit. It can be converted to the SI energy unit, joule (J), as 1 BTU = 1.0551×10^3 J.

Note that energy and power are two different quantities. Energy is an <u>amount</u>. Units of energy are, for example, BTU, joules (J), and kilowatt-hours (kWh). Power is a <u>rate</u> of energy use or transfer. Units of power are, for example, kilowatts (kW), horsepower (hp), and BTU/h.

Example 2.4

Express the power output of a 225-hp engine in BTU/h and kW.

Using conversion factors from Table 2.3:

$$225\,hp = \frac{225\,hp}{1} \times \frac{2.5444 \times 10^3\,BTU}{1\,hp \cdot h} \times \frac{1\,h}{60\,min} = 9{,}541.5 \cong \underline{\mathbf{9{,}540\ BTU/min}}$$

$$225\,hp = \frac{225\,hp}{1} \times \frac{0.74570\,kW}{1\,hp} = 167.78 \cong \underline{\mathbf{168\ kW}}$$

Example 2.5:

Students in an apartment used 985 kWh over one month. What is the equivalent amount of energy in kilojoules (kJ) and BTU? What is the average power over the month in kW?

Using conversion factors from Table 2.3:

$$985\,kWh = \frac{985\,kWh}{1} \times \frac{1\,{}^{kJ}\!/_{s}}{kW} \times \frac{3{,}600\,s}{1\,h} = 3{,}546{,}000 \cong \underline{\mathbf{3.55 \times 10^6\ kJ}}$$

$$985\,kWh = \frac{985\,kWh}{1} \times \frac{3{,}412.14\,BTU}{kWh} = 3{,}360{,}958 \cong \underline{\mathbf{3.36 \times 10^6\ BTU}}$$

$$\frac{985\,kWh}{month} \times \frac{month}{30\,day} \times \frac{day}{24\,h} = 1.3681 \cong \underline{\mathbf{1.37\ kW}}$$

EXERCISES

1. If your body temperature was 102.5°F, what would the temperature reading be on a thermometer calibrated in degrees Celsius?
2. How many cubic meters are contained in a box measuring 1.5 yd × 3.0 ft × 30.0 in?
3. If you are traveling at a speed of 65 km/h, what is your speed in furlongs per fortnight? (1 fortnight = 14 days.)
4. A beaker contains 578 mL of water. What is the volume in quarts?
5. Convert 758 acres to hectares using the following values:

   1 ac = 43,560 ft², 1 ft = 0.3048 m, and 1 ha = 10,000 m²

6. Convert 12.5 miles to kilometers using the following values:

   1 mi = 5,280 ft, 1 ft = 12 in, 1 m = 39.37 in, and 1 km = 1,000 m

7. Your car has a speedometer calibrated in kilometers per hour.
   a. What reading would appear on the speedometer if you were to drive 65 miles per hour?
   b. On a test track, a speed of 120 kilometers per hour would be how many miles per hour?

8. If the fuel efficiency of a combine harvesting machine is 0.18 kilometers per liter for non-stop harvesting, what is this in miles per gallon?
9. The power output of a particular steam boiler is rated at 150 Hp. What is this in kilowatts?
10. A student apartment uses 1,253 kWh during a typical month (30 days). What is the average power use in kilowatts?
11. The tires on your car have a recommended inflation pressure of 35 lb per square inch. What is this pressure in kilopascals (kPa)?
12. The furnace in a home is rated at 200,000 BTU/hr. What is the equivalent rating in kW?
13. Convert as indicated.
    a. 3.75 ft to mL
    b. 1775 L to ft³
    c. 58.6°C to °F
    d. 18.5 × 10³ bu to m³
    e. 79,500 BTU/h to kW

14. If the density of carbon tetrachloride is 0.793 g/mL, and a sample has a volume of 9.29 mL, what is the mass (g) of the sample?

15. Table salt (NaCl) has a density of 2.16 g/cm³. If you used 0.65 cm³ of salt on your food, how much is this in mg?

16. A solution contains 5.00 grams of glucose per 100. mL. Each mole of glucose weighs 180.2 grams. How many moles are there in 225 mL of the glucose solution?

17. On the planet Shnoidia, an average person earns 80.00 Quatloos a day. One Zerumba (a favorite food item) costs 7.00 Quatloos. How many Zerumbas can be purchased if an average Shnoidian works for 3 days?

18. You are mixing some concrete for a home project, and according to the directions, you've calcuated that you need six gallons of water for your mix. But your water bucket isn't calibrated, so you don't know how much it holds. On the other hand, you just finished a two-liter bottle of soda. If you use the bottle to measure your water, how many times will you need to fill it?

19. The average density of Styrofoam is 1.00 g/cm³. A Styrofoam cooler is made with outside dimensions of 20.0 × 14.0 × 12.0 inches and the uniform thickness of the cooler is 1.50 inches (including the lid).
    a. What is the volume of the Styrofoam used in m³?
    b. What is the mass of Styrofoam in kg?
    c. How many gallons of liquid could be stored in the cooler?

20. An ethanol plant produces 1.35×10^6 gallons of ethanol in one year. If the conversion efficiency of the plant is 2.85 gallons of ethanol per bushel of corn, how many tons of corn are processed by the plant each year?

21. How many square miles of corn must be grown each year to supply the plant in the previous problem? Assume an average yield of 175 bu/ac.

22. Geologists' observations suggest that the two most common rocks exposed at the surface of the Earth are granite (continental crust) and basalt (oceanic crust). From travel times of earthquake waves, we also know that the average density of the Earth is about 5,500 kg/m³.
    a. As an astute observer walking around on continental crust (granite), you might decide to test the hypothesis that the Earth is made entirely of granite. You weigh a 1.00 ft³ piece of granite on your home scale and find that it weighs 171 lbs. What is your granite's density in kg/m³? Given the information above, could the earth be made completely of granite?
    b. Given that basalt seems to well up when ocean crust pulls apart at Mid-Ocean ridges, you might decide that maybe the entire Earth is made of basalt. On your bathroom scale, a 64 in³ (4 in by 4 in by 4 in) block of basalt weighs 116 ounces. Use this information to calculate whether the average density of the Earth can be explained by an Earth made completely of basalt.

23. You've been watching a highway construction project that you pass on the way home from work. They've been moving an incredible amount of dirt. You go to the state highway commission's website and find out that when all the trucks are running with full crews, the

project moves approximately nine thousand cubic yards of dirt each day. You think back to the allegedly "good old days" when work was all done manually, and wonder how many wheel barrows of dirt would be equivalent to nine thousand cubic yards of dirt. You go to your garage, and see that your wheelbarrow is labeled as holding six cubic feet. Since people wouldn't want to overfill their wheelbarrows, spill their load, and then have to start over, you assume that this stated capacity is a good measurement. How many wheelbarrow loads would it take to move the same amount of dirt as those trucks in a single day?

24. Plate steel is being coated with an anti-corrosion liquid in a manufacturing process. The steel (1.38 m wide) is conveyed down the manufacturing line at a rate of 1.50 m/s. The steel passes under nozzles that evenly and completely coat the steel. The desired application rate of anti-corrosion liquid is 0.010 L/m². At what rate (L/min and gal/h) should the liquid be pumped to the nozzles?

Table Source

1.   Tbl. 2.1: Arvid Eide, Roland Jenison, Larry Northup, and Steven Mickelson, Engineering Fundamentals and Problem Solving. Copyright © 2006 by McGraw-Hill Education.

3

FUNDAMENTALS OF MECHANICAL SYSTEMS

OBJECTIVES

When you complete study of this chapter, you will be able to:

1. Write a force vector in two or three dimensions
2. Construct a free-body diagram of a rigid body at rest
3. Write and solve the equations of equilibrium for a rigid body at rest
4. Describe simple machines, and use the principle of simple machines to solve problems
5. Define force, torque, work, and power, and calculate them with the right formula
6. Describe a power train, and determine the proper size for a pulley, sprocket, or gear
7. Understand the relationship between speed, torque and power in a power train
8. Determine the speed, torque and power at any point in a power train
9. Calculate friction force, and rolling resistance; and calculate towing capacity of a vehicle

3.1 Introduction

Mechanics is the study of the effects of forces acting on bodies. The fundamental principles of classical mechanics were discovered and summarized by Sir Isaac Newton in one of the most influential scientific books ever published, *Philosophiæ Naturalis Principia Mathematica* (Mathematical

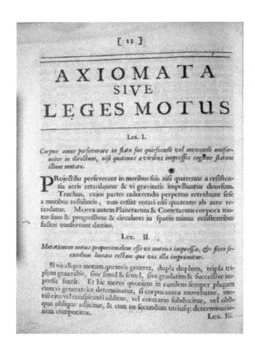

Figure 3.1: Newton's 1st and 2nd Laws, in Latin, from the Original 1687 *Principia Mathematica*.

Principles of Natural Philosophy). In the book, first published in 1687, Newton formulated three laws of motion:

1st law: An object either remains at rest or continues to move at a constant velocity, unless acted upon by an external force.

2nd law: $f = ma$. The net total force f on an object is equal to the mass m of that object multiplied by the acceleration a of the object.

3rd law: When one body exerts a force on a second body, the second body simultaneously exerts a force equal in magnitude and opposite in direction on the first body.

These three laws lay the foundation of classical mechanics. Figure. 3.1 shows the original page in the 1687 *Principia Mathematica*. The principles of mechanics have applications in the study of machines and structures utilized in several engineering and technology disciplines. Without them, modern machines and engineering would not exist.

Mechanics is divided into three general areas of application: rigid bodies, deformable bodies, and fluids. In this book, we will only cover mechanics of rigid bodies. It includes two branches: statics and dynamics. When a body is acted upon by a balanced force system, or, in other words, when the total net force acting on a body is zero, according to Newton's 1st law, the body will either remain at rest, or move with constant velocity. In mechanics this state is often referred to as an "equilibrium" state, and the mechanics of equilibrium state is called statics. The study of an unbalanced force system, or a nonzero total net force acting on a body, is called dynamics, which is governed by Newton's 2nd law, where the acceleration of the body can be calculated from the mass of the body and the total net force acting on it. It should be noted that velocity or acceleration is represented mathematically by vectors, and they are quantities that have both magnitude and direction. When a net total force is acting on a body, it can change its velocity in either magnitude, or direction, or both.

Before we start discussion on force analysis, we will first look at coordinate systems that we will use to analyze forces.

3.1.1 Cartesian Coordinate System

The Cartesian coordinate system is the basis of reference for describing the body and force system for mechanics. It is named after *Rene Descartes (Latinized name, Cartesius),* a French philosopher, mathematician, and writer.

Let's first look at two-dimensional (2-D) case, where we restrict our discussion to a 2-D plane, as shown in figure 3.2. Three elements are needed to define a 2-D Cartesian coordinate system: an origin, with a pair of coordinates of (0, 0), an x-axis where the unit length is defined, and a y-axis where the unit length is also defined. Usually the unit lengths on x- and y- axes are identical, and the two axes are orthogonal (i.e., perpendicular) to each other. Once such a coordinate system is constructed, every point on the plane can be defined by a combination of two numbers, (x, y), which is called the coordinates for the point. And this matching is exclusive; any combination of two numbers will be mapped by one, and only one point.

The coordinate system can be applied to 3-D space as well. Again, an origin (0, 0, 0) and three orthogonal axes (x-axis, y-axis and z-axis) are needed to define a 3-D Cartesian coordinate system, as shown in Figure 3.3. Any point in space is now defined by a set of three coordinates (x, y, z), and this matching is again exclusive.

3.2 Scalars and Vectors

Physical quantities that we deal with in this book are either scalars or vectors. A scalar is a physical quantity having magnitude but no direction. Examples of scalars are mass, time, temperature, energy, and power. They are represented mathematically by simply a number with proper unit.

A vector, on the other hand, is a physical quantity having both a direction and a magnitude. Some familiar examples of vectors are velocity, force, acceleration, and momentum. Vectors may be represented by either

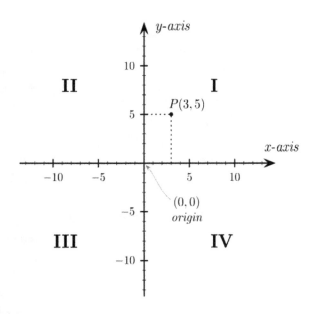

Figure 3.2: A 2-D Cartesian Coordinate System

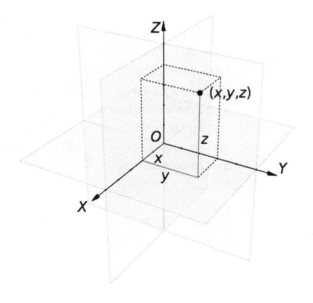

Figure 3.3: A 3-D Cartesian Coordinate System

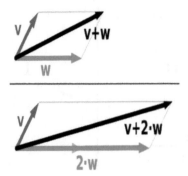

Figure 3.4: Graphical representation of vector addition

graphical or analytical methods. Graphically, a vector is represented by an arrow, where the length indicates the magnitude, and the pointing of the arrow indicates the direction. The tail of the arrow is called the initial point of the vector, and the tip of the arrow the terminal point. The following symbols are commonly used to denote a vector: $\vec{a}, \bar{a}$, or **a.**

Vectors that have the same length and same direction are called *equivalent*. Since we want to define a vector solely by its length and direction, equivalent vectors are regarded as *equal* even if they may be located in different positions. That is to say, they are regarded as equal even if their initial points are at different positions. The rule of thumb is if you can move a vector by simple lateral and/or vertical movement without turning it, so that it will perfectly match another vector, then these two vectors are equivalent, or equal.

If **v** and **w** are equivalent, or equal, we write **v** = **w**. Vector –**v** has the same length as **v**, but opposite direction.

If **v** and **w** are two vectors, then the sum **v** + **w** is a vector, too. It is determined as follows:

Position the vector **w** so that its initial point coincides with the terminal point of **v**. The **v** + **w** is represented by the arrow from the initial point of **v** to the terminal point of **w**. In a different interpretation, the **v** + **w** is the diagonal of the parallelogram determined by **v** and **w**, as shown in the Figure 3.4.

A zero vector is a vector that has a zero magnitude, and an arbitrary direction.

Once we have the coordinate system set up, we can express vectors using analytical methods. In an analytical representation, we always put the initial point of a vector at the origin of the coordinate system, that is, the (0, 0) in 2-D or (0, 0, 0) in 3-D. Since we can move vectors up and down in space as long as their magnitude and direction stay the same (i.e., equivalent), we can do these for all vectors. Once the initial point is fixed, we only need to know the terminal point to define a vector. Hence, a vector now can be easily represented by its terminal point. To use a 2-D coordinate system for vector algebra, any vector on the 2-D plane can now be defined by its terminal point, a combination of its x and y coordinates. For example, for a vector that goes from origin to P(3, 5), we can just write it as **v** = (3, 5). This simplification makes vector addition/subtraction very easy:

For $\mathbf{v} = (v_1, v_2)$, and $\mathbf{w} = (w_1, w_2)$;
$$\mathbf{v} + \mathbf{w} = (v_1 + w_1, v_2 + w_2); \mathbf{v} - \mathbf{w} = (v_1 - w_1, v_2 - w_2) \qquad \text{Eq. 3.1}$$

This is true for all vectors.

The same principle can be applied to 3-D space. Again, all vectors will have origin as their initial points, and they can be defined by the coordinates of their terminal points, which now have three coordinates (x, y, z) instead of two. In a 3-D coordinate system, a vector v will now be written as $\mathbf{v} = (v_1, v_2, v_3)$. The same simple rule applies for vector addition and subtraction.

A useful way to look at vectors in a 3-D coordinate system is through what is called "unit" vectors. In a 3-D Cartesian system, unit vectors are defined as:

$$\mathbf{i} = (1, 0, 0); \mathbf{j} = (0, 1, 0), \mathbf{k} = (0, 0, 1)$$

What does it mean? i is the vector with unit length and positive x as its direction; **j** is the vector with unit length and positive y as its direction; and **k** is the vector with unit length and positive z as its direction.

An arbitrary vector $\mathbf{v} = (v_1, v_2, v_3)$ can now be written as $v_1\mathbf{i} + v_2\mathbf{j} + v_3\mathbf{k}$.

Generally speaking, this expression is not limited to Cartesian coordinate systems. For any 3-D coordinate system, we can define unit vectors (or base vectors), $(\mathbf{e_1}, \mathbf{e_2}, \mathbf{e_3})$, and we can write any given vector in this coordinate system as a combination of the base vectors:

$\mathbf{a} = a_1\mathbf{e_1} + a_2\mathbf{e_2} + a_3\mathbf{e_3}$, where (a_1, a_2, a_3) are the coordinates of the terminal point of vector **a.**

In this book, we only use 2-D or 3-D Cartesian coordinate systems.

3.2.1 Vector Arithmetic

Basic vector arithmetic rules are defined as follows:

1. Addition and subtraction
    $\mathbf{v} = (v_1, v_2, v_3)$ and $\mathbf{w} = (w_1, w_2, w_3)$
    $\mathbf{v} + \mathbf{w} = (v_1 + w_1, v_2 + w_2, v_3 + w_3); \mathbf{v} - \mathbf{w} = (v_1 - w_1, v_2 - w_2, v_3 - w_3)$ Eq. 3.2

2. Multiplication by a scalar
    For any vector **v**, you may multiply it by a scalar, *k,* and the result is a new vector that has the same direction as **v**, but its magnitude is changed by *k* times.
    $k\mathbf{v} = (kv_1, kv_2, kv_3)$ Eq. 3.3

3. Norm, or magnitude
    The norm of a vector is equal to its magnitude, and it is designated as $||\mathbf{v}||$.
    2–D, $\mathbf{v} = (v_1, v_2)$
    $$||\vec{v}|| = \sqrt{\left(v_1^2 + v_2^2\right)}$$
    3–D, $\vec{v} = (v_1, v_2, v_3)$ Eq. 3.4
    $$||\vec{v}|| = \sqrt{\left(v_1^2 + v_2^2 + v_3^2\right)}$$

Example 3.1: $\mathbf{v} = (2, 1, 2)$, $\mathbf{w}$ is $(3, 0, 1)$, which one of these two vectors has larger magnitude?
$||\mathbf{v}|| = \sqrt{2^2 + 1^2 + 2^2} = \sqrt{9} = 3$
$||\mathbf{w}|| = \sqrt{3^2 + 0^2 + 1^2} = \sqrt{10} > 3$
$\Rightarrow$ $\mathbf{w}$'s magnitude is larger

4. Dot product → yields a scalar
   For two vectors, $\mathbf{v}$ and $\mathbf{w}$, a dot product between them can be defined.
   In graphical representation:

   $\mathbf{v} \cdot \mathbf{w} = ||\mathbf{v}|| ||\mathbf{w}|| \cos\theta$, θ being the angle between $\mathbf{v}$ and $\mathbf{w}$
   or, in analytical representation, $\mathbf{v} = (v_1, v_2, v_3)$ and $\mathbf{w} = (w_1, w_2, w_3)$
   $\mathbf{v} \cdot \mathbf{w} = v_1 w_1 + v_2 w_2 + v_3 w_3$, which is a scalar.   Eq. 3.5

   Dot product between two vectors yields a **scalar**!

   Example 3.2: $\mathbf{v} = (2, 1, 2)$, $\mathbf{w}$ is $(3, 0, 1)$, what is the dot product of them?
   $\mathbf{v} \cdot \mathbf{w} = 2*3 + 1*0 + 2*1 = 6 + 0 + 2 = 8$

5. Cross product → yields a new vector
   Cross product between two vectors will result in a new vector that is **NOT** in the same plane as the two vectors. Hence, cross product is only meaningful in 3-D space (or higher dimensions). It is not meaningful in 2-D space.
   Suppose you have two vectors, $\mathbf{a} = (a_1, a_2, a_3)$, $\mathbf{b} = (b_1, b_2, b_3)$, in graphical representation, the cross product between $\mathbf{a}$ and $\mathbf{b}$ is defined as:

   $$\mathbf{a} \times \mathbf{b} = ||\mathbf{a}|| ||\mathbf{b}|| \sin\theta \mathbf{n} \qquad \text{Eq. 3.6}$$

   where $||\mathbf{a}|| ||\mathbf{b}|| \sin\theta$ is the magnitude of the new vector, hence a scalar and can be multiplied to a vector;
   $\mathbf{n}$ is a unit vector that is orthogonal (i.e., perpendicular) to the plane of the vectors $\mathbf{a}$ and $\mathbf{b}$, as shown in Figure 3.5.
   Using analytical representation, the cross product is defined as:

   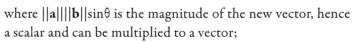

   $$\mathbf{a} \times \mathbf{b} = (a_2 b_3 - a_3 b_2)\mathbf{i} + (a_3 b_1 - a_1 b_3)\mathbf{j} + (a_1 b_2 - a_2 b_1)\mathbf{k} = (a_2 b_3 - a_3 b_2, a_3 b_1 - a_1 b_3, a_1 b_2 - a_2 b_1) \qquad \text{Eq. 3.7}$$

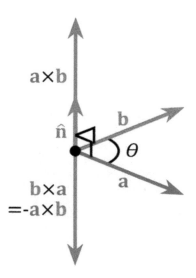

Figure 3.5: Graphical Representation of Cross Product Between Vectors **a** and **b**

where **i, j, k** are the unit vectors of the 3-D Cartesian coordinate system.

Example 3.3: v = (2, 1, 2), w is (3, 0, 1), what is the cross product of them?

v × w yields a new vector. Using equation 7, we can determine its x, y, and z coordinates.

$x = a_2b_3 - a_3b_2 = 1*1 - 2*0 = 1$

$y = a_3b_1 - a_1b_3 = 2*3 - 2*1 = 4$

$z = a_1b_2 - a_2b_1 = 2*0 - 1*3 = -3$

Hence, the answer is **v × w** = (1, 4, −3)

3.3 Forces and Force Systems

In mechanics, a force is defined as the action on a body that tends to change the motion of that body. A force is a vector, as it has both direction and magnitude. How forces alter the motion of a body can be determined by Newton's laws of motion, as introduced in 3.1.

Forces acting along the same line of actions are called collinear forces. The magnitude of collinear forces can be added and subtracted algebraically. Forces that pass through the same point in space are called concurrent forces. Forces that lay in the same plane are called coplanar forces.

3.3.1 Resolution of Forces and Free-body Diagram

In this book, we will focus on two-dimensional force systems, and work primarily with the x-y 2-D Cartesian coordinate system. As we recall, when we put the initial point of a vector at the origin of the 2-D coordinate system, any given vector can be represented by the coordinates of its terminus. Hence, in a 2-D system, it is convenient to resolve any forces into components at the x- and y-directions, represented by its (x, y) coordinates, as shown in Figure 3.6. By doing this, the force **F** can be replaced by its two components, **F**$_x$ and **F**$_y$, respectively. It means if O is a point on a rigid body, the net effect of a force **F** acting on the body is identical to the combined effect of its components **F**$_x$ and **F**$_y$.

Expressed in mathematical terms, the scalar relationship of the quantities in Figure 3.6 is:

$F_x = |\mathbf{F}|\cos\theta; F_y = |\mathbf{F}|\sin\theta;$

It is often times convenient to decompose a force into its tangential and normal components. For a force acting on a point of any curved or flat surface, it can be decomposed as a sum of two components,

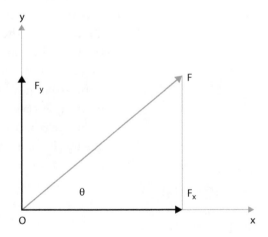

Figure 3.6: Resolution of a Force into x and y Components

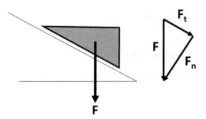

Figure 3.7: Resolution of a Force into Tangential (t) and Normal (n) Components

one tangent to the curve, or parallel to the surface, usually referred to as the tangential force; and another perpendicular to the surface, usually referred to as the normal force. Figure 3.7 shows an example of decomposing gravity into its tangential and normal components for a body sitting on a slope. We also have:

$$F_n = |\mathbf{F}|\cos\theta; \; F_t = |\mathbf{F}|\sin\theta; \qquad\qquad \text{Eq. 3.8}$$

As we will see, this decomposition will become useful when we analyze friction force that keeps a body from sliding down a slope.

Example 3.4: In Figure 3.7, suppose the weight of the block is 250.0 lbs, and the slope is at an angle of 30°. What are the tangential and normal components of the gravity?

Solution: we can decompose the weight, which is the gravity, as shown in the figure. Hence,
$F_t = |\mathbf{F}|\sin\theta = 250.0 \text{ lbs} \times \sin30° = 125.0 \text{ lbs}$
$F_n = |\mathbf{F}|\cos\theta = 250.0 \text{ lbs} \times \cos30° = 216.5 \text{ lbs}.$

Therefore, to prevent the block from sliding down, the friction between the body and the slope has to be equal to or larger than 125.0 lbs! We will take a closer look at the friction in 3.7.

As illustrated in this example, free-body diagrams are often used to show all forces acting on a body with their relative magnitudes and directions in a given situation. Typically, the size of the arrow in a free-body diagram reflects the magnitude of the force. The direction of the arrow shows the direction that the force is acting. Each force arrow in the diagram is labeled to indicate the exact type of force. It is generally customary in a free-body diagram to represent the object by a box and to draw the force arrow from the center of the box outward in the direction that the force is acting. A revisiting of example 3.4 yields a free-body diagram shown in Figure 3.8. Three forces are acting on the body sitting on a slope: gravity (F_g), normal force exerting on the body by the slope to support it (F'_n), and friction force (F_{fri}) to prevent the body from sliding downhill. For a body that is not moving, the total net force of these three forces must come to a zero. If, as shown in Figure 3.7, we decompose the gravity into its tangential and normal components respectively, we will have $F_t = F_{fri}$, and $F_n = F'_n$!

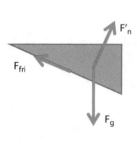

Figure. 3.8: Free Body Diagram Showing Forces Acting on a Body Sitting on a Slope

3.4 Simple Machines

In this book, a machine is defined as a device that either changes the direction or magnitude of a force. All mechanical machines are composed of combinations and modifications of two basic machines: the lever and the inclined plane. These two are also the basic simple machines, and they are the simplest mechanisms that use mechanical advantage (also called leverage) to regulate or increase the effect of a force.

Renaissance scientists defined six classical simple machines: lever, wheel and axle, pulley, inclined plane, wedge, and screw. However, if we carefully analyze their working mechanisms, we will find out that there are only two basic simple machines: the lever and the inclined plane. Wheel and axle machines and pulleys are modified forms of the lever, and wedges and screws are modified forms of the inclined plane.

In this section we will study the basic principles underlining the operation of simple machines. It should be noted that in the following discussion, two assumptions are made: losses due to friction are ignored, and the strength of the materials is always sufficient so that materials won't break under force.

3.4.1 Lever and Wheel-axle Machines

A lever is a rigid bar, straight or curved, capable of being rotated around a fixed supporting point named a fulcrum. When a fulcrum and a bar are used, two different forces can be defined: an applied force (F_a) and a resistant force (F_r). The forces, bar, and fulcrum can be used in three ways, called three classes of levers. They are summarized in table 3.1.

Table 3.1: Classes of Levers

Class	Description	Mechanical Advantage	Illustration
Class I	Fulcrum is between the applied and resistant force	MA < 1 or MA = 1 or MA > 1	
Class II	Resistant force is between applied force and fulcrum	MA > 1	
Class III	Applied force is between the resistant force and the fulcrum	MA < 1	

To analyze the lever, we define the applied arm (A_a) as the distance between the acting point of the applied force and the fulcrum, and the resistant arm (A_r) as the distance between the acting point of the resistant force and the fulcrum. The principle of levers can be expressed mathematically as:

Applied force × Applied arm = Resistant force × Resistant arm

$$F_a \times A_a = F_r \times A_r \hspace{4cm} \text{Eq. 3.9}$$

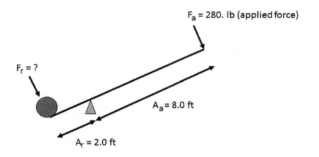

Figure 3.9: Class I Lever Example

F_a = 280. lb (applied force)

F_r = ?

A_a = 8.0 ft

A_r = 2.0 ft

The mechanical advantage (MA) is defined as the ratio between F_r and F_a. $MA = F_r/F_a = A_a/A_r$. Hence, for a lever with a mechanical advantage larger than 1, the applied force would be less than the resistant force. In other words, using such a lever, one gets to move a load that is heavier than the force being applied. This is why it is called an "advantage."

Class I levers are used primarily for their mechanical advantage. By choosing an applied arm that is longer than the resistant arm, we can gain mechanical advantage and reduce the applied force needed to move a load. Example 3.5 shows how to determine the parameters for a class I lever.

Figure 3.10: Class III Lever, Tweezers

Example 3.5: How much weight can 280.0 lb force lift with a class I lever if the applied arm is 8.0 ft, and the resistant arm is 2.0 ft long? What is the resulting mechanical advantage?

Solution: as shown in Figure 3.9, we set up our equation:

$F_a \times A_a = F_r \times A_r$ to find F_r, we re-arrange the terms to get:
$F_r = F_a \times A_a/A_r = F_a \times MA$
$MA = A_a/A_r = 8.0 \text{ ft}/ 2.0 \text{ ft} = 4.0$
Hence, $F_r = Fa^*4.0 = 280 \text{ lb}^* 4.0 = 1120 \text{ lb}$

Class II levers are also used for mechanical advantage. For a class II lever, as shown in table 3.1, its mechanical advantage is always larger than 1. It should be noted that in this class of lever, the distance moved at the applied force end and the speed of movement are both proportional to the ratio of the lengths of the two arms. With a mechanical advantage greater than 1, the applied force end would need to be moved faster than the resistant end.

Class III levers, as shown in table 3.1, have a mechanical advantage less than 1. This class of lever is used primarily to increase speed and movement. In other words, with this class of lever, a small-scale movement at the applied end can be magnified at the resistant end. Think of a pair of tweezers, which is made of two typical class III levers. By applying force at the middle of the tweezers, we can control the resistant ends to move faster, or move to a larger extent. We get to control the movement better.

The wheel and axle machine behaves as a continuous lever, or curved lever, as shown in Figure3.11. The center of the axle is the fulcrum. The radius of the axle is the resistant arm, and the radius of the wheel is the applied arm. The mechanical advantage of the wheel and axle machine is thus simply determined by:

$$MA = R_{wheel}/R_{axle}$$

The mathematics for wheel and axle machines work exactly the same as for a lever.

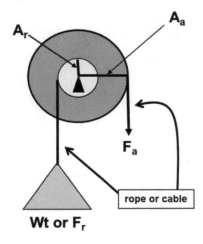

Figure 3.11: A Wheel and Axle Machine

Example 3.6: How much force will it take to lift a 20.0 lb weight with a wheel and axle if the axle is 2.0 inches in radius, and the wheel is 10.0 inches in radius?

We first calculate the mechanical advantage:

$$MA = R_{wheel}/R_{axle} = 10.0 \text{ in}/2.0 \text{ in} = 5.0$$

Then, the applied force can be determined:
$$F_a = F_r/MA = 20.0 \text{ lb}/5.0 = 4.0 \text{ lbs}$$

Hence, 4.0 lbs force can lift a 20-lb weight using this wheel and axle, so we clearly gain mechanical advantage here.

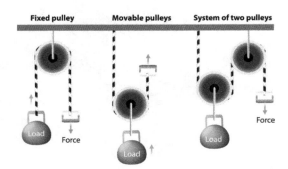

Figure 3.12: Fixed, Movable and Combination Pulleys

3.4.2 Pulleys and Pulley systems

A pulley is a modification of a class I or class II lever. A single pulley can be deployed in one of two ways: a fixed pulley, or a moving pulley, as shown in Figure 3.12 a and b. For a fixed pulley, when the fulcrum is at the center of the pulley, and the resistant and applied arms are both equal to the radius of the pulley, we will always have a mechanical advantage of 1. Although a fixed pulley does not provide any mechanical advantage, it does alter the direction of the applied force: it converts a "lifting" operation to a "pulling" operation, and often times it is more convenient for a worker. For a movable pulley, the fulcrum is indeed at the edge of the pulley, hence the applied arm has the length of the diameter of the pulley, while the resistant arm is equal to the radius of the pulley. We will always have a mechanical advantage of 2. However, a movable pulley does not alter the direction of the applied force. In most cases, to take advantage of both a mechanical advantage, and an altered

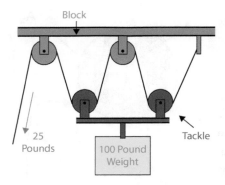

Figure 3.13: Block and Tackle Machine

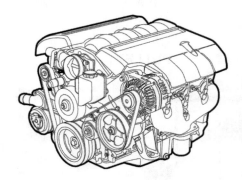

applied force direction, we use combination pulleys, as shown in Figure 3.12c. The simplest combination pulley has one fixed pulley and one movable pulley, and has a mechanical advantage of 2.

More complex block and tackle machines can be built, by introducing more pulleys. An example is shown in Figure 3.13. There is an easy way to analyze block and tackle machines. Typically, one rope is wrapped around the blocks and tackles. The tension in the rope will be the same everywhere throughout the rope when it is being pulled. Hence, if we count the rope segments that are directly used to support the load (i.e., weight), we will have a simple mathematical correlation:

$$R_n = Wt/F_a \qquad \text{Eq. 3.10}$$

Here R_n is the number of rope segments that are directly supporting the weight (Wt), and F_a is the tension throughout the entire rope, hence it is equal to the applied force.

Example 3.7: A block and tackle machine is being used to lift an engine weighing 785 lbs. The machine used a stationary double block and a movable single block as the tackle. How much pull would it take to lift the engine?

Analyzing the setup, we notice that 3 rope segments are supporting the engine. Therefore, $R_n = 3$

$F_a = Wt/R_n = 785$ lbs/ $3 = 262$ lbs.

This analysis of a block and tackle machine is based on the simple fact that only one rope is used to wrap around all the pulleys. When more than one rope is used, simple mathematics will no longer be valid. As shown in Figure 3.14, this is a design called Spanish's Burton, originated by Leonardo da Vinci. It uses 5 movable pulleys, and each will give a mechanical advantage of 2. When all are counted, it provides a mechanical advantage of $2^5 = 32$! You should notice, here each movable pulley uses a different rope!

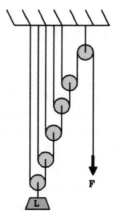

Figure 3.14: Spanish's Burton

3.4. 3 Inclined Plane and Screws

An inclined plane is an even surface sloping at an angle between 0° and 90°. The mechanical advantage of an inclined plane is determined by the ratio between the length of the plane, and the elevation. As shown in Figure 3.15, the mechanical advantage, MA, is determined by:

$$MA = AC/BC \qquad \text{Eq. 3.11}$$

Using an inclined plane, instead of lifting the entire load to the desired elevation, part of the load is supported by the inclined plane. tThe actual applied force needed to move the load, assuming that friction is neglected, is equal to the load divided by the mechanical advantage of the inclined plane. The equation to calculate the actual applied force (Fa) is:

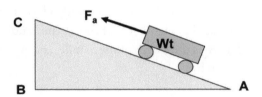

$$F_a \times AC = Wt \times BC \qquad \text{Eq. 3.12}$$

Figure 3.15: An Inclined Plane

Keep in mind that sometimes what we know is the elevation (BC) and the horizontal distance (AB), not the length of the inclined plane (i.e., the hypotenuse of the right triangle ABC). In this case, we need to use the Pythagorean Theorem first to calculate the length of the inclined plane:

$$AC^2 = AB^2 + BC^2 \qquad \text{Eq. 3.13}$$

Example 3.8: In Figure 3.15, if the weight of the cart is 200. lbs, AB is 20.0 ft, and BC is 4.0 ft, what is the minimum applied force needed to move the cart?

We first need to figure out the length of the inclined plane:

$$AC = (AB^2 + BC^2)^{1/2} = 20.4 \text{ ft}$$

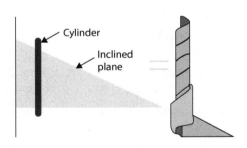

Figure 3.16: From an Inclined Plane to a Screw

Then, we calculate the applied force:

$$F_a = Wt \times BC/AC = 39.2 \text{ lbs} \approx 39 \text{ lbs}$$

The screw is a modification of the inclined plane. As shown in Figure 3.16, a screw is indeed an inclined plane wrapped around a cylinder, where the depth of the thread is equivalent to the

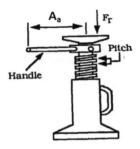

Figure 3.17: Screw Jack

elevation of the inclined plane, and the length of the thread of one cycle (i.e., approximately the circumference of the screw cross section) is equivalent to the length of the inclined plane.

Hence, the mechanical advantage of a screw is determined by:

$$MA = 2\pi R/D \qquad \text{Eq. 3.14}$$

Where R is the radius of the screw's cross-section; D is the depth of thread.

A screw can be combined with a lever to yield a powerful tool for weight lifting, a screw jack, as illustrated in Figure 3.17. Here, as the handle turns one revolution, the screw moves up by one pitch. Here A_a is the length of the handle, and A_r is the depth of the pitch. The mechanical advantage, MA, is given by:

$$MA = 2\pi Aa/A_r \qquad \text{Eq. 3.15}$$

And, the load, F_r, that can be lifted by applied force, F_a, is given by

$$F_r = F_a \times MA \qquad \text{Eq. 3.16}$$

Example 3.9: A student is using a screw jack to lift a load. He can exert 75 lbs force to turn the handle, the lever arm is 24.0 inches long, and the pitch of the thread is 0.200 inches. How much weight can the jack lift?

As we can see, $MA = 2\pi A_a/A_r = 2\pi \times 24.0" / 0.200" = 753.6$
And, $F_r = F_a \times MA = 75 \text{ lbs} \times 753.6 = 5.6 \times 10^4 \text{ lbs}$
Here we can see that a screw jack is very effective!

The same principle also applies to a bolt and nut. In this case, the lever arm would be a wrench, or a screwdriver, and the resistant force is the clamping pressure.

It should be noted that in reality, friction cannot be neglected when using an inclined plane or screws. However, with proper lubrication, it can be kept to a manageable level.

3.5 Work, Power and Torque

Mechanical systems are constructed from one or more simple machines. To evaluate their performance, physical quantities other than force are often needed. Among them, work, power, and torque are the ones that are the most important. In this section, we will look at how they are defined, and how to calculate them under different circumstances.

3.5.1 Work and Power

In section 3.3 we discussed force. Force is an action which causes and tends to cause motion, or a change in motion. To characterize motion, outside force, there are two other physical quantities that are also important, which are displacement and time.

First we will take a look at displacement. In physics, displacement is a vector. As we indicted earlier, a vector is a quantity that is characterized by both its magnitude and its direction. It is easy to see why we need a vector to describe motion. In motion, direction is as important as magnitude. Traveling south by five miles is totally different from traveling north by the same distance. Therefore, displacement vector, $\vec{D}$, is the physical quantity that is suitable for the description of motion.

The concept of time has its root in the natural cycles of the earth. One very visible cycle is the ocean tides, and another is the day/night cycles. The words time and tide both come from the same root, but end differently. The simple view on time is that it is a measurement of an interval of duration. In the context of this book, it is sufficient to use Newton's concept of absolute time: "Absolute, true and mathematical time, of itself, and from its own nature flows equably without regard to anything external." It is considered to describe the independent aspects of objective reality.

Combining the displacement vector, $\vec{D}$, with time, we can define velocity vector, $\vec{v} = \dfrac{\vec{D}}{t}$. Here, it is again clear that the nature of motion dictates that velocity needs to be a vector, in which both magnitude and direction are important.

With the definition of force, displacement and time clarified, we can now define work and power. Work is the result of a force acting (or moving) through a distance. There are two critical components in generating work, force, and movement under the influence of the force. When work is being done to an object, the object will gain mechanical energy. In essence, work is an addition (when work is being done to an object) or a subtraction (when work is being generated from an object) of mechanical energy. It is important to know that work is a scalar—only its magnitude matters (since work is the addition or subtraction of mechanical energy, this implies that energy is also a scalar).

Since force and displacement are both vectors, and work, as a result of force acting through a displacement, is a vector, it makes mathematical sense only if work is defined mathematically as the dot product between force and displacement vectors.

$$W = \vec{F} \bullet \vec{D} = |F||D|\cos\theta \qquad\qquad \text{Eq. 3.17}$$

From this definition, it is clear that when force and displacement are aligned in their directions, (i.e., when the angle between them, θ, equals to zero), a maximum amount of work will be generated. It is also clear that force acting in perpendicular to the direction of motion ($\theta = 90°$) does not generate any work.

Power is defined through work; it is the rate of work being generated. Or, mathematically, it is defined as:

Power = Work/Time, or P = W/t $\qquad$ Eq. 3.18

Not surprisingly, power is a scalar, too. It can also be considered as:

$$P = \vec{F} \bullet \vec{v} = |F||v|\cos\theta \qquad \text{Eq. 3.19}$$

Where **F** is the force vector and **v** is the velocity vector.

While work is typically defined or associated with mechanical motion, power can be defined purely from an energy standpoint. Here, power is defined as the rate of change of energy (E).

P = E/t $\qquad$ Eq. 3.20

Here, the energy can be thermal energy or electrical energy, or other forms of energy, such as wind, solar, or nuclear energy.

When it comes to work and power, there are many units that are widely used. To avoid confusion, it is worthwhile to take a look at these units.

In the SI unit system, the base units are: Newton (N) for force, meter (m) for distance/displacement, and second (s) for time. Hence, the base unit for work is N-m, which is defined as Joule (J), where 1 J = 1 N-m, and the base unit for power is Watt (W), where 1 W = 1 J/s.

In the US customary unit system, the base units are: pound (lb) for force, foot (ft) for distance/displacement, and second for time. Hence, the base unit for work is ft-lb, where one-foot displacement is created under the influence of one-pound force. The base unit for power is therefore ft-lb/s.

In the US customary unit system, another unit is used for thermal energy—the British thermal unit (BTU). Hence, power is also often measured by BTU/min, or BTU/hr, as far as thermal energy is concerned.

Special attention should be paid to another widely used power unit, the horsepower (hp). Horsepower is an arbitrarily created unit, which has a story behind its origin. When James Watt (1736–1819) was asked by customers about "how many horses your new steam engine can replace," he estimated that an average horse could exert 150 lbs of pull at a speed of 2.5 mph. Hence, he gave the following definition of a horsepower:

$$1hp = (150lb) \times \left(\frac{2.5\,mi}{h}\right) \times \left(\frac{5{,}280\,ft}{mi}\right) \times \left(\frac{h}{60\,min}\right) = 33{,}000\,\frac{ft-lb}{min} \qquad \text{Eq. 3.21}$$

And this definition has been used ever since. Keep in mind this is completely arbitrary!

Example 3.10: How much work (in ft-lb) is done when a 250.0 lb box is moved 14.5 ft up a slope of 30°?

Figure 3.18: Work Example

We first need to figure out the force needed to move the the box uphill. Assuming there is no friction between the the box and the slope, then the force that we need to overcome to move the box is determined by the gravity component that is dragging the box downhill (recall from example 3.4, this is the tangential component of gravity).

$F_p = wt \times sin\theta = 250.0 \text{ lbs} \times sin30° = 125.0 \text{ lbs}$

Then we need to calculate the distance under the influence of this force that the box moves:

$$D = 14.5 \text{ ft}$$

The force and the displacement are aligned, hence the angle between the two is 0°.

Therefore, $W = FD = 1812.5$ ft-lb, to keep three significant figures, as dictated by the displacement, we have:

$$W = 1810 \text{ ft-lb}$$

Example 3.11: A person with a mass of 105 kg climbs up a wall, a vertical distance of 4.55 m in 8.6 seconds. How much power (in watts) is developed?

Here, we also need to first determine how much force is being exerted to generate the power, because the force needs to at least overcome the person's body weight, therefore:

$F = Wt = m \times g$, where m is the mass, and g is the gravitational acceleration, $g = 9.8 \text{ m/s}^2$

Hence, $F = 105 \text{ kg} \times 9.8 \text{ m/s}^2 = 1029 \text{ N}$

$P = \mathbf{F \cdot v} = Fvcos\theta$, where $\theta = 0°$, $v = 4.55 \text{ m}/8.6 \text{ s} = 0.53 \text{ m/s}$

We have $P = 1029 \text{ N} \cdot 0.53 \text{ m/s} = 544 \text{ W} = 540 \text{ W}$ (why keep only two significant figures?)

Example 3.12: A boat is cruising on open water. The boat weighs 1500. lbs, and it covers a distance of 10,000. ft in 5.0 mins. How much work is being done? How much power is developed?

To solve for work or power, we need to know the force that is doing the work, and the distance traveled under the influence of the force. Here, we know the boat traveled 10,000. ft, however, we have no information about the force being exerted to move the boat! We know the weight of the boat, but that does not translate into the force needed to drive it, because the boat is moving horizontally! We do not have enough information to solve this problem!

Figure 3.19: Power Example

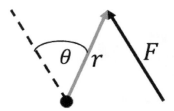

Figure 3.20. Torque

3.5.2 Torque

Another important physical quantity in analyzing mechanical systems is torque. Torque is generated when force is being applied through a torque arm, which causes or tends to cause a twisting or rotary movement. We experience torque when we use a wrench to either tighten or loosen a screw. From our experience, we know that even if we apply exactly the same magnitude of force, depending on the direction that we apply it, the effect on the screw could be exactly opposite. Which suggests that when talking about torque, both magnitude and direction may matter. From a mathematical standpoint, that makes torque a vector.

Torque is defined as the cross product between a force and a position vector, which is a vector that describes the torque arm. As shown in Figure 3.20, the magnitude of the torque is determined by the magnitude of the force, the magnitude of the torque arm, and the angle between the two vectors.

$$T_o = FR\sin\theta \hspace{4cm} \text{Eq. 3.22}$$

When written in vector format, we have:

$$\mathbf{T_o} = \mathbf{F} \times \mathbf{R} \hspace{4cm} \text{Eq. 3.23}$$

Where the direction of the new vector, To, is determined by the "right hand rule." Here is how it works: Let the four fingers of your right hand point to the direction of the force, then make a fist by turning the four fingers towards the direction of the second vector, the position vector. The direction that your thumb ends up pointing is the direction of the torque

Example 3.13: As shown in Figure 3.21, 125 lb force was applied to pull the rope, which is in turn causing the wheel to turn. How much torque is being applied to the wheel?

We now have two pieces of information. The force that is generating the torque is 125 lbs, and the torque arm, as shown in the figure, is equal to the radius of the wheel (why?), which is $1.20/2 = 0.600$ ft. Also as shown, the force is along the tangential direction of the wheel, hence the angle θ between the force and the torque arm is $90°$ (why?).

Therefore, in this case,

$$T_o = F^*R^*\sin\theta = 125\ lb * 0.600\ ft * \sin(90°) = 75.0\ \text{lb-ft}$$

Figure 3.21: Torque Example

It should be noted, that in the SI unit system, the unit for torque is N-m; while in the US customary unit system, to distinguish the unit for torque and work, we use lb-ft as a unit for torque, with ft-lb as a unit for work!

Now we need to determine the direction of the torque. Using the right hand rule, let your four fingers point to the direction of the force (to the right), then turn them towards the torque arm, with your thumb pointing into this page, and that would be the direction of the torque!

3.6 Power Trains

A power train is a system used to transfer mechanical power through a machine. Most common power train systems are constructed using pulleys, sprockets, shafts, bearings, gears, belts, and chains. Power is transferred throughout a power train to each individual component. During this process, speed, direction of rotation, and torque can be changed to meet different requirements.

Figure 3.22: Pulley-Belt Power Train Torque Example

3.6.1 Pulleys and Belts

Pulleys are usually used with V-belts, where the belt fits in well with the V-shaped grooves of the pulleys. A typical pulley-belt power train is illustrated in Figure 3.22. The friction between the belt and the pulleys is usually significant, so that no slip will occur. But for the sake of simplification in our discussion of the power train, we will assume that no power loss will result from this friction.

The simplest pulley-belt system has only two pulleys, the driver pulley and the driven pulley. If torque is applied to the driver pulley to make it rotate, a tension or force will be created in the belt. If the tension exceeds the load (i.e., the required torque) of the driven pulley and the friction of the power train, it will cause the driven pulley and shaft to turn, at the same direction as the driver pulley.

A pulley-belt power train system can certainly have more than two pulleys. In this case, there is still only one driver pulley; all the others in the system connected by the same belt are driven pulleys.

To analyze the pulley-belt power train, we first focus on the moving belt. Obviously, the belt can only move at one speed, no matter where we measure it. When there is no slip between the belt and pulleys, which is the precondition for the whole system to work properly, we can calculate the belt speed, S, based on the rotational speed of the pulleys. For any pulley in the system, with a rotational speed of N, we have:

$S = N \times$ circumference $= \pi ND$
where: D = pulley diameter.   Eq. 3.24

In other words, since the belt speed is the same throughout the power train system, when comparing any pair of pulleys in our system, we should always have:

$D_1N_1 = D_2N_2$ Eq. 3.25

Where D_1, and D_2 are the diameter of pulley 1 and 2, and N_1 and N_2 are the rotational speed of pulley 1 and 2, respectively. The rotational speed is routinely measured in revolutions per minute, or RPM. This equation is applicable to any two pulleys in a pulley-belt power train system, as long as they are connected by the same belt. When the pulleys are of different sizes, they will rotate at different speeds. Hence, the speed of pulleys can be controlled by changing their sizes.

Example 3.14: What is the speed of the driven pulley in the system diagrammed below?

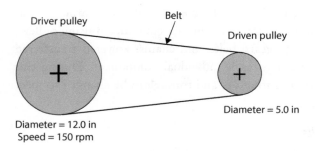

Driver pulley

Belt

Driven pulley

Diameter = 5.0 in

Diameter = 12.0 in
Speed = 150 rpm

This is a system of two pulleys connected by one belt, hence,

$$D_1 N_1 = D_2 N_2$$
$$N_2 = N_1 D_1 / D_2 = 150 \text{ rpm} * 12.0 \text{ in} / 5.0 \text{ in} = 360 \text{ rpm}$$

Example 3.15: The motor pictured drives a fan. The motor rotates at 1725 rpm. We wish the fan to rotate at 500. rpm. The fan pulley is 20. cm diameter. What diameter pulley should be on the motor?

This is a system of two pulleys connected by one belt, hence,

$$D_1 N_1 = D_2 N_2$$
$$N_2 = N_1 D_1 / D_2 = 500. \text{ rpm} * 20. \text{ cm} / 1750 \text{ rpm} = 5.7 \text{ cm}$$

Note that it's usually difficult for us to find a pulley exactly 5.7 cm. Normally, you'd choose one that's close, as long as the small change in speed is acceptable. Alternatively, perhaps a different size pulley on the fan would give a result closer to a more available size.

A useful parameter often used to characterize a pulley-belt power train system is the speed ratio (SR). It is defined as follows:

$$SR = \frac{N_{driver}}{N_{driven}} = \frac{D_{driven}}{D_{driver}}$$

Eq. 3.26

It is analogous to the mechanical advantage in simple machines. In example 3.15, we will have a SR = 1750 rpm/500. rpm = 3.50.

A pulley-belt system is simple, cheap, and easy to assemble. The pulleys don't need to be aligned. However, it is not without its weakness: There can be slip between the belt and pulleys, which will render the power train system ineffective. The pulleys are not synchronized, (i.e., the rotational positions of each pulley are somewhat independent of each other). If you need the rotation of every moving part to be synchronized, a pulley-belt system would not be your choice. Also, pulley-belt systems are not suitable to transmit large torque, due to possible slip, and breaking of the belt when tension becomes too high. To make a pulley-belt system function properly, care needs to be taken to ensure proper tension and installation; belts that are too loose will slip, causing excessive belt and sheave wear; sagging belts can snap during start-up or during peak loads; and belts that are too tight can also damage bearings on the pulleys.

3.6.2 Sprockets and Chains

Roller chains and sprockets used in a power train system can overcome two weaknesses of the pulley-belt system. They are capable of transmitting greater torque and power, because the chain will not slip under any circumstance, and the sprockets are synchronized, which will always move in sync.

The underlying principle governing a sprocket-chain power train system is the same as the pulley-belt system; the chain moves at the same speed throughout the power train. Here, instead of calculating the circumferences of the sprockets from their diameters, it is the number of teeth at the periphery of each sprocket that is used as a measure of the size of the sprocket. The bigger the sprocket, the more teeth. Keep in mind that a number obtained through counting is an exact number. Hence, the number of teeth in a sprocket-chain calculation is considered an exact number.

The sprocket-chain system hence is characterized by:

$$T_1 N_1 = T_2 N_2$$

Eq. 3.27

Figure 3.23: Sprocket-Chain Power Train

where T_1, T_2 are the number of teeth of sprocket 1 and 2, and N1 and N2 are the rotational speeds of sprocket 1 and 2, respectively. The rotational

Figure 3.24: Gear Power Train

speed is routinely measured in revolutions per minute, or RPM. Just as in the case of pulley-belt system, a speed Ratio (SR) can be defined as:

$$SR = N_{driver}/N_{driven} = T_{driven}/T_{driver} \qquad \text{Eq. 3.28}$$

Example 3.16: In the sprocket-chain system shown in Figure 3.23, the driver sprocket has 12 teeth, and the driven sprocket has 20 teeth. The driver sprocket is rotating at 480 rpm. What is the speed ratio? What is the speed of the driven sprocket?

$$SR = T_{driven}/T_{driver} = 20/12 = 1.67$$
$$N_{driven} = N_{driver}/SR = 280 \text{ rpm}$$

3.6.3 Gears

In a power train, when the shafts are very close together, we can take out the chains from sprocket and chain systems, and allow the teeth of the sprockets to directly intermesh with each other, and this will give us a gear system, as illustrated in Figure 3.24. The principle that governs gears is exactly the same as that for sprocket-chain, so $T_1 N_1 = T_2 N_2$ is also applicable.

Figure 3.25: Direction of Rotation in a Gear Power Train

Gears can be used to transmit very large amounts of power and torque, and unlike in pulley-belt and sprocket-chain systems, in a gear system, the driver gear and the driven gear have opposite direction of rotation. If the driver is rotating clockwise, then the driven gear will be rotating counterclockwise. Because of this, if you need to maintain the direction of rotation, then an intermediate gear needs to be used. As shown in Figure 3.25, the gear nos. 1, 3, 5, and 7 will be rotating at the same direction, while No. 2, 4, 6 will be rotating at the opposite direction.

Gear ratio (Gr) is often used to compare sizes of different gears. Gr is defined as the ratio between the numbers of teeth of two gears. Keep in mind, when it comes to significant figures, gear ratios are considered exact numbers, because it is the ratio between two exact numbers that are obtained through counting.

Example 3.17: Consider two gears as shown in the figure, with a driver gear that has 10 teeth, and driven gear that has 20 teeth. The driver turns clockwise, at a speed of 225 rpm. What is the speed and direction of the driven gear?

$$(T_1)(N_1) = (T_2)(N_2)$$
$$N_2 \frac{(T_1)(N_1)}{T_2} = \frac{(10)(225\,rpm)}{20} = 112.5 \approx 113\,rpm \quad (3\,sigfig)$$

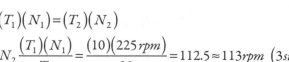

Gears reverse the direction of rotation, hence, the driven gear will revolve counterclockwise (CCW).

Example 3.18: Consider these gears: Gear 1 (driver): 16 teeth, 185 rpm, CCW. Gear 2: 24 teeth. Gear 3: 12 teeth. What is the speed and direction of gear 3?

$$(T_1)(N_1) = (T_2)(N_2) = (T_3)(N_3)$$
$$N_3 \frac{(T_2)(N_2)}{T_3} = \frac{(T_1)(N_1)}{T_3} = \frac{(16)(185)}{12} = 246.67 \approx 247\,rpm \;\; (3\,sigfig)$$

Gear 3 will be rotating CCW.
The number of teeth on gear 2 doesn't really matter!

3.6.4 Speed and Torque

As shown in Figure 3.26, suppose the tension or force in the belt is 85 lbs. Because the tension or force in the belt is constant along its entire length, there is 85 lbs of force pulling at the edge of both the driver and the driven pulleys. From the definition of torque, if we only consider the magnitude of the torque being applied to each pulley, we will have:

$$T_o = F \times R \hspace{5cm} \text{Eq. 3.29}$$

Where F is the force acting at the edge of each pulley, which is the same force in the belt; and R is the radius of the pulley being studied. From this equation, it is obvious the torque changes throughout the pulley-belt power train system depend on the size of the pulleys. Large size translates into large torque. This is true for sprocket-chain and gear systems as well—the torque changes, depending on the size of the sprockets or gears.

As we have seen, the speed of the pulleys depends on their sizes, too. However, for the torque, it changes proportionately as the size of the pulley increases; but for the speed, it is inversely proportional to the sizes.

The point of a power train is to transmit power. In our analysis, we assume that the loss of power due to friction is negligible, hence, the amount of power

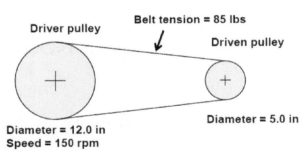

Figure 3.26: Speed and Torque

that is being transmitted throughout the power train remains a constant. Now, let's take a look at how power, torque, and speed are correlated.

First, as we discussed earlier, power is defined as the dot product of force and velocity. In the power trains that we discussed so far, the force acting on all moving parts, regardless of pulleys, sprockets, or gears, is always at the same direction as the velocity, as both are along the tangential lines. Hence, power can be simply described by,

$P = FV$, where F and V are the magnitude of the force and velocity, respectively.
In power trains, the magnitude of the velocity, V, is
$V = \pi N D$, where N is the rotational speed, and D is the diameter of each pulley/sprocket/gear.
Substitute V into the power expression, and we will have:

$$P = 2\pi N \times FR = 2\pi N T_o$$

Taking into unit conversions, we can reach an equation that is widely used to correlate power, torque and speed in machinery analysis.

$$P = \frac{(T_0)(N)}{5252.1131} \approx \frac{(T_0)(N)}{5252}$$

Eq. 3.30

Where P is measured in horsepower (hp), To is measured in lb-ft, and N is measured in rpm.

As we have assumed that the power being transmitted throughout a power train will remain constant, as the loss of power due to friction is neglected, we can then have:

$$(T_0)_1(N_1) = (T_0)_2(N_2)$$

Eq. 3.31

Where T_{o1}, N_1, T_{o2}, N_2 are torque and speed of the driver, and any of the driven parts of the power train.

Combine this with the gear speed equation, $T_1 N_1 = T_2 N_2$, and we have

$$T_{o1} T_2 = T_{o2} T_1$$

Eq. 3.32

Since gear ratio is defined as $Gr = T_2/T_1$, we have

$$T_{o2} = T_{o1} * Gr$$

Eq. 3.33

Example 3.19: A 2008 Nissan Pathfinder with a 5-speed auto transmission has the following gear ratios in the transmission:

Gear	1st	2nd	3rd	4th	5th
GR	3.842:1	2.353:1	1.529:1	1.000:1	0.839:1

In 1st gear, the engine, which is at the driver end, makes 3.842 revolutions for every revolution of the transmission's output (driven end). In 4th gear, the gear ratio of 1:1 means that the engine and the transmission's output are moving at the same speed. 5th gear is known as overdrive gear, in which the output of the transmission is revolving faster than the engine.

The above Pathfinder has a differential ratio of 2.220:1. This means that for every 2.22 revolutions of the transmission's output, the wheels make one revolution. The differential ratio multiplies with the transmission ratio, so in 1st gear, the engine makes 8.529 (2.22*3.842) revolutions for every revolution of the wheels. The Pathfinder is equipped with tires having a diameter of 33.7 inches.

1. Given the engine is running at 2500. RPM, on 3rd gear, what is the speed of the car (in mph)?

   On 3rd gear, from the engine to the wheels, through the differential, the total gear ratio, Gr, is:

   $Gr_{tot}. = 3.39438$
   Now, $N_1 T_1 = N_2 T_2 \rightarrow N_2 = N_1/Gr_{tot}. = 2500.$ rpm$/3.39438 = 736.5$ rpm
   Linear speed $= N\pi D = 736.5$ rpm$*3.14*33.7$ ins $= 77934.96$ in/min $= 77934.96$ in/min $* 1$ ft$/12$ in$* 1$ mile$/5280$ ft $* 60$ min$/ 1$ hr $= 73.8$ mph

   We keep three significant figures, because the number that has the least significant figures is the radius of the wheel, which only has three.

2. Suppose the engine is running at 2000. rpm and its power output is 185 hp. What is the torque output at the wheels on 3rd gear?

   Step 1. Torque at the engine
   To $=$ P$*5252/$N $= 185$ hp$*5252/2000.$ rpm $= 485.8$ lb-ft
   Step 2. Gear ratio from engine to wheels
   Gr $= 1.529*2.22 = 3.39438$
   Step.3. Torque at the wheels
   $(T_o)_{wheel} = (T_o)_{engine}*$Gr $= 485.8$ lb-ft $* 3.39438 = 1649$ lb-ft ≈ 1650 lb-ft

   We again keep three significant figures, because the horsepower output of the engine, 185 hp, has only three significant figures.

3.7 Friction

Up to this point in our discussion, we have always neglected friction. In reality, friction is omnipresent. Hence, it is worthwhile to take a look at friction, and understand how to take it into account when necessary.

Friction, in general, is the force resisting relative motion between contacting objects. It can be categorized into dry friction, fluid friction, and lubricated friction. Dry friction resists lateral motion, or trend to have lateral motion, between two solid surfaces in contact. It is further subdivided into static friction between non-moving surfaces, and kinetic friction between moving friction. Fluid friction resists relative motion between layers of a viscous fluid. Lubricated friction is a fluid friction, where a lubricant fluid separates between solid surfaces. Here, we will focus on dry friction.

When surfaces in contact move relative to each other, the friction between the two surfaces converts kinetic energy into thermal energy. Another important consequence of many types of friction is wear and tear on the materials, which may lead to performance degradation and/or damage to parts, (e.g., gears).

Friction arises from interatomic and intermolecular forces between the two contacting surfaces. Its origin lies in the electromagnetic interaction between charged fundamental particles, such as electrons and protons. The complexity of these interactions makes the calculation of friction from first principles impractical. Hence, empirical methods are developed for the analysis of friction.

3.7.1 Laws of Dry Friction

Three empirical laws have been used to characterize dry friction. They are:

Amontons' First Law: The force of friction is directly proportional to the applied load. The applied load is characterized by the normal force acting perpendicular to the contacting surface. This law can be expressed mathematically as Coulomb friction (named after French physicist Charles-Augustin de Coulomb, 1736–1806). An approximation (F_f) is used to describe dry friction.

$$F_f \leq \mu N \hspace{6cm} \text{Eq. 3.34}$$

F_f is the force of friction exerted by each surface on the other. It is always parallel to the surface, in a direction that is opposite to the net applied force. Remember, friction is always resistant to the relative motion of the contacting surfaces.

N is the normal force exerted by each surface on the other, directed perpendicular (normal) to the surface. The normal force is defined as the net force compressing two parallel surfaces together, and its direction is perpendicular to the surfaces. Now let's look at the simplest case first, when an object is sitting or moving on a horizontal plane, as shown in Figure 3.27. The normal force N is equal to the weight (or the load) of the object. When the object is on a slope, as shown in Figure 3.27, we need to decompose weight (Wt, red arrow) first. Wt is decomposed into two components: $F_{parallel}$ is parallel to the slope (purple), and $F_{perpendicular}$ is perpendicular to the slope (green).

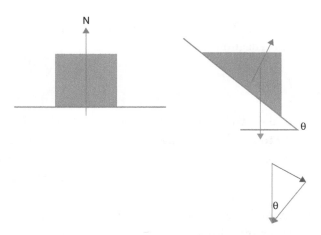

Figure 3.27: Normal Force Analysis

We always have:

$$F_{parallel} = \text{Wt}*\sin(\theta); \text{ and } F_{perpendicular} = \text{Wt}*\cos(\theta)$$

Normal force N is always equal to the perpendicular component $F_{perpndicular}$
Hence, $N = \text{Wt}*\cos(\theta)$, where θ is the angle of the slope.

Example 3.20: If a block with a mass of 10 kg is sitting on a floor, what is the normal force acting on the contacting surface?
Remember if we only know the mass of the object, we need to calculate the weight from the mass.
N = Wt = mg = 10 kg * 9.8 N/kg = 98 N = 22 lbf (1 N = 0.2248 lbf)

Example 3.21: If a block with a mass of 10 kg is sitting on a 30° slope, what is the normal force acting on the contacting surface?
We first calculate Wt from mass, Wt = mg = 10 kg*9.8 N/kg = 98 N
Then, $N = \text{Wt}*\text{con}(\theta) = 98 \text{ N} * \cos(30°) = 98 \text{ N} * 0.866 = 85 \text{ N}$

μ is the coefficient of friction (COF). This is an empirical property of the contacting materials. It may vary greatly from material to material. It is a dimensionless scalar value that describes the ratio of the force of friction between two bodies, and the force pressing them together. The coefficient of friction depends on the materials used. For example, ice on steel has a low coefficient of friction, while rubber on pavement has a high coefficient of friction. Coefficients of friction range from near zero to greater than one.

As dry friction is subdivided into static friction and kinetic friction, there are two COFs for static and kinetic conditions, too. For surfaces at rest relative to each other, μ_s is the coefficient of static

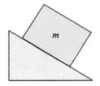

A block on a ramp

Free body diagram
of just the block

Figure 3.28: Static Friction

friction. This is usually larger than its kinetic counterpart. For static friction, equation 3.34 is now expressed as:

$$F_f \leq \mu s N \qquad \text{Eq. 3.35}$$

F_f may take any value from 0 up to $\mu_s N$. Keep in mind, static friction is the force of friction that is resistant to the trend of relative motion; since there is no motion, the net force always equals to zero. From the analysis of the net force, we can find out about the force of static friction.

Example 3.22: What is the static friction force acting on the block sitting on a ramp without sliding, as shown in Figure 3.28?

From looking at the free body diagram, we know that the weight of the block (wt = mg) can be decomposed into $F_{parallel}$ and $F_{perpendicular}$. Since the block is not sliding, this $F_{parallel}$ must be balanced by the static friction force, F_f. From this analysis, we can concluded that $F_f = F_{parallel} = \text{wt}\sin\theta = \text{mg}\sin\theta$! Also keep in mind that $N = F_{perpendicular} = \text{wt}\cos\theta = \text{mg}\cos\theta$

If the tilt angle of the ramp is being increased, then $F_{parallel}$, and in turn F_f, will both go up. Until to a point that the F_f reaches its maximum value, $F_{f\_max} = \mu_s N = \mu_s \text{mg}\cos\theta$.

Hence, the condition for the sliding to occur is when $F_{parallel} > F_{f\_max} = \mu_s \text{mg}\cos\theta$, hence,
$\text{Mg}\sin\theta > \mu_s \text{mg}\cos\theta \rightarrow \tan\theta > \mu_s$
This is the tilt angle at which sliding will occur! When $\mu_s \geq \tan\theta$, the block will remain static.

Once the sliding, or relative motion, starts to occur between the contacting surfaces, the static friction will be replaced by the kinetic friction. The COF for kinetic friction, μ_k, is slightly smaller than that of static friction. Equation 3.34 now becomes:

$$F_f = \mu_k N \qquad \text{Eq. 3.36}$$

Where N is still the normal force acting at the contacting surfaces, the frictional force on each surface is exerted in the direction opposite to its motion relative to the other surface.

Example 3.23: A block is sliding on a horizontal surface. The weight of the block is 10. Lbf, and the kinetic friction coefficient between the surfaces is 0.2. How much is the friction force?
On a horizontal surface, N = Wt = 10. lbf
$F_f = \mu k*N = 0.2*10$ lbf = 2.0 lbf (two sig figs), the COF is considered to be a physical constant, hence an exact number!

Example 3.24: The same block traveled 10.0 ft at constant speed. How much work is done?
The block travels at constant speed, hence net force acting on it must be zero.
The driving force at the horizontal direction hence must equal to the friction force.
$F_{drive} = F_f = 2.0$ lbf

$W = FD = 2.0$ lbf* 10 ft = 20. Ft-lb (2 sig figs)

Amontons' Second Law: The force of friction is independent of the apparent area of contact.

At first look, this law is a bit against intuition. We tend to feel that larger contact areas would result in a larger friction force. But that is not true. The friction force is only dependent on the load, or normal force; it does not depend on the contact area.

Coulomb's Law of Friction: Kinetic friction is independent of the sliding velocity.

No matter how fast the relative motion is, as long as the same normal force is applied, the kinetic friction will remain the same.

Static and lubricated friction coefficients for common materials are listed in table 3.2.

Table 3.2: COF of Common Materials

MATERIALS		STATIC FRICTION	
		Dry & clean	Lubricated (wet)
Aluminum	Steel	0.61	
Copper	Steel	0.53	
Brass	Steel	0.51	
Cast iron	Copper	1.05	
Cast iron	Zinc	0.85	
Concrete	Rubber	1.0	0.30
Concrete	Wood	0.62	
Copper	Glass	0.68	
Glass	Glass	0.94	
Metal	Wood	0.2-0.6	0.2
Polythene	Steel	0.2	0.2
Steel	Steel	0.8	0.16
Steel	Teflon	0.04	0.04
Teflon	Teflon	0.04	0.04
Wood	Wood	0.25-0.5	0.2

3.7.2 Rolling Resistance

Rolling resistance, sometimes called rolling friction or rolling drag, is the force resisting the motion when a body (such as a ball, tire, or wheel) rolls on a surface. It is mainly caused by deformations of the object (e.g., tire) or the surface (e.g., soil). Another cause of rolling resistance lies in the slippage between the wheel and the surface.

In analogy with dry friction, rolling resistance is often expressed as a coefficient times the normal force.

This coefficient of rolling resistance is generally much smaller than the coefficient of kinetic friction.

$$F_{rr} = C_{rr}N$$

Eq. 3.37

Where F_{rr} is the rolling resistance, and C_{rr} is the rolling resistance coefficient.

Table 3.3: Gives a List of C_{rr} Values for Various Conditions

C_{RR}	DESCRIPTION
0.0002 to 0.001	Railroad steel wheel on steel rail
0.0002-0.001	Steel ball bearings on steel
0.0025	Special Michelin solar car tires
0.005	Tram rails
0.0055	BMX bicycle tires
0.006-0.01	Truck tires on smooth road
0.01-0.015	Ordinary car tires on concrete
0.02	Car tires on stone plates
0.03-0.035	Ordinary car tires on tar or asphalt
0.055-0.065	Ordinary car tires on grass, mud
0.3	Ordinary car tires on sand

With rolling resistance, we can do some simple estimation on towing capacity of a car. As shown in Figure 3.29, the forces acting at the trailer can be decomposed into towing force, F_{tow}, weight, which equals the normal force when driving on a flat road, and rolling resistance, F_{fric}.

We have:

$$F_{fric} = C_{rr}N = C_{rr}Wt$$

$$\therefore Wt = \frac{F_{fric}}{C_{rr}} \leq \frac{F_{tow}}{C_{rr}}$$

Therefore, once we know the towing force of a car, we can estimate the maximum weight the car can tow, based on the rolling resistance coefficient of the road conditions.

Example 3.24: A car is traveling at a constant speed of 14 m/s on a flat road. The car weighs 1,500 kg. What is the power the engine needs to provide to drive the car, given the rolling resistance between the tires and the road is 0.030?

First, let's analyze the question; we need to calculate power, P. We know $P = FV$, hence we need to figure out both the driving force and the speed.

We know the speed is 14 m/s, furthermore, we also know that the speed is constant, which means that the driving force must equal to the rolling resistance. Now, the problem becomes to find the rolling resistance, F_{rr}.

In order to find F_{rr}, we need to know the C_{rr} and normal force N.

We have $C_{rr} = 0.030$, so what is the Normal force N then?

On a flat road, $N = Wt = mg = 1,500$ kg*9.8 N/kg $= 14,700$ N
Hence, $F_{rr} = C_{rr}*N = 0.030*14,700$ N $= 441$ N
Therefore, $P = FV = 441$ N *14 m/s $= 6,174$ N-m/s $= 6,174$ J/s $= 6,174$ W $= 6.2$ kW $= 8.3$ hp

In reality, the engine provides way more than 8.3 hp. Unfortunately, most of the power is wasted!

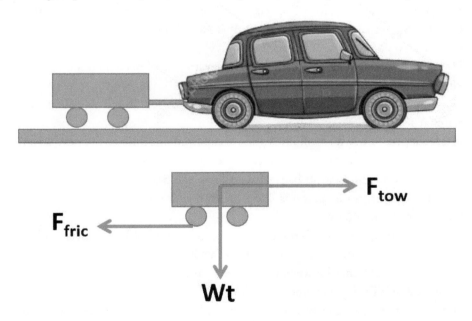

Trailer free body diagram

Figure 3.29: Towing Analysis

EXERCISES

1. Explain what is wrong with each of the following expressions (**u, v, w** are all vectors in 3-D Cartesian coordinate system, k is a scalar).
    a. **u·(v·w)**
    b. **(u·v) + w**
    c. **u × v × w**
    d. **k·(u + v)**

2. In each part, find a vector orthogonal to both u and v (hint: cross product between two vectors will yield a new vector that is orthogonal to both of them)
    a. **u** = (−7, 3, 1); **v** = (2, 0, 4)
    a. **u** = (−1, −1, −1); **v** = (2, 0, 2)

3. As we discussed in class, a screw is considered as an inclined plane wrapped around a cylinder. Suppose you are driving a screw into a piece of wood. The diameter of the handle of the screw driver is 0.50 inches, and the pitches of the thread on the screw is 0.0156 inches. If you are applying 10.0 lbf to turn the screw driver, estimate the resistant force of the wood to the screw.

4. A wagon carrying 2500. lb of goods is pulled up a hill. The wagon is pulled through a vertical rise of 15.0 feet, and the slope of the hill is 30°. Neglecting friction, what force (in lbf) is necessary to pull the wagon up the hill?

5. How much work (in kJ) is done when an elevator (total mass including passengers is 1685 kg) goes up 15 stories, at a distance of 60.5 m?

6. How much work (in ft-lb) is done when a boat of 2500.0 lb travels 1400 yards across open water at sea level?

7. A fast elevator with a mass of 500. kg moves up from one floor to the next, a vertical distance of 4.55 m in 0.50 seconds. How much power (in watts) is needed to drive the elevator?

8. A person moves 50 20.0 lb bags of seed from the floor to a bed of a truck (35.0 inches from the ground) in 85 seconds. How much power is developed? Express your answer in horsepower (hp) and kW.

9. What is the torque of a 65 lb force applied at the end of a 10.0 cm lever (in lb-ft and N-m)?

10. How much power (in hp) is needed to move a 450 lb crate 100.0 m vertically in 1.2 minutes?

11. Describe the difference between work, power, and torque.

12. Convert 225 BTU/h to hp and kW.

13. Determine the missing information for the roller chain and sprocket drive chain below. Hint: $N_B = N_C$

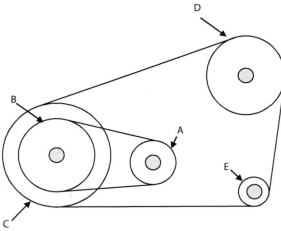

SPROCKET	TEETH	SPEED	TORQUE
A	15	525 rpm	28 lb-ft
B	25		
C	42		
D		355 rpm	
E	12		

14. A stationary engine is operating a stand-by emergency electrical generator. The engine is delivering 525 lb-ft of torque at 1250 rpm.
    a. How much power (in hp) is being delivered to the generator?
    b. If the generator is 65% efficient in turning mechanical energy into electrical energy, what is the generator's output power (in kW)?

15. A 2008 Nissan Pathfinder with a 5-speed auto transmission has the following gear ratios in the transmission:

Gear	1st	2nd	3rd	4th	5th
GR	3.842:1	2.353:1	1.529:1	1.000:1	0.839:1

In 1st gear, the engine makes 3.842 revolutions for every revolution of the transmission's output. In 4th gear, the gear ratio of 1:1 means that the engine and the transmission's output are moving at the same speed. 5th gear is known as overdrive gear, in which the output of the transmission is revolving faster than the engine.

The above Pathfinder has a differential ratio of 2.220:1. This means that for every 2.22 revolutions of the transmission's output, the wheels make one revolution. The differential ratio multiplies with the transmission ratio, so in 1st gear, the engine makes 8.529 revolutions for every revolution of the wheels.

The Pathfinder is equipped with tires having a diameter of 33.7 inches.

a. Given the engine is running at 3500. RPM on 2nd gear, what is the speed of the car?

b. The engine is running at 3000. rpm and its power output is 185 hp. What is the torque output at the wheels on 1st gear?

c. The maximum torque output of the engine is 288 lb-ft at 4000 rpm. What is the maximum towing capacity of this vehicle on a flat road? Use $C_{rr} = 0.3$ for your towing capacity calculation.

Figure and Table Sources

1. Fig. 3.1: Isaac Newton, Philosophiæ Naturalis Principia Mathematica, pp. 12. 1687.
2. Tbl. 3.2: Source: https://en.wikipedia.org/wiki/Friction.
3. Fig. 3.2: Copyright © Gustavb (CC BY-SA 3.0) at https://commons.wikimedia.org/wiki/File:Cartesian_coordinates_2D.svg.
4. Fig. 3.3: Source: https://commons.wikimedia.org/wiki/File:Coord_system_CA_0.svg.
5. Fig. 3.4: Copyright © Jakob.scholbach (CC BY-SA 3.0) at https://commons.wikimedia.org/wiki/File:Vector_addition_ans_scaling.png.
6. Fig. 3.5: Source: https://commons.wikimedia.org/wiki/File:Cross_product_vector.svg.
7. Fig. 3.6: Source: https://www.hk-phy.org/contextual/mechanics/for/add_force/3-03.gif
8. Fig. 3.10: Copyright © 2016 Depositphotos/Juliarstudio.
9. Fig. 3.12: Copyright © 2015 Depositphotos/edesignua.
10. Fig. 3.13c: Copyright © 2011 Depositphotos/Chisnikov.
11. Fig. 3.14: Source: https://www.lhup.edu/~dsimanek/TTT-fool/span-com.gif.
12. Fig. 3.16: Dr. Vasanthi Vasudev, Eureka! Science. Copyright © 2007.
13. Fig. 3.17: Harry L. Field and Lawrence O. Roth, An Introduction to Agricultural Engineering, pp. 25. Copyright © 1991 by Aspen Publishers.
14. Fig. 3.19b: Copyright © 2013 Depositphotos/leremy.
15. Fig. 3.22a: Copyright © 2014 Depositphotos/spatesphoto.
16. Fig. 3.22c: Copyright © 2013 Depositphotos/bentaboe.
17. Fig. 3.23: Copyright © 2015 Depositphotos/enterphoto.
18. Fig. 3.24: Copyright © Jared C. Benedict (CC BY-SA 3.0) at https://commons.wikimedia.org/wiki/File:Gears_large.jpg.
19. Fig. 3.25a: Source: https://www.rethinkingourstory.com/wp-content/uploads/2010/06/gears-300x184.gif.
20. Fig. 3.25b: Source: https://commons.wikimedia.org/wiki/File:Gears.png.
21. Fig. 3.25c: Copyright © 2014 Depositphotos/bluebright.
22. Tbl. 3.3: Source: https://en.wikipedia.org/wiki/Rolling_resistance.
23. Fig. 3.29b: Copyright © 2016 Depositphotos/xenia_ok.

4

FUNDAMENTALS OF ELECTRICAL SYSTEMS

OBJECTIVES

When you complete your study of this chapter, you will be able to:

1. Define the nature of electricity and basic electrical parameters
2. Understand and be able to use Ohm's law
3. Analyze and calculate series and parallel circuits
4. Understand electrical energy use and power, and the principle of transformers
5. Analyze and calculate three wire circuits
6. Understand the basic principle of electric power generation
7. Size conductors

INTRODUCTION

Modern society and technology heavily depend on electricity, which is crucial in everything from lighting, to electrically powered machines, equipment and tools. As a technologist, one needs to have a basic understanding of electricity, and its generation and applications, to be able to use electricity more effectively and safely.

4.1 Electric Charge, Electric Current, Electric Potential and Electric Power

Electricity is a physical phenomenon that involves movement of electrons. Understanding electricity starts with the atoms. As shown in

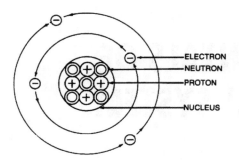

Figure 4.1: Atomic Structure

Figure 4.1, in atoms, a cloud of electrons are traveling on orbits around the nucleuses composed of protons and neutrons. The electron carries negative electrical charge, and the proton carries positive electrical charge. The neutron carries no charge. When an atom has the same numbers of electrons and protons, the atom has no net electrical charge, and hence it is *neutral*. When an atom has more electrons than protons, the atom is *negatively charged*, and when an atom has more protons than electrons, it is *positively charged*. Charged atoms are also called ions. Depending on the charges they carry, they can be categorized as anions (negatively charged) or cations (positively charged).

When electrons move from one atom to another, a microscopic electric current is produced. If by some means an abundance of electrons is created at one end of a material and a scarcity of electrons is created at the other end, a flow of electrons will travel from one end to the other resulting in a macroscopic electric current, as shown in Figure 4.2. The relative abundance and scarcity can be created by electromagnetic induction (e.g., a dynamo), electrochemical effect (e.g., a battery), thermoelectric effect, piezoelectric effect, photoelectrical and photovoltaic effect (e.g., a solar cell), or some other means. As electrons flow, they can be made to produce mechanical work (e.g., a motor), generate heat in the filament of a light bulb to incandescence (e.g., a light), transmit data to a computer, or illuminate a video screen.

To understand electricity, first we need to get to know a few important parameters and terms.

Resistance (symbol, R): Resistance characterizes how much a certain material impedes the flow of electricity. All materials have a varying amount of resistance at ambient temperature, but metals usually have a low resistance compared to other materials. At extremely low temperature, resistance of some materials drops to zero, in a phenomenon called superconductivity. Resistance is measured in Ohms (Ωs). When electrons flow through a material with nonzero resistance, heat will be generated, and electrical energy is converted to thermal energy. In electrical power transmission, this is considered as a waste of the electrical power. Hence, when electrical power is transmitted, we want to use materials with low resistance.

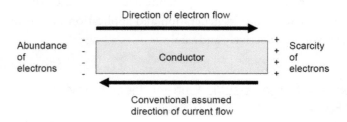

Figure 4.2: Flow of Electrical Current

Conductors and Insulators: Conductors are materials with low resistance. Most metals are conductors and the most commonly used ones are copper and aluminum. In comparison, insulators are materials with high resistance, hence electrons do not flow easily in insulators. Rubber, glass and many plastics are good insulators.

Current (symbol: I): Current is a measure of the rate of electron flow. I is the symbol for current. The unit of current is the ampere or amp (A). Here is a definition of the amp:

1 amp = 6.3×10^{18} electrons/second moving past a point. Electrical current is a flow of electrons, and it is somewhat analogous to the flow of a fluid-like water expressed in liters per second or gallons per minute.

There are two types of electrical current: direct current and alternating current. This classification is based on whether the direction of the current changes with time. A direct current (DC) system has a current that always flows at the same direction. Figure 4.3 shows a DC current which is constant with time. Although the electrical current is the flow of negatively charged electrons that goes from the negative end of a conductor (abundance of electrons) to the positive end (scarcity of electrons), the convention, due to historical reasons (the concept of electrical current was developed long before the discovery of electron!), has it that the electrical current flows from the positive end to the negative end. It should be noted though most mathematical relationships presented in this text are valid regardless of the direction of the actual electrical current.

Alternating current (AC) continually varies with time and periodically reverses direction, as shown in Figure 4.4, which usually follows a sinusoidal pattern. AC current in the USA operates at 60 Hz where it completes 60 cycles per second. Most discussion in this text will involve 60 Hz AC. It should be noted that 50 Hz AC is also widely used throughout the world, including European, African and most Asian countries.

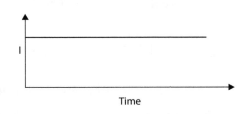

Figure 4.3: DC Current

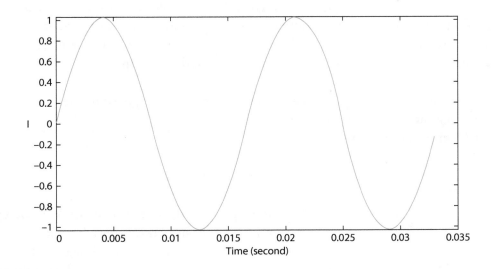

Figure 4.4. AC Current

Example 4.1: How many minutes does it take for 60 Hz AC current to complete 1 million cycles?

1,000,000 cycles*1 s/60 cycles*1 min/60 s = 278 min

Voltage (symbol, E; unit, volt, or V): voltage measures the electromotive force that drives electrons to flow through a conductor. Voltage is a measure of the potential for current flow. A voltage potential may exist between two objects without a flow of current, just like water stored in an elevated tank does not have to flow to a lower tank unless the two tanks are connected with an open channel, or a pipe. For current to flow between two objects with a voltage potential, they need to be connected by a conductor. As we discussed before, even conductors have nonzero resistance against electrical current; voltage is needed to overcome this resistance. When current flows through a resistant material, the voltage is decreased, which is usually referred to as voltage drop, or ΔE. It is necessary to maintain a ΔE across two objects if a sustained current flow is to be generated between the two objects.

Circuit: A continuous path for electrical current to flow from the source, to the load (e.g., lights, machines, appliances), and back to the source.

4.2 Simple DC Electric Circuits

4.2.1 Ohm's Law, Electrical Power and Electrical Energy

In 1823, Simon Ohm set down this relationship among the factors I, ΔE, and R:

$$I = \Delta E/R \hspace{4cm} \text{Eq. 4.1}$$

This relationship, called Ohm's Law, indicates that the current flowing in a circuit is proportional to the voltage drop between any two given points in a circuit, and inversely proportional to the resistance of the current path between the same two points. Since the three parameters are interconnected, once we know two of them, we can always find the third one.

Example 4.2: As shown in Figure 4.5, a voltage drop of 100 V is applied to a resistor of 100 Ω, what is the current flows through the resistor?

From Ohm's law, we will have:

$$I = \Delta E/R = 100\ V/100\ \Omega = 1\ A$$

By definition, power is the rate of doing work. In electricity, work is being done by the moving electrons. It is the result of the electrical potential, measured by the voltage, and the flow of the electrons. As we have seen before, the current, which is the rate of the flow of electrons, is measured by amp. Since the dot product

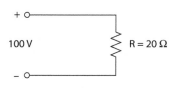

Figure 4.5: Ohm's Law

of force (i.e., the electrical potential) and velocity (i.e., the current) yields power, in electricity the product of voltage and amp yields power, with a unit of Watt (W) or kilowatt (kW). It is:

$$P = \Delta E * I \qquad\qquad \text{Eq. 4.2}$$

Using Ohm's law, we have

$$P = \Delta E^2 / R = I^2 R \qquad\qquad \text{Eq. 4.3}$$

1 watt (W) = 1 volt-amp (VA)

Electrical energy is an equivalent to work being done by the electrical current. Therefore, it equals to the electrical power multiplied by the duration of time. The most widely used unit for measuring electrical energy is kwh, or kilowatt-hour. In the power industry, kwh is the base unit on which electrical energy usage is measured and priced.

4.2.2 Series and Parallel Circuit

Electrical circuit is the path or paths of electrical current flows from the source, to loads, and back to the source. It is very useful to model actual electrical circuit with lines and symbols drawn on paper (called a circuit schematic) without having to actually construct the circuit system. figure 4.5 shows the simplest example of a circuit. It is a "close" circuit, which means that current flows through the circuit from the source, which then provides 100 V voltage to a load of 20 Ω, and back to the source. Here, a "load" means an electrical component that draws electrical power. For AC circuits, there are different types of loads: resistive, inductive, and capacitive; But for DC circuit, only resistive loads are used, called resistors, and these are electrical components that have a defined resistance. In the above mentioned example, the load has a resistance of 20 Ω. We will look at the inductive and capacitive loads in AC circuits later.

Figure 4.6 shows an example of an open circuit. Here, a switch is open, and no current flows. It needs to be noticed that for DC circuit, it is necessary for the circuit to be closed in order to have actual current.

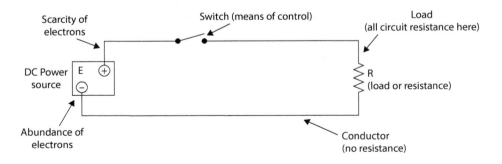

Figure 4.6: Open Circuit

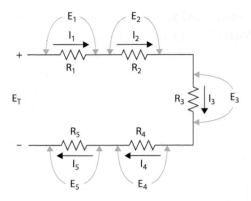

Figure 4.7: Series Circuit

In a typical circuit schematic, lines represent conductors with zero resistance. Any two points on a circuit schematic that are connected by a line are equivalent points, meaning that current runs between them with no change, and there is no voltage difference between them as well.

Two types of circuits are commonly used to supply electrical power: series and parallel.

In a series circuit, there is only one single path for the electrical current to flow; it passes every load in sequence before it comes back to the source. Hence, the current must pass through the total resistance of all the loads added together, as shown in Figure 4.7. Therefore, in a series circuit, the total resistance is the sum of the individual resistance:

$$R_T = R_1 + R_2 + R_3 + R_4 + R_5$$

A single resistor with R_T total Ohms would look exactly the same to the source as R_1 through R_5 in series put together.

As to the current, since there is no branch on its path, the same current flows through each resistor. It is the same everywhere, so we will have:

$$I_T = I_1 = I_2 = I_3 = I_4 = I_5$$

There is a voltage drop across each resistor in a series circuit. For resistor R_1, if we apply Ohm's law, we have $E_1 = I_1 R_1 = I_T R_1$. The same rule applies to each of the resistors. $E_2 = I_2 R_2 = I_T R_2, E_3 = I_3 R_3 = I_T R_3, E_4 = I_4 R_4 = I_T R_4, E_5 = I_5 R_5 = I_T R_5$. The total voltage drop, E_T, equals the sum of the voltage drops across each resistor.

$$E_T = E_1 + E_2 + E_3 + E_4 + E_5 = I_T (R_1 + R_2 + R_3 + R_4 + R_5) = I_T R_T$$

In general, for series circuit, we have:

$$E_T = E_1 + E_2 + \cdots + E_n$$
$$I_T = I_1 = I_2 = \cdots = I_n$$
$$R_T = R_1 + R_2 + \cdots + R_n$$

Eq. 4.4

And for power used, we have:

$$P_T = P_1 + P_2 + \dots + P_n = I_T^2 R_1 + I_T^2 R_2 + \dots + I_T^2 R_n = E_1^2/R_1 + E_2^2/R_2 + \dots + E_n^2/R_n \qquad \text{Eq. 4.5}$$

Loads are seldom arranged in series on power circuits in actual applications because problems encountered are as follows:

Control difficulty: If the circuit is opened to shut off one load, all the circuit loads are shut off as well. You cannot shut off just one load in a series circuit.

Load voltage: The voltage drop across any load in a series circuit is dependent on the size (resistance) of all the other loads in the circuit. Placing an additional load in a series circuit will lower the current through, the voltage across, and the power used by, all the other loads in the circuit. Removing a load will have the opposite effect. Hence, it is difficult to maintain consistent performance from loads if they are connected in series to a source.

Example 4.3: Four resistors are connected in a circuit across 230 V as shown in Figure 4.8. Calculate the total resistance and the current, the voltage drop on resistor No.2, and power used by resistor No.4.

From Eq. 4.4, $n = 4$

$R_T = R_1 + R_2 + R_3 + R_4$
    $= 60\ \Omega + 20\ \Omega + 40\ \Omega + 10\ \Omega$
    $= 130\ \Omega$
$I_T = E_T/R_T = 230\ \text{V}/\ 130\ \Omega = 1.77\ \text{A}$
$E_2 = I_T R_2 = 1.77\ \text{A} \times 10\ \Omega = 17.7\ \text{V}$
And use Eqn. 5
$P_4 = I_T^2 R_4 = (1.77\ \text{A})^2 \times 60 = 188\ \text{W}$

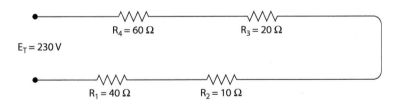

$E_T = 230\ \text{V}$

$R_4 = 60\ \Omega$ $R_3 = 20\ \Omega$

$R_1 = 40\ \Omega$ $R_2 = 10\ \Omega$

Figure 4.8: Series Circuit

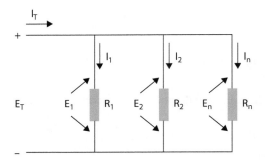

Figure 4.9: Parallel Circuit

Another type of circuit, a parallel circuit, is shown in Figure 4.9. An electron only passes through one resistor on its way from the negative electrode (−) to the positive electrode (+) of the source, since there are parallel paths available. Each resistor has the total voltage E_T across it. We have:

$$E_T = E_1 = E_2 = E_3$$

To find the current flows through each resistor, we again apply Ohm's low to each of them:

$$I_1 = E_1/R_1 = E_T/R_1$$
$$I_2 = E_2/R_2 = E_T/R_2$$
$$I_3 = E_3/R_3 = E_T/R_3$$

As the total current branches off into each of the parallel paths, and then flows back to the source, we have:

$$I_T = I_1 + I_2 + I_3 = E_T(1/R_1 + 1/R_2 + 1/R_3)$$

Now let's look at the equivalent total resistance, R_T. As seen from the source, $I_T = E_T/R_T$, where R_T is the resistance of a single resistor that is equivalent to the entire parallel circuit. Hence, $E_T/R_T = E_T(1/R_1 + 1/R_2 + 1/R_3)$, which leads to:
$1/R_T = 1/R_1 + 1/R_2 + 1/R_3$

In general, for parallel circuit, we have:

$$E_T = E_1 = E_2 = \cdots = E_n$$
$$I_T = I_1 + I_2 + \cdots + I_n$$
$$\frac{1}{R_T} = \frac{1}{R_1} + \frac{1}{R_2} + \cdots + \frac{1}{R_n}$$

Eq. 4.6

And for power used by each load, we have:

$$P_T = P_1 + P_2 + \ldots + P_n = E_T^2/R_1 + E_T^2/R_2 + \ldots + E_T^2/R_n = I_1^2 R_1 + I_2^2/R_2 + \ldots + I_n^2 R_n \quad \text{Eq. 4.7}$$

Example 4.4: Two resistors are connected in parallel to a source of 100 V as shown in Figure 4.10. Calculate I_1, I_2, I_T, R_T and P_1

$I_1 = E_T/R_1 = 100\text{ V}/20\ \Omega = 5\text{ A}$
$I_2 = E_T/R_2 = 100\text{ V}/50\ \Omega = 2\text{ A}$
$I_T = I_1 + I_2 = 7\text{ A}$
$1/R_T = 1/R_1 + 1/R_2 = 1/20\ \Omega + 1/50\ \Omega = 7/100\ \Omega$
$\Rightarrow R_T = 100\ \Omega/7 = 14.3\ \Omega$
$P_1 = E_T{}^2/R_1 = 100\ V^2/20\ \Omega = 500\text{ W}$

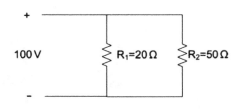

Figure 4.10. Parallel Circuit

4.2.3 Terminal Voltage

The work done by the electrical current when it passes through a resistor results in the conversion of the electrical energy into heat. During this process, a voltage drop occurs across the resistor. A resistor converts electrical energy into heat regardless of the direction of the current. This means when it comes to generating heat, there is no difference between DC and AC currents.

Current can travel in either direction through a voltage source, such as a battery. When the current moves from the negative to the positive terminal, some other forms of energy (e.g., mechanical, chemical) is converted into electrical energy. If a higher potential is being imposed in the external circuit to force the current to flow backward through the voltage source, the electrical energy would be converted to some other form. For instance, in rechargeable batteries, when current is sent backward through the batteries, electrical energy is converted back into chemical energy, that at a later time can be reconverted back into electrical energy, and this is the recharging process for the battery.

In a battery or a generator, with current flowing negative to positive, the potential at the positive terminal will be E added to the potential at the negative terminal, minus the voltage drop due to internal resistance between terminals. There always will be some energy converted to heat inside a battery or generator, which is unrecoverable.

When a voltage source is driving the circuit, the internal current passes from the negative to the positive terminal. If the internal current is at I, with an internal resistance R, then the voltage being applied to the external circuit would be E-IR, where E is the voltage of the source.

Figure 4.11 shows a circuit wherein a battery is being charged by a generator. E_G, E_B, R_G and R_B indicate the potentials and internal resistances of the generator and battery, respectively. Electrons gaining energy E_G from the generator will lose E_B to the battery, and along the way heat is generated at IR_G, IR_1, IR_B and IR_2 as well.

4.2.4 Kirchhoff's Laws and Combination Circuits

Series and parallel circuits can be combined to create circuit networks, or combination circuits. To analyze

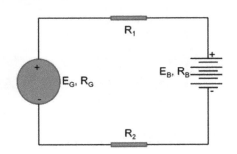

Figure 4.11: Generator Charging a Battery

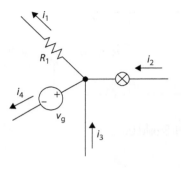

Figure 4.12: Current Entering a Node Must Equal to Current Leaving the Node $i_2 + i_3 = i_1 + i_4$

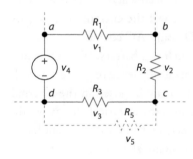

Figure 4.13: The Sum of All the Voltages Around the Loop is Equal to Zero. $v_1 + v_2 + v_3 - v_4 = 0$

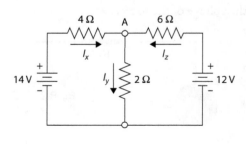

Figure 4.14: Application of KCL and KVL

such a network, we will use Kirchhoff's network laws. There are two laws, addressing current and voltage, respectively.

Kirchhoff's Current Law (KCL):
The sum of all of the currents coming into a node (junction point on a circuit path) must be equal to the currents coming out of the same node.

Kirchhoff's Voltage Law (KVL):
The sum of the voltages around any closed loop in a network equals zero.

Using these two laws, DC circuit networks can be analyzed and calculated.

Example 4.5: Given the circuit illustrated in Figure 4.14, determine the currents I_x, I_y, and I_z

At point A, using KAL, we have: $I_y = I_x + I_z$

Apply KVL at the left loop, in a clockwise fashion;
$I_x * (4\Omega) + I_y * (2\Omega) = 14$ V (this is the voltage of the left loop source)

Apply KVL at the right loop, again in a clockwise fashion;
$-I_z * (6\Omega) + 12$ V $-I_y * (2\Omega) = 0$ (the right loop source is at 12 V)

When we solve these three equations for three unknowns, we will find:
$I_x = 2$ A, $I_y = 3$ A, $I_z = 1$ A

Note: you may choose counterclockwise direction to analyze the voltage, as it will not change the results!

Example 4.6: Given the circuit illustrated in Figure 4.15, determine i_1, i_2, and i_3, where $R_1 = 100\Omega$, $R_2 = 200\Omega$, $R_3 = 300\Omega$; $e_1 = 30$ V, and $e_2 = 40$ V
At the node, using KCL, we have $i_1 = i_2 + i_3$
Apply KVL at the top loop, in a clockwise fashion;
$i_2 *(200\Omega) + i_1 *(100\Omega) = 30$ V $(e1)$
Apply KVL at the bottom loop, in a clockwise fashion;
$I_3 * (300\Omega) + 40$ V $(e2) + 30$ V $(e1) = i_2 * (200\ \Omega)$

Solving the three equations, we have:

$I_1 = 1/110$ A

$I_2 = 16/110$ A

$I_3 = -15/110$ A

According to this result, the direction of i_3 is actually the opposite of what is showing (assumed) in Figure 4.15!

4.3 AC Circuits and Transformers

4.3.1 AC Circuits

For an AC circuit, the flow of electric charges periodically reverses direction. In addition to resistive loads, there can be inductive and capacitive components as well.

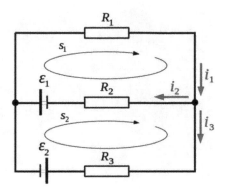

Figure 4.15: Application of KCL and KVL

An inductive component, or an inductor, is an electrical component that resists changes in electric current passing through it. It consists of a conductor such as a wire, usually wound into a coil. Figure 4.16 shows typical inductors. For DC current, because the current flowing through an inductor is not changing, an inductor behaves just like a regular conductor, with usually very small resistance that can be neglected in circuit analysis. However, in an AC circuit, the current is changing over time. When a current flows through an inductor, energy is stored temporarily in a magnetic field in the coil. As the current changes, the time-varying magnetic field induces a voltage in the conductor, which opposes the change in current that created it.

An inductor is characterized by its inductance, the ratio of the voltage to the rate of change of current, which has units of henries (H). Inductors have values that typically range from 1 μH (10^{-6}H) to 1 H. Many inductors have a magnetic core made of iron or ferrite inside the coil, which serves to increase the magnetic field and thus the inductance. Inductors are widely used in alternating current (AC) electronic equipment, particularly in radio equipment. They are used to block AC while allowing DC to pass. They are also used in electronic filters to separate signals of different frequencies, and in combination with capacitors to make tuned circuits, which are used to tune radio and TV receivers.

A capacitive component, or a capacitor, is another electrical component that is used to store energy electrostatically in an electric field. The forms of practical capacitors vary widely, but all contain at least two electrical conductors (plates) separated by a dielectric (i.e. insulator), as shown in Figure 4.17. In a DC circuit, after the initial charging stage, capacitors are just open circuits with no

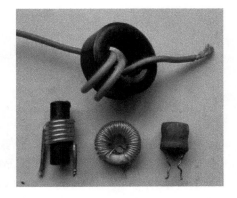

Figure 4.16: Inductors

Fixed Capacitor   Polarized Capacitor   Variable Capacitor

Figure 4.17: Capacitors

current flowing. In an AC circuit, the change of the current direction results in capacitors being charged or discharged with alternating ± charge accumulation on both conductors, and a current flowing through it.

An ideal capacitor is characterized by a single constant value for its capacitance. Capacitance is expressed as the ratio of the electric charge Q on each conductor, to the potential difference V between them. The SI unit of capacitance is the farad (F), which is equal to one coulomb per volt (1 C/V). Typical capacitance values range from about 1 pF (10^{-12} F) to about 1 mF (10^{-3} F). Capacitors are widely used in electronic circuits for blocking direct current, while allowing alternating current to pass. In analog filter networks, they smooth the output of power supplies. In resonant circuits, they tune radios to particular frequencies. In electric power transmission systems, they stabilize voltage and power flow.

Resistors, inductors, and capacitors are the three basic passive linear circuit elements that make up electric circuits. In AC circuit, when there are inductors and capacitors, not all the energy delivered to loads will be used, because part of it will be stored in the inductors and capacitors. Therefore, a power factor (PF) is often used as a characteristic of the load and is always between 0 and 1. It is the fraction of the total power carried by the conductors to the load, which is used by the load. (The power not used is momentarily stored by the load and then passed back to the generator). If the load is resistive, PF = 1.

$$PF = P/IE \hspace{8cm} \text{Eq. 4.8}$$

Where P is the power being used by the load, I is the current flowing through the load, and E is the voltage across the load.

Figure 4.18 will help to explain the concept of power factor. Both voltage and current vary with time in AC. If the load is a resistor, voltage and current peaks are in sync and they occur at the same time, as shown in Figure 4.18a. Since peaks are in sync, at any time the instantaneous voltage and instantaneous current always have the same sign (positive or negative) and their product, p, (the instantaneous power) is always positive. Positive power is power going from the source to loads. A load like a motor (which is also inductive) causes current to fall behind voltage (Figure 4.18b), because a magnetic field is produced by the inductive component of the motor. The building and collapsing of this field at a frequency of 120 Hz is what causes current to lag voltage. When this happens, the

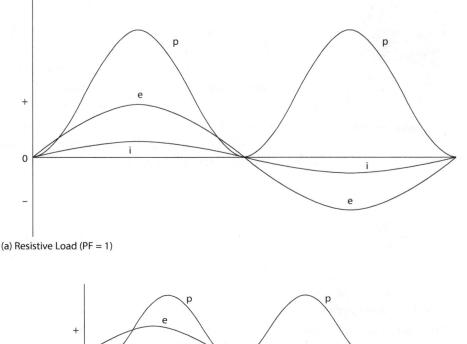

(a) Resistive Load (PF = 1)

(b) Motor Load (PF < 1)

i = instantaneous current
e = instantaneous voltage
p = instantaneous power = ie

Figure 4.18: AC Time Relations

voltage and current peaks are no longer in sync. Hence, during a portion of the cycle, instantaneous voltage and instantaneous current have different signs. Since the product of two numbers of different signs is negative, this means p is negative, indicating that power is going from the load back to the source during this portion of the cycle. During periods of negative power, energy stored in the magnetic field is flowing back toward the source. A power factor less than 1.0 indicates that more current is flowing to the load than is required to supply the actual power used by the load. If the power factor of a load is increased (with no other change), the power used by the load stays the same, but the current to the load is reduced.

Example 4.7: What is the power factor of a load which draws 900. W and 15 A when connected across 110 V?

$PF = P/IE = 900 \text{ W}/(15 \text{ A}*110 \text{ V}) = 0.55$
For an AC circuit, at any given time, and on average, Ohm's law holds for resistive loads.

Figure 4.19. Electromagnetic Induction

4.3.2 Electromagnetic Induction and Faraday's Law

Electromagnetic induction is the production of an electromotive force across a conductor when it is exposed to a varying magnetic field. It is described mathematically by Faraday's law of induction, named after Michael Faraday, who discovered electromagnetic induction in 1831. As shown in Figure 4.19, when a magnet is being moved into and out of a closed circuit loop, a voltage will be generated between the two terminals of the loop.

Faraday's law of induction can be expressed as:

$$Voltage\ generated = -N\frac{\Delta(BA)}{\Delta t}$$

Eq. 4.9

Where N is the winding number of the circuit loop (i.e., how many turns of conductors are wrapped around the core), B is the intensity of the magnetic field. When B is multiplied by the cross section area (A) of the circuit loop, a quantity called magnetic flux is created. The magnetic flux describes essentially how much of a magnetic field is going through a given surface. Faraday's law of induction allows us to calculate how much electricity can be generated by altering the magnetic flux going through a closed loop. It is the governing principle of how an electrical generator works.

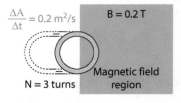

Figure 4.20: Electromagnetic Induction

Example 4.8: As shown in Figure 4.20, a closed loop with a winding number of 3 is moving into a magnetic field with $B = 0.2$ T. If the across area of the loop exposed to the magnetic field is changing at 0.2 m²/s, what is the voltage being generated inside the loop?

Here B is constant, and A is changing at 0.2 m²/s, hence, $\Delta(BA)/\Delta t = B\Delta A/\Delta t = 0.04$ Tm²/s

Using Faraday's law of induction, $N = 3$, we have
$E = -3*0.04$ V $= -0.12$ V

4.3.3 Transformers

Today most electric power is produced and transmitted as AC. One reason for this is the ease of changing AC voltage using transformers. This convenience arises from the electromagnetic induction. A transformer is a device that transfers energy between two or more circuits through electromagnetic induction. A simple transformer circuit is illustrated in Figure 4.21. The winding connected to the AC power source is usually called primary winding, and the winding used to deliver power to loads is called secondary winding. The windings are electrically insulated, so that there is no current conducted to the iron core, or from one winding to the other. However, the magnetic flux is running through the iron core. In other words, the magnetic flux at the primary winding side and the secondary winding side is the same, and it changes in sync with the AC current flowing in the primary winding. According to Faraday's law of induction, when the change of magnetic flux, $\Delta BA/\Delta t$, is the same, and the voltage generated is only dependent on the winding number, N. This simple fact dictates how a transformer works.

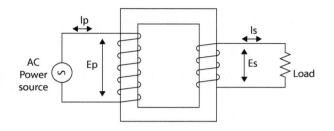

Figure 4.21: Transformer

$$\frac{E_p}{E_s} = \frac{N_p}{N_s}$$

Eq. 4.10

Where, E_p and E_s are the voltage in the primary and secondary windings; and N_p and N_s are the winding numbers of the primary and secondary windings, respectively.

The power being transmitted from the primary winding to the secondary winding, if we neglect the small portion that is being converted to heat due to the resistance of the conductors, remains a constant, a 100% power efficiency. Hence, we have

$$P = I_p E_p = I_s E_s$$

Eq. 4.11

Where I_p and I_s are the current in the primary and secondary windings. For transformers, the power efficiency is usually about 97% to 99%.

Example 4.9: Given a transformer has 72,000 turns at the primary winding, it is used to transform the 7200 V from the power grid at the primary side to 120 V at a consumer service panel. A load of 20 Ω is connected to the service panel.

1. What should the winding number be at the secondary side?
2. What is the current at the primary side?

Solution: We first decide the winding number of the secondary side, using equation 10.

$$\frac{E_p}{E_s} = \frac{N_p}{N_s} \Rightarrow \frac{7200}{120} = \frac{72000}{N_s} \Rightarrow N_s = 1200 \text{turns}$$

Now, let's take a look at the current at the secondary side, using Ohm's law:

$$I_s = E_s / R_s = 120 \text{ V}/20 \text{ }\Omega = 6 \text{ A}$$
$$\text{Hence, we have } P_s = E_s I_s = 120 \text{ V}*6 \text{ A} = 720 \text{ W}$$

Using Equation 11, we have:

$$P_p = P_s = 720 \text{ W}$$
$$\text{And } I_p = P_p / E_p = 0.1 \text{ A}$$

In the US, the commonly used voltages in a power grid are 7,200 V, 12,470 V, 25,000V, and 34,500 V. The advantage of using higher voltage for power transmission over long distance is better illustrated by an example:

Example 4.10: 1.0 kW power is to be transmitted from a power distribution station to consumers over a long distance. Resistance of the conductor wire is 3.2 Ω (10 km of size 0 copper wire). What is the power being wasted by the wire itself, if:

1. 7,200 V AC is used?
2. 120 V AC is used?

First, we calculate current through the wire:

$$I_1 = P/E_1 = 1000 \text{ W}/7200 \text{ V} = 0.13 \text{ A}$$
$$I_2 = P/E_2 = 1000 \text{ W}/120 \text{ V} = 8.3 \text{ A}$$

The conductor wire is connected to the load via series circuit, hence, the power consumed by the wire is:

$$P_1 = I_1^2 R_{wire} = (0.13 \text{ }A^2)*3.2\Omega = 0.054 \text{ W}$$
$$P_2 = I_2^2 R_{wire} = (8.3 \text{ }A^2)*3.2\Omega = 220 \text{ W}$$

Apparently, using higher voltage for power transmission dramatically reduces the power wasted on the conductor wire! This is why AC is chosen over DC for power transmission. With the help of transformers, we can easily increase the voltage for transmission, and then bring it down again for consumer usage.

4.3.4 Three-Wire Circuits

The most common type of electrical service provided by electric power companies in the US is the 3-wire, 120/240 V type. A schematic illustration of the 3-wire setup is shown in Figure 4.22. A

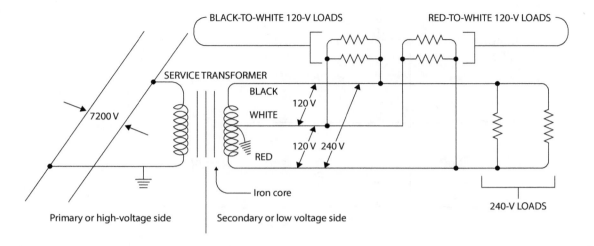

Figure 4.22: Three-Wire Circuit

transformer is used to bring the voltage from the power grid (e.g., 7,200 V as shown) down to the desired values. At the user's end, either 120 V or 240 V can be obtained depending on the actual need of the appliance and device being used.

Notice:
- The service originates from a distribution line which typically operates with 7200 V to ground.
- The service transformer cuts this voltage to 240-volts.
- A wire or lead call a center tap is brought out half-way between the ends of the secondary side of the transformer, providing two voltages of 120-volts each.
- If the secondary side wires are colored, they are BLACK, RED and WHITE.
- The WHITE (center tap) is called a neutral conductor, since it is connected to and at the same voltage as the ground.
- The BLACK and RED conductors are "hot" since there are 240-volts between them, and 120-volts from either of them to the WHITE or neutral.
- 240-volt loads connect between the BLACK and the RED.
- 120-volt loads connect between either the BLACK and WHITE, or RED and WHITE.

To analyze a 3-wire circuit, we need to realize a few facts:
1. All appliances/devices (i.e., loads) are connected into 3-wire circuits in parallel. This significantly simplifies our analysis. Depending on the way that a load is being connected, it will draw either 120 V or 240 V across it.
2. To obtain current in black, red and white wires, we apply Kirchhoff's current law (KCL); at each junction point, the total current flows into it always equal to the total current flows out of it.

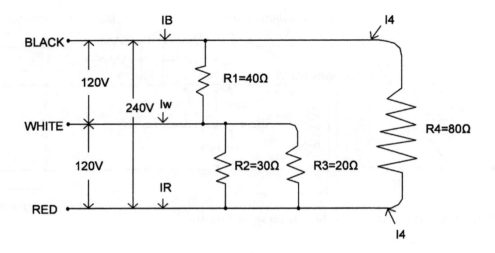

Figure 4.23: Three-wire Circuit

Example 4.11: Consider the circuit in Figure 4.23, and find the currents in the black, white and red wires.

Solution: First, we calculate the current in all four loads:

$$I_1 \frac{E_1}{R_1} = \frac{120}{40} = 3A \quad I_2 = \frac{E_2}{R_2} = \frac{120}{30} = 4A \quad I_3 = \frac{E_3}{R_3} = \frac{120}{20} = 6A \quad I_4 = \frac{E_4}{R_4} = \frac{120}{80} = 3A$$

Next, the black wire is the only source of current for loads 1 and 4, hence,

$$I_B = I_1 + I_4 = 3 + 3 = 6A$$

Similarly, the red wire is the only source of current for loads 2, 3 and 4, hence,

$$I_R = I_2 + I_3 + I_4 = 4 + 6 + 3 = 13A$$

To find the current in the white, we need to assign current directions. The service transformer winding is the source of all load currents. This winding carries AC current. We'll look at it at the instant when current is flowing up, as shown in the figure:

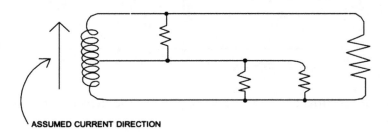

ASSUMED CURRENT DIRECTION

With the current flowing up, currents through all loads must be as shown:

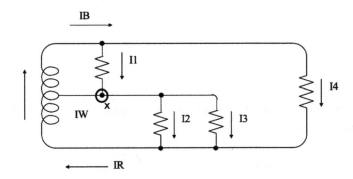

Now, examine what happens at point X, and apply Kirchhoff's current law (KCL). We can hypothetically assign a direction to I_w, and supposing it flows out of point x, we will have:

$$I_W + I_2 + I_3 = I_1$$
$$I_W = I_1 - I_2 - I_3 = 3 - 6 - 4 = -7\,A$$

The negative sign means the actual direction of I_w is the opposite of what we have assigned. It flows into point *x*, not out of it.

Now, we have another solution:

$$I_B = 6\,A\ \ I_R = 13\,A\ \ I_W = 7A$$

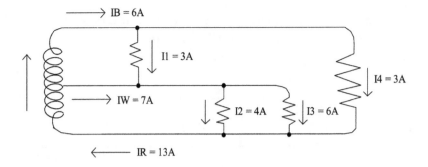

It should be noted that current in the white wire equals to the difference between I_B and I_R. Or, we can write it as:

$$I_W = |I_R - I_B|$$
Eq. 4.12

When current in the red and black wires is equal, there is no current in the white wire. In this case, the circuit is called balanced, which is desirable.

4.4 Electric Power Generation

There are seven methods based on different physical principles that can be used to transform other forms of energy into electricity:

- Static electricity, from the physical separation and transport of charge (examples: triboelectric effect and lightning)
- Electromagnetic induction, where an electrical generator, dynamo or alternator transforms kinetic energy (energy of motion) into electricity. This is the most used form for generating electricity and is based on Faraday's law of induction. In its simplest form, rotating a magnet within closed loops of a conducting material (e.g. copper wire) will create a current running through the loop.
- Electrochemistry, the direct transformation of chemical energy into electricity, as in a battery, fuel cell or nerve impulse.
- Photovoltaic effect, the transformation of light into electrical energy, as in solar cells.
- Thermoelectric effect, the direct conversion of temperature differences to electricity, as in thermocouples, thermopiles, and thermionic converters.
- Piezoelectric effect, from the mechanical strain of electrically anisotropic molecules or crystals.
- Nuclear transformation, the creation and acceleration of charged particles.

- Among these methods, large-scale electricity generation can be produced via electromagnetic induction or photovoltaic effect. These are the two methods we will discuss in more details here.

4.4.1 Electricity Generation through Electromagnetic Induction

According to Faraday's law of induction, when a relative motion exists between a closed circuit loop and a magnetic field that creates a continuous change of magnetic flux through the circuit loop, an electrical current will be generated in the loop. This is the basic principle of electricity generation

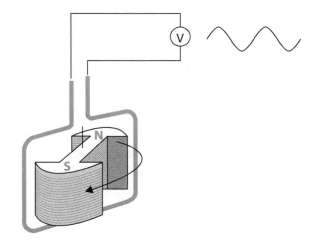

Figure 4.24: Mechanism of an AC Generator

through electromagnetic induction. When a permanent magnet is moved relative to a conductor, or vice versa, an electromotive force is created. If the wire is connected through an electrical load, current will flow, and thus electrical power is generated, converting the mechanical energy of motion to electrical energy. An example is illustrated in Figure 4.24 as an AC generator (i.e., an alternator). Here, a permanent magnet rotates at an angular velocity of ω inside a closed wire loop. The motion of the magnet creates a relative motion between the wire loop and the magnet, causing the wire loop to cut through the magnetic field, which creates electromotive force that drives electrons to flow.

To keep the wire loop in motion, mechanical work needs to be done to overcome the resistant force that will be created due to the induced electromagnetic field. When a current flows, it will generate a magnetic field. In the generator example shown in Figure 4.24, the interaction between the permanent magnetic field and the induced magnetic field will cause the motion of the wire loop to slow down and eventually stop. In order to maintain the relation motion, mechanical work needs to be done to the wire loop to keep it going. This mechanical work can be generated in a variety of ways: in a gas turbine, burning of natural gas produces steam that drives the relative motion; in a hydroelectric generator or wind generator, it is the hydropower or wind that drives the relative motion; in nuclear reactors, it is the nuclear fission reaction that heats up water to produce steam that drives the relative motion. No matter how the relative motion is driven, the basic principle remains the same: Through electromagnetic induction, kinetic (mechanical) energy is transformed into electrical power.

Both DC and AC current can be generated using electromagnetic induction. In AC generation, an alternator is usually used with a moving magnet as shown in figure 4.24. As the magnet rotates, a voltage is generated that has alternating directions in sync with the motion of the magnet. The frequency of the AC voltage/current is determined by the rotational speed of the magnet.

$$f = N \times P/120 \hspace{5cm} \text{Eq. 4.13}$$

Where N is the rotational speed of the magnet measured in RPM, P is the number of poles of the stationary wire loop (e.g., in Figure 4.24, $P = 2$). With equation 12, we can determine that to produce a 60 Hz AC, with a simple setup as shown in Figure 4.24, the magnet needs to be rotated at 3,600 RPM.

4.4.2 Photovoltaic Effect and Solar Panel

As the world is paying more attention to renewable electricity generation to mitigate climate change, photovoltaic electricity generation has become more widely adopted. The photovoltaic effect is the creation of voltage or electric current in a material upon exposure to light. The standard photovoltaic effect is directly related to the photoelectric effect. When the sunlight or any other light is incident upon a material surface, the electrons present in the material absorb energy and become free. These free electrons diffuse, and some reach a junction where they are accelerated, and enter into a different material by a built-in potential (Galvani potential). This generates an electromotive force, and thus some of the light energy is converted into electric energy. The photovoltaic effect can also occur when two photons are absorbed simultaneously in a process called two-photon photovoltaic effect.

Besides the direct excitation of free electrons, a photovoltaic effect can also arise simply due to the heating caused by absorption of the light. The heating leads to an increase in temperature, which is accompanied by temperature gradients. These thermal gradients, in turn, may generate a voltage through the Seebeck effect. Whether direct excitation, or thermal effects dominate the photovoltaic effect will depend on the properties of the material.

In most photovoltaic applications the radiation is sunlight, and the devices are called solar cells. In the case of a p-n junction solar cell, illuminating the material creates an electric current as excited electrons and the remaining holes are swept in different directions by the built-in electric field of the depletion region, as shown in Figure 4.25.

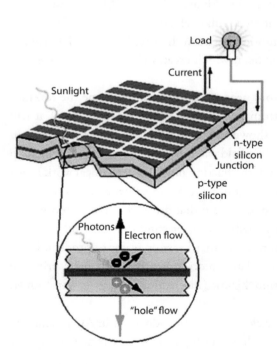

Figure 4.25: Mechanism of a Solar Panel

4.5 Conductor Design

4.5.1 Conductor and Insulator Materials

In the previous section when we discussed circuit analysis, we assumed that the resistance of the conductor itself is negligible. While in circuit analysis this approach is appropriate, in practical applications we will have to take the small but nonzero resistance of the conductors into consideration. This section discusses the real world scenario and how to select conductors to meet your needs.

Conductors made of materials having atoms with loosely held outer-orbit electrons exhibit the least resistance to electron flow. These electrons are called in the conducting band. Most metals are in this category, being characterized by having only one or two electrons in their outer-most orbits and can move into conducting band easily.

The resistance of a length of conductor depends on the physical properties of the material, the length, and the cross-sectional area of the conductor (Equation 4.14):

$$R = \rho\, L\, /A \qquad\qquad\qquad \text{Eq. 4.14}$$

Where R is the resistance of the conductor (Ωs), ρ is a material property called resistivity of the material, (it is usually measured in Ω-cmil/ft), L is the length of the conductor (ft), and A is the cross-sectional area of the conductor measured by circular mil, or cmil. A circular mil is a unit of area, equal to the area of a circle with a diameter of one mil (1 mil = 1/1000 inch). It corresponds to 5.067×10^{-4} mm^2. It is a unit intended for referring to the area of a wire with a circular cross section. As the area in circular mils can be calculated without reference to π, the unit makes conversion between cross section and diameter of a wire considerably easier. The area in circular mils, A, of a circle with a diameter of d mils, is given by the formula:

$$A = d^{2} \qquad\qquad\qquad \text{Eq. 4.15}$$

Electricians in Canada and the United States are familiar with the circular mil because the National Electrical Code (NEC) uses the circular mil to define wire sizes larger than 0000 AWG.

Equation 4.14 indicates that, once the material is set, the longer a conductor, the larger the resistance; and the thicker the conductor, the smaller the resistance. This is the basic rule for conductor selection.

Table 4.1 shows the resistivity of common conducting materials at 20°C. Taking into account the cost of and availability of materials, copper and aluminum are the mostly widely used conducting materials for wiring applications. Silver and gold sometimes are also used in high-end electrical products.

Example 4.12: Calculate the resistance of an aluminum rod 50. ft long, and 1.0 in in diameter. We first calculate the across sectional area in cmil:

$A = (1.0 \times 10^3 \text{ mil})^2 = 1.0 \times 10^6 \text{ cmil}$
Then, using equation 13, with $L = 50.$ ft, and $\rho = 17.01$ Ω-cmil/ft
$R = 17.01$ Ω-cmil/ft $\times 50.$ ft $/ (1.0 \times 10^6 \text{ cmil}) = 8.5 \times 10^{-4}$ Ω

In addition, to provide a low resistance path for electric current, a good conductor design must also employ a high resistance covering or barrier to prevent electric current from leaving its intended path. The high resistance of this insulating material also arises from its atomic structure. In this case, the outer orbits are nearly full, and electrons may be drawn out of orbit only with difficulty.

Table 4.1: Resistivity of Common Conducting Materials at 20 °C

MATERIALS	RESISTIVITY, Ω-CMIL/FT
Silver	9.55
Copper	10.37
Gold	14.7
Aluminum	17.01
Tungsten	33.10
Platinum	66.9
Steel	100
Lead	129
Cast Iron	360
Mercury	577

The resistivity of insulating materials is much greater than that of conductors. Common values are on the order of 10^7 ohm cmil/ft. The quality of an insulating material, however, is usually not measured by its resistivity since this property varies greatly from sample to sample, and also varies according to what voltage is impressed across the material. Insulating materials are usually compared by their dielectric strength (Table 4.2). This is the voltage per mil of thickness at which their resistance suddenly reaches a breakdown point and they become conductors.

Example 4.13: A piece of Bakelite 0.012 inches thick separates two conductors in a switch. Voltage between the two conductors is 240 V. Will the Bakelite conduct current?

The Bakelite will conduct current if it reaches its breakdown point. From Table 4.2, we have the dielectric strength of Bakelite is 500 V/mil. Hence, for a piece that is 12 mil thick, its breakdown voltage E can be determined as:

$$E = 500 \text{ V/mil} \times 12 \text{ mil} = 6000 \text{ V}$$

Here, the voltage is only 240 V, far less than the breakdown voltage of 6000 V. Therefore, the Bakelite won't conduct current and the two conductors are safely insulated from each other.

Table 4.2: Dielectric Strength of Some Common Insulating Materials

MATERIALS	DIELECTRIC STRENGTH, V/MIL
Air	80
Bakelite	500
Glass	200
Mica	2000
Paraffined paper	1200
porcelain	750
Poly-vinyl chloride (PVC)	375

4.5.2 Conductor Sizes

Conductor sizes in the US are specified by an AWG or kcmil size designation (Tables 4.3 and 4.4) AWG stands for American Wire Gauge. AWG numbers run from 40 to 0000, with the larger the AWG gauge number, the thinner the conductor. The AWG gauges commonly used in electrical wiring are listed in tables 3 and 4, for copper and aluminum, 14 through 0000.

Table 4.3: Conductor Reference Table, Copper (Bern and Olson, 2002)

SIZE (AWG)	AREA (CM)	USUAL NUMBER OF STRANDS	DIAMETER EACH STRAND, (INCHES)	AMPACITY (AMPS)	WEIGHT (LB/1000 FT)	RESISTANCE (Ω/1000 FT)
14	4110	1	0.064	15	12.5	3.07
12	6530	1	0.081	20	19.8	1.93
10	10380	1	0.102	30	31.4	1.21
8	16510	1	0.128	40	50.0	0.764
6	26240	1	0.061	50	79.4	0.491
4	41740	7	0.077	70	126	0.308
3	52620	7	0.087	80	159	0.245
2	66360	7	0.097	90	205	0.194
1	83690	7	0.066	100	259	0.154
0	105600	19	0.074	115	326	0.122
00	133100	19	0.084	130	411	0.0967
000	167800	19	0.094	150	518	0.0766
0000	211600	19	0.106	175	653	0.0608

Table 4.4: Conductor Reference Table, Aluminum (Bern and Olson, 2002)

SIZE (AWG)	AREA (CM)	USUAL NUMBER OF STRANDS	DIAMETER EACH STRAND, (INCHES)	AMPACITY (AMPS)	WEIGHT (LB/1000 FT)	RESISTANCE (Ω/1000 FT)
14	4110	1	0.064	10	3.8	5.06
12	6530	1	0.081	15	6.0	3.18
10	10380	1	0.102	25	9.6	2.00
8	16510	1	0.128	30	15.2	1.26
6	26240	1	0.061	40	24.6	0.808
4	41740	7	0.077	50	38.4	0.508
3	52620	7	0.087	60	48.4	0.403
2	66360	7	0.097	70	62.3	0.319
1	83690	7	0.066	80	78.6	0.253
0	105600	19	0.074	100	99.1	0.201
00	133100	19	0.084	115	125	0.159
000	167800	19	0.094	130	157	0.126
0000	211600	19	0.106	150	199	0.100

4.5.3 Conductor Design

To select a conductor to meet specific needs, three factors need to be considered:

- Environment in which the conductor will be placed. This is mostly related to what type of insulator needs to be used to coat the conductor;
- Amperage capacity (i.e., ampacity) of the conductor. This is to ensure that the conductor selected has enough capacity to sustain required current;
- Voltage drop: This is to ensure that when the voltage drop that occurred on the conductor is taken into account, enough voltage can still be delivered to the loads.

We will now look at these three requirements in more details.

4.5.3.1 Environment Requirement

The environment determines what kind of insulator coating the conductor needs. This is specified by the conductor or cable type designation. In most cases, this is printed on the insulator coat.

Table 4.5: Common Insulated Conductor and Cable Types (Bern and Olson, 2002)

INSULATOR DESIGNATION	TRADE NAME	TEMPERATURE RATING*	DESCRIPTION
YHHN	Heat resistant thermoplastic	90 °C	Flame retardant, heat resistant thermoplastic insulated individual conductors. For use in conduit, dry and damp locations. Available in several colors.
THWN	Moisture and heat resistant thermoplastic	75 °C	Flame retardant, moisture and heat resistant, thermoplastic insulated individual conductors. For use in conduit, dry and wet locations. Available in several colors.
NM**	Non-metallic sheathed cable	60 °C	Two or three conductors (plus bare grounding conductor) in a moisture-resistant, flame-retardant non-metallic sheath. For use in normally dry locations. Cannot be embedded in poured concrete or used as service entrance cable. Use in family dwellings not exceeding 3 floors above grade and other structures. Can be used exposed or concealed.
SE	Service entrance cable	75 °C	Commonly 3 conductors in a flame retardant, moisture-resistant covering. The neutral is braided around the two energized conductors. Type SE is used primarily between an above-ground point of attachment and the service entrance panel.
USE	Underground service entrance cable	75 °C	Single conductors cabled into an uncovered assembly for direct burial as a feeder or branch circuit or service lateral. Covering is moisture resistant but not necessarily flame retardant, or protective against mechanical abuse.
UF**	Underground feeder cable	60 °C	Two or three conductors (plus bare grounding conductor) with a flame-retardant moisture-, fungus-, corrosion-resistant covering for direct burial as a feeder or branch circuit. Also used for interior wiring in wet, dry, or corrosive locations. Used in livestock buildings. Cannot be exposed to direct sunlight unless label specifies "Sunlight Resistant." Cannot be used as service entrance cable. Cannot be embedded in poured concrete.
Multiplex	Overhead feeder	90 °C	Two or three insulated aluminum conductors wound around a bare stranded messenger which serves as a neutral, and supports the assembly. The messenger contains one steel strand for strength. For use as overhead feeders. Conductors are usually XHHW (Surbrook and Mullin 1985).

* Highest temperature that the conductor can be safely used for extended period of time without insulator degradation
** NM and UF may be marked as NM-B and UF-B. This marking means the conductors within the cable are rated at 90 °C. For the purpose of ampacity, the temperature rating of the cable remains 60°C.

Common conductor types, along with their uses and temperature ratings, are listed in table 4.5. Many, many more are available for particular applications.

It is possible that the environment will dictate conductor size for overhead spans, mainly due to the tensile strength needed to sustain the weight of the cable. The National Electrical Code (NFPA 1998) rules are simple: Conductors for overhead spans shall not be smaller than AWG 10 copper or AWG 8 aluminum for spans up to 50 feet, and not smaller than AWG 8 copper or AWG 6 aluminum for longer spans, unless supported by a messenger wire (NEC 225-6).

Selection of conductor type and insulation is very important since the life of the conductor or cable almost always corresponds to the life of the insulator coat. Conductors never wear out or run out of electrons as long as they are protected by insulation. Insulator coat, however, deteriorates over time. Insulator reacts with oxygen and other chemicals in its surroundings, like ammonia and other manure gases, oil, gasoline, salts, and water. Some of these materials can also react with and corrode conductors if insulator is broken. For example, buried aluminum cable rapidly corrodes and fails if its insulator coat is punctured. The rate of reaction increases with temperature, and approximately doubles when temperature rises 10°C. Direct solar radiation also can speed up deterioration. In choosing insulator, the least expensive type which meets environmental requirements is desired from an economic standpoint.

4.5.3.2 Ampacity Requirement

The ampacity of a conductor is its current carrying capacity in amps. Ampacity depends on conductor resistance, the allowable operating temperature of the insulation, and the heat dissipation capability of the conductor. All conductors carrying current produce heat as their own resistance converts electrical energy into heat. The heat generated must be transferred to the environment. Conductors which carry currents at or below their ampacities will operate at a temperature cool enough to ensure a full, useful life. Ampacities of several conductor and cable types are listed in Table 4.3 (copper) and 4.4 (aluminum).

Several things can be noted from these tables. Refer to the ampacity section of Table 4.3:

- Ampacity increases with conductor size (AWG 14 can carry 15 amps, while AWG 0000 can carry 175 amps).
- Ampacity for copper is higher than ampacity for aluminum in the same wire size (AWG 14 copper) will carry 15 amps, but AWG 12 is required for 15 amps if the conductor is aluminum.

You might wonder, at this point, what the result would be if the ampacity of a conductor is exceeded. Consider an AWG 14 copper conductor. From Table 3, its ampacity is 15 amps. If this conductor carried, say, 18 amps for a long period of time, probably the only effect would be a significant decrease in the insulator life due to an increased operating temperature. If its current was increased to, say, 25 amps, the insulation would probably become warm to the touch. At a current of 50 or 60 amps, the insulation would begin to melt and smoke within a few seconds.

The time factor is important; the ampacity can be exceeded for a very short time without any adverse effects.

Specific requirements may be applicable to further reduce the table ampacity values. The National Electrical Code (NEC) regulation should be checked for these special requirements when a wiring task is being conducted.

4.5.3.3 Voltage Drop Requirement

Voltage drop occurs due to the resistance and current in the conductor. As shown in Figure 4.26, when power is being delivered to the load over a distance, the conductors are indeed connected to the load through a series circuit. Hence, voltage will be drawn by the conductors themselves, and the actual voltage delivered to the load is less than the 120 V coming from the source.

If we calculate how much voltage drop is occurring, we need to first calculate the resistance of the conductors:

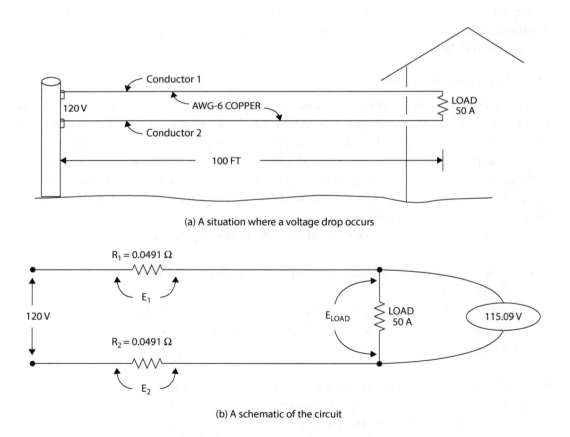

(a) A situation where a voltage drop occurs

(b) A schematic of the circuit

Figure 4.26: Voltage Drop Over Conductors

The resistance of AWG-6 copper is 0.491 Ω/1000 ft. 100 ft has a resistance of 0.0491 Ω. Now we can represent the situation in a schematic shown in figure 4.26b.

$E_T = 120\text{ V} = E_1 + E_{load} + E_2$ (series circuit)
$E_1 = I_1 R_1 = (50\ A)(0.0491\ \Omega) = 2.5\text{ V}$
$E_2 = I_2 R_2 = (50\ A)(0.0491\ \Omega) = 2.5\text{ V}$
$E_{load} = 120\text{ V} - 2.5\text{ V} - 2.5\text{ V} = 115\text{ V}$

Hence, a total of 5 V voltage drop occurs over the entire conductor, and only ~115 V is delivered to the load. This voltage drop is typically expressed as a percentage voltage drop:

$\%_{voltage\ drop} = 5.0\text{ V}/120\text{ V} * 100\% = 4.2\%$

As a result of the voltage drop, the load performance will be reduced.

Excessive voltage drop is obviously undesirable. Since all conductors regardless of size have resistance, we cannot eliminate voltage drop completely. However, voltage drop is proportional to the resistance of the conductors, hence it is proportional to the size of the conductors. By selecting the proper size, we can control the voltage drop to be within an acceptable range. The National Electrical Code states that these voltage drop limits will provide "reasonable efficiency of operation (NEC 210–19, FPN No. 4):

- 3% maximum voltage drop in branch circuit at farthest power outlet
- 5% maximum voltage drop in the feeder and branch circuit combined

Branch circuit designs for 2% voltage drop are common. It is necessary to meet ampacity requirements for safety. It is desirable to meet voltage drop guidelines for proper load performance.

The smallest conductor size allowed for building wiring by the NEC is AWG 14 copper, and AWG 12 for aluminum or copper-clad aluminum (NEC 310-5).

An equation for calculating the conductor size needed for a specified voltage drop can be derived from equation 4.14:

$A = \rho L/R$ 　　　　　　　　　　　　　　　　　　　　　　　　　　　　　Eq. 4.16

Where A is the cross sectional area (i.e., conductor size), ρ is the resistivity of the conductor, and R is the resistance of the conductor.

From Ohm's law, we have:

$R = E_{drop}/I_{line}$ 　　　　　　　　　　　　　　　　　　　　　　　　　　Eq. 4.17

Where E_{drop} is the maximum allowable voltage drop on the conductor, and I_{line} is the current in the conductor. Substitute 4.16 into 4.15, and we have:

$$A = \rho \times I_{line} \times L/E_{drop}$$

L is the total length of conductor. It is more convenient to use one-way length in the equation, called it l

$$2l = L \hspace{4cm} \text{Eq. 4.18}$$

Usually, to add some buffer to our calculation, a 10% add-on can be added to the one-way length.

Since $\rho_{Cu} = 10.37$ Ω-cmil/ft, $\rho_{Al} = 17.01$ Ω-cmil/ft, substitute these values and equation 17 to 16, we will have:

For copper, $A = 22 \times I_{line} \times l/E_{drop}$ Eq. 4.19
For aluminum, $A = 34 \times I_{line} \times l/E_{drop}$ Eq. 4.20

Once the cross section area is calculated, the AWG gauge table can be consulted to find the proper conductor size.

Example 4.14: A service panel (120 V) is 91 feet away from a 10 Ω load, which uses 1440 W power. If a 2% voltage drop is allowed, what is the size of conductor to use, supposing you are using copper cable?
First, we calculate the current running in the line:
$I_{line} = I_{load} = (P_{load}/R)^{1/2} = (1440 \text{ W}/10 \text{ }\Omega)^{1/2} = 12 \text{ A}$
$l_{one-way} = 91 \text{ ft} \times (100\% + 10\%) = 100 \text{ ft}$
$E_{drop} = 2\% \times 120 \text{ V} = 2.4 \text{ V}$

Hence, for copper, we use equation 4.19, and we have:
A = 22 Ω-cmil/ft*12 A*100 ft/2.4 V = 11000 cmil
Checking Table 3, this would require an AWG-8 copper cable.

In practice, when a decision needs to be made on conductor selection, all three factors (environment, ampacity and voltage drop) need to be considered. The final selection must satisfy all three requirements.

Example 4.15: Conductor design.
Design a feeder line to a building with these specs:
Load: 78 amps@230 V.

Aluminum conductors to be strung overhead

One-way length: 273 ft

Voltage drop: 2%

1. Environment consideration says that multiplex is the proper choice. It is available only in aluminum, hence, ampacity and voltage drop requirements will be considered for aluminum.

2. Ampacity

   For 78 amps, AWG 1 is the minimum size that can carry 78 amps.

3. Voltage drop

   For aluminum, equation 4.20 is to be used.

   I_{line} = 78 amps

   $l_{one-way}$ = 273 ft × (100% + 10%) = 300 ft

   E_{drop} = 2%*230 V = 4.6 V

   Hence, A = 34 Ω-cmil/ft *78 A *300 ft/4.6 V = 179,061 cmil

   From table 3, this requires an AWG 0000.

Taking into account both ampacity and voltage drop requirements, AWG 0000 must be used. Therefore, the final selection would be AWG 0000 multiplex cable.

EXERCISES

1. Determine the resistance R (in ohms) of a circuit operating at E = 19.0 volts with 4.3 amps of current.

2. Determine the current flow (in amps) in a series circuit with resistances of R_1 = 7.3, R_2 = 32.7, and R_3 = 17.8 ohms, when the total voltage is 240 volts.

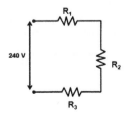

3. Determine the voltage drop (in volts) across the R_1 resistor (24.8 ohm) when it is in series with $R_2 = 7.9$ and $R_3 = 18.3$ ohm resistors. The total voltage is 240 volts.

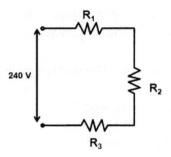

4. Determine the total current (in amps) in a circuit with four (4) parallel resistors of $R_1 = 25.3$, $R_2 = 52.9$, $R_3 = 31.0$, and $R_4 = 76.0$ ohms, when the total voltage is 240. volts.

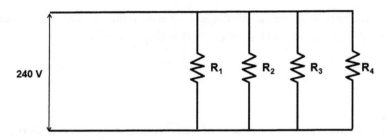

5. Determine the current (in amps) across resistor of $R_1 = 10.0$ ohms in the circuit below, where $R_2 = 25.0$ ohms, $R_3 = 50.0$ ohms, when the total voltage is 240. volts.

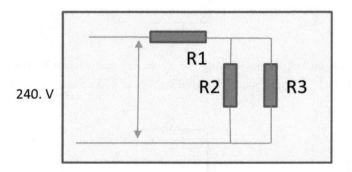

6. For the circuit shown to the right, find:

   a. The equivalent resistance (R_T)
   b. Current through R_1
   c. Power used by entire circuit

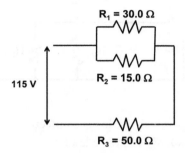

$R_1 = 30.0\ \Omega$

$R_2 = 15.0\ \Omega$

115 V

$R_3 = 50.0\ \Omega$

7. Consider the circuit shown to the right. The current in R_3 is measured to be 2.0 A. $E_T = 120.$ V, $R_1 = 50.0$ ohms, $R_2 = 100.$ ohms, Find:

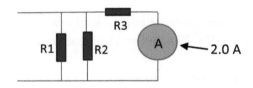

R3

R1   R2   A   ← 2.0 A

   a. R_3
   b. the equivalent total resistance of the circuit
   c. the total current
   d. the current through R_1, R_2

   Note that the "A" with a circle is an ammeter, a device to measure the current at a single point, where its own resistance is negligible ($R_A = 0$). Treat it as a wire in your calculation.

8. A service transformer is used to step down 7200 V to 240 V. The transformer is rated at 25 kVA.

   a. (1 pt) If there are 500 turns on the secondary, how many turns are on the primary?
   b. (2 pts) At rated load, what is the primary and secondary current? (1 kVA = 1 kW = 1000 VA)

9. Consider this three-wire circuit. $R_1 = 40$ ohms, $R_2 = 29$ ohms, $R_3 = 30$ ohms, and $R_4 = 77$ ohms. What is the current (in amps) in the black, red, and white wires?

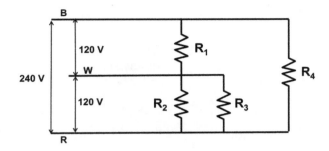

10. A three-wire service has these resistive loads connected:
    - 120-V: Black to white: 800W, 400W (2 loads)
    - 120-V: Red to white: 900W, 200W, 600W (3 loads)
    - 240V: 4kW, 10kW (2 loads)
      a. (2 pts) Draw the circuit diagram.
      b. (5 pts) Compute the current in the black, red and white wires.

    Note: You need to calculate resistance of each load first. For instance, for a 120-V, 800 W load, its resistance $R = E^2/P = 120^2/800 = 18$ ohm. Do the same for all loads.

11. A shop with a three-wire service has these resistive loads connected:
    - 120-V: Black to white: 2 outlets (1.5A each), lighting (10A)
    - 120-V: Red to white: 1 outlets (15A), exhaust fan (5A)
    - 240V: Welder (50A), drill press (20A), air compressor (25A), outlet (30A)
    Draw the schematic of the circuit (2 pts), and compute the current in the black, red and white wires.

12. You will be supplying electricity from a transformer mounted on a power pole to the shop mentioned in problem No.11. Using the results you obtain from problem No. 11, please specify the type and size of wire to use. Consider the environment, ampacity, and voltage drop. State any assumptions you might make.
    - The shop is 125-ft from the transformer.
    - The cable is overhead.
    - A maximum of 3% voltage drop is allowed.
    -

Figure and Table Sources

1. Fig. 4.1: Source: https://commons.wikimedia.org/wiki/File:Atom_(PSF).png.
2. Fig. 4.6: Adapted from Carl J. Bern and Dean I. Olson, Electricity for Agriculture Appliances. Copyright © 2002 by John Wiley & Sons, Inc.
3. Fig. 4.7: Adapted from Carl J. Bern and Dean I. Olson, Electricity for Agriculture Appliances. Copyright © 2002 by John Wiley & Sons, Inc.
4. Fig. 4.8: Adapted from Carl J. Bern and Dean I. Olson, Electricity for Agriculture Appliances. Copyright © 2002 by John Wiley & Sons, Inc.
5. Fig. 4.10: Adapted from Carl J. Bern and Dean I. Olson, Electricity for Agriculture Appliances. Copyright © 2002 by John Wiley & Sons, Inc.
6. Fig. 4.11: Arvid Eide, Roland Jenison, Larry Northup and Steven Mickelson, Engineering Fundamentals and Problem Solving. Copyright © 2007 by McGraw-Hill Education.
7. Fig. 4.12: Copyright © Pflodo (CC BY-SA 3.0) at https://commons.wikimedia.org/wiki/File:KCL_-_Kirchhoff%27s_circuit_laws.svg.
8. Fig. 4.13: Copyright © Kwinkunks (CC BY-SA 3.0) at https://commons.wikimedia.org/wiki/File:Kirchhoff_voltage_law.svg.
9. Fig. 4.14: Adapted from Arvid Eide, Roland Jenison, Larry Northup and Steven Mickelson, Engineering Fundamentals and Problem Solving. Copyright © 2007 by McGraw-Hill Education.
10. Fig. 4.15: Source: https://commons.wikimedia.org/wiki/File:Kirshhoff-example.svg.
11. Fig. 4.16: Copyright © FDominec (CC BY-SA 3.0) at https://commons.wikimedia.org/wiki/File:Electronic_component_inductors.jpg.
12. Fig. 4.17: Copyright © Eric Schrader (CC BY-SA 2.0) at https://commons.wikimedia.org/wiki/File:Capacitors_(7189597135).jpg.
13. Fig. 4.18: Adapted from Carl J. Bern and Dean I. Olson, Electricity for Agriculture Appliances. Copyright © 2002 by John Wiley & Sons, Inc.
14. Fig. 4.19: Source: https://faculty.ksu.edu.sa/eltamaly/Pages/EE205.aspx.
15. Fig. 4.21: Adapted from Carl J. Bern and Dean I. Olson, Electricity for Agriculture Appliances. Copyright © 2002 by John Wiley & Sons, Inc.
16. Fig. 4.22: Adapted from Carl J. Bern and Dean I. Olson, Electricity for Agriculture Appliances. Copyright © 2002 by John Wiley & Sons, Inc.
17. Fig. 4.23a: Adapted from Carl J. Bern and Dean I. Olson, Electricity for Agriculture Appliances. Copyright © 2002 by John Wiley & Sons, Inc.
18. Fig. 4.23b: Adapted from Carl J. Bern and Dean I. Olson, Electricity for Agriculture Appliances. Copyright © 2002 by John Wiley & Sons, Inc.
19. Fig. 4.23c: Adapted from Carl J. Bern and Dean I. Olson, Electricity for Agriculture Appliances. Copyright © 2002 by John Wiley & Sons, Inc.
20. Fig. 4.23d: Adapted from Carl J. Bern and Dean I. Olson, Electricity for Agriculture Appliances. Copyright © 2002 by John Wiley & Sons, Inc.
21. Fig. 4.24: Copyright © Egmason (CC BY-SA 3.0) at https://commons.wikimedia.org/wiki/File:Alternator_1.svg.
22. Fig. 4.25: Source: https://www.maproyalty.com/images/_pv.jpg.
23. Tbl. 4.1: Adapted from Carl J. Bern and Dean I. Olson, Electricity for Agriculture Appliances. Copyright © 2002 by John Wiley & Sons, Inc.
24. Tbl. 4.2: Adapted from Carl J. Bern and Dean I. Olson, Electricity for Agriculture Appliances. Copyright © 2002 by John Wiley & Sons, Inc.
25. Tbl. 4.3: Adapted from Carl J. Bern and Dean I. Olson, Electricity for Agriculture Appliances. Copyright © 2002 by John Wiley & Sons, Inc.
26. Tbl. 4.4: Adapted from Carl J. Bern and Dean I. Olson, Electricity for Agriculture Appliances. Copyright © 2002 by John Wiley & Sons, Inc.
27. Tbl. 4.5: Adapted from Carl J. Bern and Dean I. Olson, Electricity for Agriculture Appliances. Copyright © 2002 by John Wiley & Sons, Inc.
28. Fig. 4.26: Adapted from Carl J. Bern and Dean I. Olson, Electricity for Agriculture Appliances. Copyright © 2002 by John Wiley & Sons, Inc.

5

FUNDAMENTALS OF THERMAL SYSTEMS

OBJECTIVES

When you complete the study of this chapter, you should be able to:

1. Understand the fundamentals of heat flow and insulation
2. Determine heat loss from a building
3. Determine the properties of air-water vapor mixtures
4. Analyze situations in which air is heated, cooled, humidified and de-humidified
5. Determine ventilations rates to maintain air quality, humidity and temperature
6. Understand the fundamentals of drying

5.1. Heat Flow and Insulation

Heat is something everyone knows about. It is felt on a sunny day. It is added to keep houses and apartments warm. It is removed to keep houses and apartments cool. It is also a vitally important topic to technologists. For example, it can be part of a process that must be managed, or the expense of controlling heat can impact a company's financial bottom line.

In this section, the basics of heat flow and insulation are discussed as they relates to maintaining or predicting temperatures in a structure.

5.1.1 Definitions

Heat is a form of energy that is transferred from an object to another due to a difference in temperature. Heat flows from "warm" to "cold."

Temperature is a measure of the degree or intensity of heat present in an object or its ability to transfer or receive heat from its surroundings. It is an indication of molecular activity. Temperature is expressed relative to some standard condition, e.g., absolute zero (–273.15°C or 459.67°F) or the freezing/boiling point of water (0°C/100°C or 32°F/212°F). Technologists usually deal with two scales of temperature: Fahrenheit and Celsius. The relationship between the two is:

$$T_c = (T_F - 32) \div 1.8 \qquad\qquad \text{Eq. 5.1}$$

$$T_F = (1.8 \times T_C) + 32 \qquad\qquad \text{Eq. 5.2}$$

where: T_C = temperature in degrees Celsius (°C)
T_F = temperature in degrees Fahrenheit (°F)

Ambient temperature is the temperature of an object or system's surroundings.

Quantity of heat is measured in units that are the same as other units of energy or work. One British Thermal Unit (BTU) is the amount of energy it takes to raise the temperature of one pound of 59°F water by 1°F at atmospheric pressure. A kilocalorie (kCal) is the amount of energy it takes to raise one kilogram of water by 1°C at atmospheric pressure.

In the SI system of units, the joule is normally used – one joule (J) is equal to the work done by a force of one newton when its point of application moves one meter in the direction of action of the force. 1 BTU = 1,055.06 J and 1 kJ = 0.947817 BTU. The symbol often used in an equation for the quantity of heat is a lower case "*q.*"

Specific Heat or Specific Heat Capacity is the amount of heat per unit mass required to raise the temperature of an object or material by one degree Celsius (SI) or one degree Fahrenheit. The symbol used for specific heat capacity is c_p.

Sensible heat is a measure of the amount of heat that accompanies a temperature change (but no change in phase, e.g., water evaporation). The relationship between sensible heat and temperature is:

$$q = c_p m \Delta T \qquad\qquad \text{Eq. 5.3}$$

where: q = amount of sensible heat (BTU or J)
c_p = specific heat capacity (BTU / lb·°F or J / kg·°C)
m = mass of an object (lb or kg)
ΔT = change in temperature (°F or °C)

Latent heat is a measure of the amount of heat that accompanies a change in phase. The three phases are solid, liquid and gas.

Latent heat of fusion is the amount of heat that accompanies a solid-liquid phase change. When ice melts or water freezes, 144 BTU/lb or 335 kJ/kg, is absorbed or released.

Latent heat of vaporization is the amount of heat that accompanies a liquid-gas phase change. When water evaporates or water vapor condenses, 970.4 BTU/lb or 2257 kJ/kg is absorbed or released. This value changes depending on the temperature of the water or water vapor. A common value used for animals and humans under typical ambient conditions is 1044 BTU/lb or 2428 kJ/kg.

5.1.2 Heat Transfer

Heat is transferred in three different ways: radiation, convection, and conduction.

Radiation

Radiation is the exchange of thermal energy between two objects via electromagnetic radiation due to a difference in temperature. You notice that you gain heat radiantly on a hot summer day when the sun shines on you. You notice that you lose heat radiantly when you stand in front of a picture window when the outside temperature is below zero degrees Fahrenheit. Radiant heat loss affects human or animal comfort even if the temperatures within a room or structure are correct.

Radiant heat follows the same physical laws as light. It follows a straight-line path, it is transmitted through space, and it can be reflected, transmitted, or absorbed. Physical bodies can be transparent, translucent, or opaque to radiation, depending on the nature of the body's material and the wavelength of the radiation.

Convection

Convection is the transfer of heat to or from an object to a fluid (a gas or a liquid) when they are at different temperatures. Heat is removed from a running engine by liquid convection (the relatively cooler anti-freeze circulating through the engine block) and gas convection (air passing through the radiators). Convective heat transfer can either be natural (fluid motion due to gravity and differences in fluid density) or forced (fluid motion created by a fan or pump). The convective heat transfer rate is generally much higher for forced conditions than natural convection when other conditions are the same.

The rate of heat transfer due to convection is a function of the temperature difference between the fluid and the body's surface, the surface area, the surface area conditions, the fluid properties, and the rate of fluid flow.

Conduction

Conduction is the exchange of heat between two bodies touching each other due to a temperature difference. The handle of a frying pan becomes warm due to conduction of heat from the bottom of the pan to the handle. Your hands are warmed by conduction when you place them on a hot water bottle.

Conductive heat loss through a material, or series of materials, (e.g., the wall of your house) is described by the following equation:

$$q = \frac{A}{R}\Delta T = UA\Delta T \qquad\qquad \text{Eq. 5.4}$$

where: q = rate of heat transferred through the material via conduction (BTU / h or W)
  A = surface area (ft^2 or m^2)
  R = R-value (h·ft^2·°F / BTU or m^2·°C / W)
  U = U-value = 1/R (BTU / h·ft^2·°F or W / m^2·°C)
  ΔT = temperature difference across the material (°F or °C)

Note the difference in units of q in Equations 5.3 and 5.4. In Equation 5.3, the units of q are BTU or J. In Equation 5.4, the units are BTU/h or W. When using the variable q, be sure to always state the units so there is no confusion about whether it is an amount of heat or a rate of heat transfer.

R-value is a property of the material. The English unit equivalent (BTU/h·ft^2·°F) is what you commonly see on insulating materials you purchase. The higher the R-value, the better the material is as an insulator (reducing the amount of heat flow).

5.1.3. Insulation

There are at least two reasons heat insulating materials are used: (1) to control heat loss or gain; and (2) to control surface temperatures.

In controlling heat loss or gain, temperature of a space can be maintained. This might be necessary for maintaining conditions for a particular industrial process, maintaining human, plant or animal comfort, or minimizing the amount of money spent to add or remove heat from a space.

Controlling surface temperatures is important, particularly in cold climates. For example, insulated walls provide warmer surfaces on the inside of exterior walls in cold climates, thereby reducing or eliminating condensation or "sweating." Warmer surfaces also lower the amount of radiant heat loss from objects in the building to the exterior walls.

Insulating materials

Insulating materials are any material that reduces the amount of heat flow via conduction. Every material has some amount of resistance to heat flow, but some materials have more resistance than others. Materials with a high amount of resistance are commonly referred to as just "insulation." Resistance to heat flow is commonly measured by "R-value" as discussed previously.

Materials with a high amount of resistance typically are of low density. These materials often trap countless small pockets of air within the material, which makes the material less dense and provides a large amount of insulating value. Air (when it isn't moving) has a high resistance to heat flow. An example of a material with a high insulating value would be a building board made out of Styrofoam. It is not very dense because of the air trapped within material, yet it is a good insulator. Fiberglass insulation (sometimes the color pink) is another example of a good insulator with low density that traps air.

Manufactured insulation comes in several common forms: batt or blanket, loose-fill, rigid, or foam.

Batt insulation comes in variable thickness (1" to 8") and widths to fit into spaces between wall studs and ceiling joists (e.g., 16" or 24"). A common batt length is 8 ft. **Blanket insulation** comes in long rolls and can be as long as 100 ft. The batt or blanket could be faced with paper or foil to aid in installation and/or to provide a partial vapor barrier. (See section 5.1.4.4 for more information about vapor barriers.) Fiberglass and glass wool are common materials.

Loose-fill insulation is just as it says—loose. It comes packaged in bags and must be poured or blown into walls, ceilings, and concrete block cores. Poor quality loose-fill insulation can settle, thereby leaving the top of a space inadequately insulated. Common materials are mineral wool, cellulose fiber, vermiculite, and/or polystyrene.

Rigid insulation comes in panels, typically 4 ft in width, and ½" to 2" thick. It can have aluminum foil or other vapor barriers attached to one or both faces. Rigid insulation can be used for roofs, walls, along foundations, or buried under concrete floors. Common materials are polystyrene and polyurethane, although other materials can also be used. Rigid insulation does not have a great deal of structural strength, so it must be supported. Joints between panels are often sealed with tape or caulk to prevent water vapor from passing through the joints.

Foamed insulation is applied by foaming organic materials with air or an inert gas and spraying it into place, either to be made into pre-cut board stock or directly into the space being insulated. Many foams must be covered with fire-resistant materials.

Sometimes a reflective material like aluminum foil is used as part of an insulating material or system to reduce the amount of radiant heat transfer. By itself, a thin foil does a poor job of reducing conductive heat transfer.

Air spaces provide insulating value. Consider a double-paned window: the air (or inert gas) trapped between the two panes acts as an insulator. A dead air space of between ¾" and 4" does have some insulating value, but in construction, it is better to fill those spaces with insulating material. Convective air currents occur in these spaces and decrease the insulating value of the air.

Insulation performance

Table 5.1 lists some R-values of common building materials. The higher the R-value, the better the material is as an insulator (reducing the amount of heat flow).

Conductive heat flow is analogous to the flow of electrons in an electrical circuit. The R-value of a wall made of multiple materials can be determined in either series (similar to Equation 4.5) or parallel (similar to Equation 4.9).

Table 5.1. R-values of Selected Building Materials

MATERIAL	R-VALUE (H·FT²·°F/BTU)	
	PER INCH THICKNESS	FOR THICKNESS LISTED
Batt or blanket insulation, glass or mineral wool, fiberglass	3.00–3.80	
Fill-type insulation		
Cellulose	3.13–3.70	
Glass or mineral wool	2.50–3.00	
Vermiculite	2.20	
Shavings or sawdust	2.22	
Hay or straw, 20"		30+
Rigid insulation		
Expanded polystyrene		
Extruded, plain	5.00	
Molded beads, 1 lb/ft³	5.00	
Molded beads, over 1 lb/ft³	4.20	
Expanded rubber	4.55	
Expanded polyurethane, aged	6.25	
Glass fiber	4.00	
Wood or cane fiberboard	2.50	
Polyisocyanurate	7.04	
Foamed-in-place insulation, polyurethane		6.00
Building materials		
Concrete, solid	0.08	
Concrete block, 3 hole, 8"		1.11
Lightweight aggregate, 8"		2.00
Lightweight, cores insulated		5.03
Common Brick	0.20	
Metal siding	0.00	
Hollow-backed		0.61
Insulated-backed, 3/8"		1.82
Softwoods, fir and pine	1.25	
Hardwoods, maple and oak	0.91	
Plywood, 3/8"	1.25	0.47
Plywood, ½"	1.25	0.62
Particleboard, medium density	1.06	
Hardboard, tempered, ¼"	1.00	0.25

Insulating sheathing, 25/32"	2.06
Gypsum or plasterboard, ½"	0.45
Wood siding, lapped, ½" x 8"	0.81
Asphalt shingles	0.44
Wood shingles	0.94
Windows (includes surface conditions)	
Single glazed	0.91
With storm windows	2.00
Insulating glass, ¼" air space	
Double pane	1.69
Triple pane	2.56
Doors (exterior, includes surface conditions)	
Wood, solid core, 1 ¾"	3.03
Metal, urethane core, 1 ¾"	2.50
Metal, polystyrene core, 1 ¾"	2.13
Air space, ¾" to 4"	0.90
Surface conditions, inside surface	0.68
Surface conditions, outside surface	0.17

Taken from Table 631–1 of MWPS Structures and Environment Handbook ISBN 0-89373-057-2. Reprinted with permission.

Example 5.1

What is the total R-value of a wall made of the following material: metal siding on the outside surface, 3-1/2" fiberglass blanket insulation, and ½" plywood on the inside surface?

In this example, add the R-values of each component using the values from Table 5.1:

MATERIAL	R-VALUE (H·FT²·°F/BTU)
Outside surface	0.17
Metal Siding	0.00
Fiberglass 3.5 in @ 3.5/in	12.25
½-in plywood	0.62
Inside surface	0.68
TOTAL	13.72

In this case, the R-values are summed, similar to a series electrical circuit. Only one "path" of heat flow is considered, through each of these materials in sequence.

Note the R-values for "outside surface" and "inside surface." On any surface, there is a small but not insignificant layer of stagnant air that has some insulating value. An "average" R-value of 0.68 for inside conditions (likely little airflow) is used. For outside conditions where there is likely more airflow, the stagnant layer is thinner and thus a smaller R-value of 0.17 is used. Note that these values are for "typical" conditions—useful in getting an approximate, but not exact, result.

Example 5.2

Assume the wall in the previous example has an area of 100 square feet. A triple-paned window is installed in the wall, 6.00 square feet in area. What is the equivalent R-value for the entire wall with the window installed?

There is 94.0 square feet of wall with an R-value of 13.72. The 6.00 square feet of window has an R-value of 2.56 (from Table 5.1, includes surface conditions). Analogous to parallel electrical circuit resistance, relative areas of each component are accounted for:

$$\left(\frac{A}{R}\right)_{total} = \left(\frac{A_{total}}{R_{equivalent}}\right) = \frac{A_1}{R_1} + \frac{A_2}{R_2} + \ldots + \frac{A_n}{R_n} = \sum_{i=1}^{n} \frac{A_i}{R_i} \qquad \text{Eq. 5.5}$$

where: $R_{equivalent}$ = equivalent R-value of the combined surface (h·ft²·°F/BTU or m²·°C/W)
A_{total} = total surface area (ft² or m²)
R_i = R-value of the individual component (h·ft²·°F/BTU or m²·°C/W)
A_i = surface area of the individual component (ft² or m²)

In this case:

$$\left(\frac{100}{R_{equivalent}}\right) = \frac{94.0}{13.72} + \frac{6.00}{2.56} = 9.20 \implies R_{equivalent} = \underline{\mathbf{10.88}}$$

A wall of 100 sq. ft. with an R-value of 10.88 is equivalent to a wall of 94.0 square feet of wall with an R-value of 13.72 and 6.00 square feet of window with an R-value of 2.56.

Protecting insulation from water condensation

Under certain conditions, moisture can condense on or inside building insulation, causing damage and other serious problems. How can this happen? How does liquid water appear where there was none? How can water get inside insulating materials?

First, consider the first situation—condensation. Air in buildings contains moisture in the form of water vapor (discussed in the next section). Condensation on building surfaces results from warm, moist air contacting a cold surface. Water vapor condenses into liquid water, just like on a cold can of soda or glass of ice water. This occurs when the surface temperature is below the dew point temperature of the air, which is also discussed in the next section. If the surface is cold enough, the liquid water freezes and appears as frost. Condensation and/or frost appears first on poorly insulated surfaces as colder outside temperatures approach. A proper amount of insulation will result in warm, not cold, surfaces and will eliminate condensation under most circumstances.

Now, let's examine condensation inside the building insulation, such as insulation within a wall. Water vapor in the often warmer, more humid inside air tries to get to the other side of the wall where a lower amount of water vapor is present. Warm air holds more water vapor than cold air, so water vapor will naturally try to move from an area of higher concentration (or higher vapor pressure) to an area of lower concentration (or lower vapor pressure) until the concentration (or vapor pressure) is equal.

Most building materials are permeable to water vapor, (i.e., water vapor can move freely through the material). If the water vapor encounters the temperature where condensation occurs (the dew point), the water will change from vapor to liquid. Wet insulation has little insulation value and will soon cause rot if not taken care of.

In order to prevent moisture problems in building sections, a material called a vapor barrier is installed. Placed on the warm side of the wall, just below the surface material, it prevents water vapor from entering the wall and possibly condensing. **Permeability** is the measure of a material to allow water vapor to pass through it. Most building materials have a high permeability value (e.g., 2 to 90 perms, where 1 perm = 1 grain of water per hour per square foot per inch of mercury pressure difference). Vapor barrier materials (e.g., aluminum foil and polyethylene film) have a permeability of 0.00 to 0.06. Polyethylene is almost universally used as a vapor barrier.

5.1.4 Determining Heat Loss in a Building

The rate of heat loss (BTU/h or W) through each building component is a function of the difference in temperature (inside versus outside), the area, and the component composition (R-value). This rate can be calculated using Equation 5.4.

Calculating overall heat loss from a building can be quite complicated, particularly if different components have different temperatures both inside and out. For example, in a house, the drop in temperature across a basement wall (inside condition vs. soil temperature) will be different than the heat loss from an upstairs wall (inside conditions vs. outside temperature). In this text, cases of different temperature differences across a building's various components will not be considered.

However, we will consider the condition of a perimeter where there is no basement but the building is built on an insulated concrete slab and an insulated perimeter and foundation wall.

Example 5.3
Consider the building constructed in Figure 5.1. The inside temperature is 70°F and the outside temperature is O°F. The building has two 3′×7′ doors, each with an R-value of 7.99. Assume that the temperature above the ceiling (attic) is the same as the outside temperature. What is the amount of heat loss (in BTU/h) from the building?

First, list the dimensions and R-values of the building components.

BUILDING DIMENSIONS (FT)		SURFACE AREA (FT²)		R-VALUES (H·FT²·°F/BTU)	
Length	36	Ceiling	864	Ceiling	13.47
Width	24	Windows	0	Windows	n/a
Frame wall height	6	Doors	42	Doors	7.47
Concrete wall height	2	Frame less windows & doors	678	Frame Wall	12.47
				Concrete wall	11.58
Perimeter	120	Concrete wall	240	Perimeter	2.22

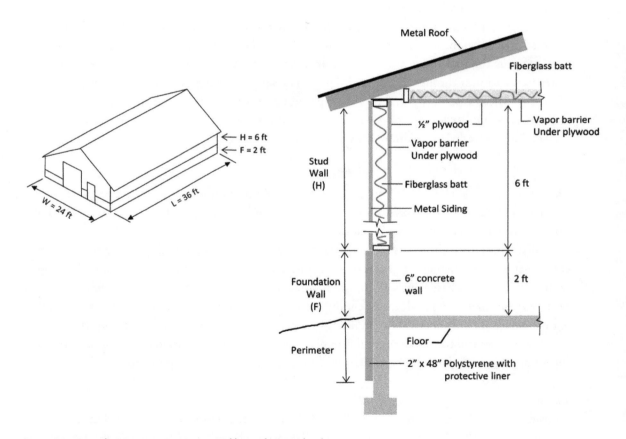

Figure 5.1: Example 5.3 — Heat Loss From a Building with an Insulated Perimeter

Now, apply equation 5.4 for each of the components:

$$q = \frac{A}{R}\Delta T \qquad\qquad\qquad \text{Eq. 5.4}$$

$$q_{ceiling} = \frac{864}{13.47}(70) = 4490\frac{BTU}{h}$$

$$q_{windows} = 0\frac{BTU}{h}$$

$$q_{doors} = \frac{42}{7.99}(70) = 368\frac{BTU}{h}$$

$$q_{frame\ walls} = \frac{678}{12.47}(70) = 3806\frac{BTU}{h}$$

$$q_{concrete\ wall} = \frac{240}{11.58}(70) = 1451\frac{BTU}{h}$$

The only component left is the perimeter. It does not face the same temperature difference as the rest of the building. Additionally, the perimeter is a length, not an area, so equation 5.4 won't apply. To solve this situation, engineers have developed an approximation for perimeters so that equation 5.4 can be used. From table 5.1, for an insulated perimeter, an equivalent R-value of 2.22 (per foot of exterior wall) can be used.

For building perimeters, the following can be used:

$$q_{perimeter} = \frac{L}{R_{perimeter}}\Delta T \qquad\qquad\qquad \text{Eq. 5.6}$$

where: $q_{perimeter}$ = amount of conductive heat transferred through the material (BTU/h or W)
L = perimeter length (ft or m)
$R_{perimeter}$ = Perimeter R-value (h-ft-°F/BTU or m-°C/W)
ΔT = temperature difference $T_{inside} - T_{outside}$ (°F or °C)

For this example:

$$q_{perimeter} = \frac{120}{2.22}(70) = 3784\frac{BTU}{h}$$

Now:

$$q_{total} = q_{ceiling} + q_{wndow} + q_{door} + q_{frame\ wall} + q_{concrete\ wall} + q_{perimeter} = 13{,}899 \cong \underline{\mathbf{14{,}000\ BTU/h}}$$

5.2. Psychrometrics

The properties of air affect many things with which technologists will work. In drying systems, air is used to carry moisture away from grain, biological products, and other materials. Building temperature and humidity are maintained with ventilation. Ventilation also maintains air quality in buildings by removing gases and aerosols that could potentially cause problems for the building's occupants or processes. The properties of air (actually air / water vapor mixtures, since air almost always contains water vapor) must be known in order to design and understand mechanical systems that move air for a variety of purposes.

There is a branch of science called *psychrometrics* that is concerned with the physical and thermodynamic properties of air / water vapor mixtures. The term comes from the Greek *psuchron* (ψυχρόν) meaning "cold" and *metron* (μέτρον) meaning "means of measurement."

Air is a mixture of many gases, but the two main ones are nitrogen (71%) and oxygen (20%). Water, in vapor form, is part of the remaining 9%. The amount of water vapor air can hold is determined by air temperature; in general, the warmer the air, the more water it can hold. The mathematical relationships between air temperature and other air properties are represented graphically by a *psychrometric chart*. It shows the water holding capabilities of air at different temperatures. It also gives several other properties of air such as its density, the amount of energy stored in it, and its relative humidity. Figure 5.10 at the end of the chapter is a complete psychrometric chart for air temperatures 20°F to 110°F.

5.2.1 Physical Properties of Air-Water Vapor Mixtures

<u>Dry-bulb temperature and absolute humidity</u>
The two properties that define the psychrometric chart are temperature and water content. Dry bulb temperature (what is normally thought of as air temperature) forms the horizontal scale of the chart; water content is the vertical scale. Figure 5.2 shows these scales with the rest of the lines removed.

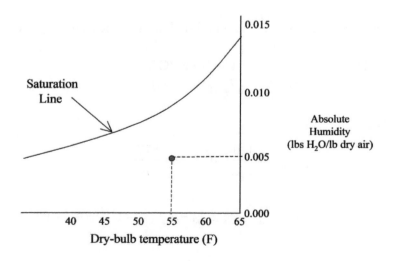

Figure 5.2: A Psychrometric Chart with Dry-Bulb Temperature (*x*-axis) and Absolute Humidity (*y*-axis)

The water content of air is called absolute humidity (or sometimes the humidity ratio). It is the weight ratio of water vapor to air, and its units are lb of water per lb dry air (or kg of water per kg of dry air). Absolute humidity is sometimes expressed in the units of grains per pound of dry air. There are 7000 grains per pound. The usual symbol for absolute humidity is "w."

There is a maximum weight of water that air will hold at a particular temperature. Connecting the points of maximum absolute humidity forms the saturation line, or the line of maximum water content. For example, air at 60°F can hold a maximum of 0.012 lb of water per pound of dry air.

Air conditions can be represented on the psychrometric chart as a "state point." A state point of 55°F dry-bulb temperature and 0.005 lb water/lb dry air absolute humidity is shown in Figure 5.2.

Relative humidity

Water content of air is often described by the term relative humidity. This is not the same as the absolute humidity discussed previously. Relative humidity is the ratio of the absolute humidity of the air to the maximum possible absolute humidity of that air, at the same temperature. Mathematically:

$$RH = \frac{w}{w_{max}} \times 100\%$$
Eq. 5.7

where RH = relative humidity (%)

w = absolute humidity (lb H_2O / lb dry air)

w_{max} = absolute humidity at saturation at the same T_{DB} (lb H_2O / lb dry air)

Example 5.4
What is the relative humidity of the air at 55°F and 0.005 lb water/lb. dry air?

w_{max} = 0.0093 lb water/lb dry air; found by reading the absolute humidity scale for saturation at 55F dry-bulb

$$RH = \frac{w}{w_{max}} \times 100\% = \frac{0.005}{0.0093} \times 100\% = \underline{\textbf{54\%}}$$

Lines of constant relative humidity can be drawn on the psychrometric chart. They are below the saturation line. Figure 5.3 shows the chart with one line (50% RH) added. This line represents all air state points where the air contains 50% of its maximum possible water. The 50% relative humidity line lies, at all dry bulb temperatures, halfway between the horizontal axis and the saturation line.

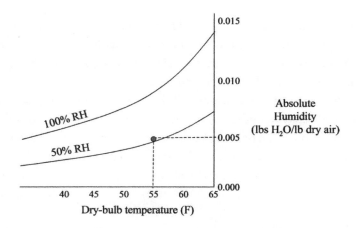

Figure 5.3: A Psychrometric Chart with a 50% Relative Humidity (RH) Line.

Figure 5.10 has multiple lines of relative humidity on it, from 100% (saturation) to below 10%. If temperature and relative humidity are known, a state point is determined, and absolute humidity can be read from the vertical scale. Actually, any two properties of air will determine the state point, and the rest can be read directly from the psychrometric chart.

Energy content and wet-bulb temperature

All temperature scales start at a theoretical minimum temperature called absolute zero. At this temperature all materials lose all internal energy. This temperature is about −460°F − it has never actually been reached experimentally. A material at any temperature greater than absolute zero will contain energy; the energy that would be required to heat it from absolute zero to the measured temperature. Thus air contains heat energy, called *enthalpy*. The symbol "*h*" is used to represent enthalpy, and its units are BTU/lb dry air.

Here are some useful conversions:

$$1 \text{ kW (electrical energy)} = 3{,}413 \text{ BTU/h}$$
$$1 \text{ hp (mechanical energy)} = 2{,}545 \text{ BTU/h}$$
$$1 \text{ kcal (nutritional energy)} = 3.97 \text{ BTU}$$

The energy content, in BTU/lb dry air, of air at any state point can be read from the psychrometric chart. The enthalpy scale is inclined left to right as shown in Figure 5.4. For the air at 55°F, $w =$ 0.005, the enthalpy value (h) is 18.7 BTU/lb. dry air.

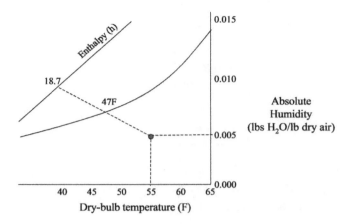

Figure 5.4: A Psychrometric Chart with Enthalpy and Wet-Bulb Temperature Scales

Closely related to energy content is *wet-bulb temperature*, T_{WB}. If the bulb of an ordinary mercury thermometer is wrapped with a wet cloth, the thermometer will read a lower value than if the bulb was dry. If the air is not saturated, water will evaporate from the wet cloth. There is only one place the energy can come from to change from a liquid to a vapor—the air itself. Evaporation is a cooling process; in exchange for more water vapor, the air will give up temperature. The temperature to which the air will come when water is evaporated is called the wet-bulb temperature. This is the temperature from a thermometer with a wet cloth on it in a moving stream of air.

The difference between the dry-bulb temperature and the wet-bulb temperature is called the *wet-bulb depression*. If the air is completely saturated (RH = 100%), the wet-bulb depression is zero. The larger the spread between the wet-bulb and dry-bulb temperatures, the larger the wet-bulb depression, and the more evaporation is taking place.

On the psychrometric chart, the wet-bulb temperature for a given state point is found by moving to the left and up, along an enthalpy line, until the saturation line is reached. The air with T_{DB} = 55°F, w = 0.005 will have T_{WB} = 47°F, and wet-bulb depression of 8°F.

Air density (specific volume)
Another important property of air that can be found on the psychrometric chart is *specific volume*, in units of cubic feet per pound (ft³ / lb dry air). The symbol for specific volume is "V." Specific volume is the reciprocal of density (lb / ft³) and is a measure of air density.

Solids and liquids maintain relatively constant density over normal temperature ranges, but gasses (like air) change density dramatically when temperature changes. Gases expand when heated. Therefore, the specific volume of air in ft³/lb dry air will increase as temperature increases. At high temperatures, more cubic feet are required to contain a pound of air than at lower temperatures. Figure 5.5 shows the location of the specific volume information on the psychrometric chart.

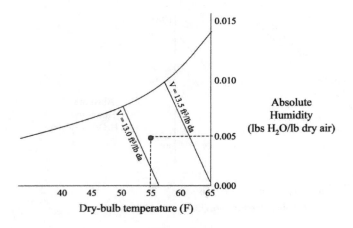

Figure 5.5: Psychrometric Chart with Specific Volume

Dew Point Temperature

Dew point temperature (T_{DP}) is the surface temperature at which water vapor will condense from air. It is a measure of the absolute quantity of water vapor in the air. As such, it is read horizontally on the same line as absolute humidity, but using the scale on the saturation line instead. This is illustrated in Figure 5.6.

Summary of psychrometric properties and symbols

The air properties found on the psychrometric chart are summarized in table 5.2. If any two air properties are known, the state point is determined and the other properties can be read off the psychrometric chart. There are two exceptions: the pairs h and T_{WB}, and w and T_{DP}.

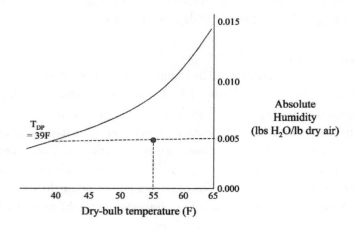

Figure 5.6: Psychrometric Chart with Dew-Point Temperature

Table 5.2. Summary of Psychrometric Properties

PROPERTY	SYMBOL	UNITS
Dry-bulb temperature	T_{DB}	°F or °C
Wet-bulb temperature	T_{WB}	°F or °C
Dew-point temperature	T_{DP}	°F or °C
Absolute humidity	w	lb H_2O / lb dry air OR kg H_2O / kg dry air
Relative humidity	RH	%
Enthalpy	h	BTU / lb dry air OR kJ / kg dry air
Specific volume	V	ft³ / lb dry air OR m³ / kg dry air

5.2.2 Changes in Air Conditions

A single state point will represent air conditions at any given time. But in ventilation and drying, of interest is what happens when air is heated, cooled, passed through a building space, or passed through a material for drying. Drying involves the movement of moisture from a material into the air, so changes in absolute humidity will determine how much drying can be done by a given amount of air. Ventilation involves the movement of heat and moisture, so changes in both temperature and absolute humidity will determine whether ventilation can control air conditions within a building space.

There are two processes of importance in grain conditioning: evaporation of water and heating. Both of these can be represented on the psychrometric chart.

Sensible Heating

Air is often sensibly heated before being used in ventilation or for drying. (Remember that sensible heat is a measure of the amount of heat that accompanies a temperature change, but no change in moisture content.) Why? For drying, it increases the water holding capacity of the air. For ventilating, it increases the dry-bulb temperature of the air.

The key point in sensible heating is that no water is removed or added. Energy is added, but the absolute humidity remains constant.

Example 5.5

Suppose that air at 55°F and a relative humidity of 50% (point A in Figure 5.7) is sensibly heated to 85°F (point C in Figure 5.7). How much energy was required to heat the air?

Refer to Figure 5.7. The properties of air at states A and C are:

PROPERTY	STATE A	STATE C
Dry-bulb temperature, T_{DB} (°F)	55	85
Wet-bulb temperature, T_{WB} (°F)	46	60
Absolute humidity, w (lb H_2O/lb dry air)	0.0046	0.0046
Relative Humidity, RH (%)	54	18
Specific Volume, V (ft³/lb dry air)	13.1	13.7
Enthalpy, h (BTU/lb dry air)	18.2	25.8

Note that the relative humidity of the air decreases from 54% to 18% because the maximum water content (w_{max}) is much greater at 85°F than at 55°F.

The energy required to heat the air can be calculated as:

$$\Delta h = h_C - h_A = 25.8 - 18.2 = \underline{\textbf{7.6 BTU/lb dry air}}$$

There is another, simpler way to determine the amount of sensible heat added to the air. The specific heat capacity (c_p) of air is approximately 0.24 BTU/lb dry air ·°F, although it varies somewhat with temperature. Equation 5.3 can be used.

$$q = c_p m \Delta T \hspace{4cm} \text{Eq. 5.3}$$

where: q = amount of sensible heat (BTU)
c_p = specific heat capacity = 0.24 (BTU / lb·dry air ·°F)
m = mass of air (lb dry air)
ΔT = change in temperature (°F)

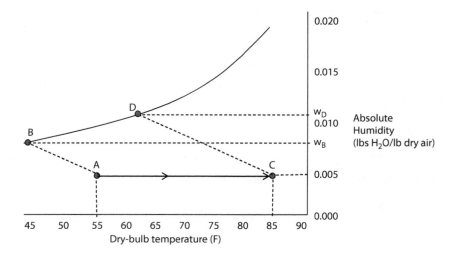

Figure 5.7: Example 5.5 — Sensible Heating

Example

In the previous example, determine the amount of energy required to sensibly heat the air using the specific heat capacity of air.

Using Equation 5.3, and ignoring the mass of air (m):

$$q = c_p \Delta T = \left(0.24 \frac{BTU}{lb\ dry\ air \cdot °F} \right)(85°F - 55°F) = \underline{\textbf{7.2 BTU/lb dry air}}$$

This result is similar to, but slightly different from the previous result. In most calculations determining required heat or ventilation rates, the difference is insignificant.

Evaporative Cooling

The water content of unsaturated air will increase when the air is bubbled through water, or passed through a mist of water, or passed through a mass of moist grain. The air will be cooled at the same time, because the heat necessary for the phase change from water liquid to water vapor comes from the air. This process is called evaporative cooling.

At the instant that evaporation takes place, no energy is being put into the air—the energy content is constant. Any increase in water content of the air must be accompanied by a decrease in temperature, with the total energy level of the air remaining the same. Sensible heat (heat associated with temperature) is being converted into latent heat (heat associated with a change in phase).

Since total energy remains constant in evaporation, an evaporation process takes place up a line of constant enthalpy and constant wet-bulb temperature on a psychrometric chart. The maximum amount of cooling that can be accomplished is equal to the wet-bulb depression, (i.e., air can at most be cooled to the dew point and no farther via evaporative cooling).

Evaporative cooling is a very popular way to cool air in dry climates. Devices commonly called "swamp coolers" humidify dry air and thereby lower the air's temperature. Typically, air passes through a fibrous pad that is saturated with water. The maximum amount of temperature change that can be accomplished is equal to the wet-bulb depression, which can be very large in dry climates. Evaporative cooling is not very effective in humid climates where the wet-bulb depression can be small.

The amount of energy required to evaporate water is somewhat dependent on temperature. This energy is called the latent heat of vaporization or *LHV*. At ambient temperatures LVH is about 1035 BTU/lb of water. The exact formula for LHV is:

$$LHV = 1094 - (0.57)(T_{DB}) \hspace{3cm} \text{Eq. 5.8}$$

where: LHV = the latent heat of vaporization of water (BTU / lb H_2O)

T_{DB} = dry-bulb temperature (°F)

Example 5.6

Consider air at state A in Figure 5.7. Suppose air passes through a water mist until the air is entirely saturated (state B, 100% RH). How much water does the air gain?

As before, the psychrometric conditions at states A and B are:

PROPERTY	STATE A	STATE B
Dry-bulb temperature, T_{DB} (°F)	55	46
Wet-bulb temperature, T_{WB} (°F)	46	46
Absolute humidity, w (lb H_2O/lb dry air)	0.0046	0.0066
Relative Humidity, RH (%)	54	100
Specific Volume, V (ft³/lb dry air)	13.1	12.8
Enthalpy, h (BTU/lb dry air)	18.2	18.2

On a psychrometric chart (Figure 5.7), the process will follow the line of constant energy ($h = 18.2$ or $T_{WB} = 46°F$) until it reaches the saturation line. At that point, it has picked up all the water it can; it is saturated at state point B.

The wet-bulb and dry-bulb temperatures are equal at state B, which is always true at saturation. The air was cooled from 55°F to 46°F, for a total of 9°F, but it also picked up water. The amount of water picked up, per pound of air, is the change in absolute humidity:

$$\Delta w = w_B - w_A = 0.0066 - 0.0046 = \underline{\mathbf{0.0020\ lb\ H_2O/lb\ dry\ air}}$$

Sensible Cooling or Air Conditioning

Sensible cooling is the opposite of sensible heating. Air is cooled (e.g., by passing it over the cold coils of an air conditioner). On a psychrometric chart, the process is a horizontal movement to the left, with no change in absolute humidity.

If the air is cooled so much that the dry-bulb temperature is equal to the wet-bulb temperature, then condensation will begin to occur. You may notice that this happens with a window air conditioning unit; water can often be seen dripping from the unit. Once the wet-bulb temperature is reached, the dry-bulb temperature can only be decreased by an accompanying condensation of water. On a psychrometric chart, the process continues towards a decreasing dry-bulb temperature by following the saturation line.

5.3. Ventilation

Ventilation is the process of supplying or moving air to or from any space. Houses, offices, factories, and livestock buildings are ventilated for three purposes: (1) air quality, (2) temperature control, and (3) moisture control. Applying the principles of psychrometrics, calculating ventilation rates can be easily calculated for a given set of inside and outside conditions.

5.3.1. Specifying Air Flow Rates

Before progressing too far along with ventilation, the basis for expressing the amount of air that is being moved must be understood. The typical unit of airflow is ft³/min or cfm. In SI units, it is often expressed as m³/s.

Expressing airflow using volume can be a problem, however. Airflow devices (fans, blowers, compressors, etc.) are often rated on a volume flow basis. However, air expands and contracts depending on the temperature and other psychrometric properties. The changes in air properties due to heating (enthalpy change or Δh) and humidification (absolute humidity change or Δw) are expressed on the basis of a pound of dry air—a weight not a volume.

The parameter of specific volume (V) is used to compensate for changes in volume and the amount of air being moved:

$$Q_m = \frac{Q \times 60}{V} \qquad\qquad \text{Eq. 5.9}$$

where: Q_m = mass airflow rate (lb dry air / h)
 Q = volumetric airflow rate (ft³/min or cfm)
 V = specific volume (ft³/lb dry air)
 60 = conversion factor (60 min = 1 h)

Example 5.7
Find the mass flow rate of 10,000 cfm of air at state A in figure 5.7.
From the earlier example, V_A = 13.1 ft³/lb dry air. Using equation 5.9:

$$Q_m = \frac{Q \times 60}{V} = \frac{(10,000)(60)}{13.1} = 45,802 \approx \underline{\textbf{45,800 lb dry air / h}}$$

In ventilation and drying problems, air can be at various states throughout the process. Which state is used to determine the specific volume (V)? Similarly, at what point in the process is the volumetric airflow rate (Q) measured?

Volumetric airflow rate (or sometimes, the airflow rate) is always measured at the <u>inlet</u> to the fan, blower, or device that is moving the air. Thus the conditions at the device input determine the psychrometric properties, including the value of the specific volume.

5.3.2. Determining Ventilation Rates

<u>Ventilating for Air Quality</u>
Ventilating for air quality maintains minimum standards for dust, carbon dioxide, and other gases. This is the minimum rate that must be maintained regardless of inside or outside temperature. It is often designated as $Q_{minimum}$.

Minimum ventilation rates have been developed for offices, factories, and residential housing. Often, they are expressed in terms of the number of air exchanges (building volume) per unit time. In many situations, the minimum ventilation rate is designed so as not to exceed certain levels of gases or airborne particulates, so there is no single minimum ventilation rate that can be quoted. A great reference for these is the *ASHRAE Handbook – Fundamentals* (in the library or www.ashrae.org). It has more information about ventilation than you can possible imagine, as it is the standard reference book for engineers designing ventilation systems for almost any type of application.

Minimum livestock ventilation rates were determined from research data. A good reference for these rates is Table 633-2 of the *Structures and Environment Handbook*, MWPS-1 by the Midwest Plan Service.

Ventilating for Temperature Control

The ventilation rate for temperature assumes that temperature can be controlled with ventilation only. No supplemental heating or cooling is used. This rate is found by performing a "heat balance" where the sources of heat (people, animals, equipment, etc.) are exactly equal to the heat losses (evaporation, building heat loss, ventilation heat loss). The heat balance equation, is:

$$q_m + q_s + q_{sr} = q_e + q_b + q_v \qquad \text{Eq. 5.10}$$

where: q_s = sensible heat from people and/or animals (BTU / h)

q_{sr} = supplemental heat (BTU / h, assumed =0 for calculating $Q_{temperature}$)

q_m = mechanical heat gain from motors, equipment, etc. (BTU / h)

q_e = heat loss to water evaporation (BTU / h, assumed =0 for many situations)

q_b = building heat loss = $(A/R)\Delta T$ (BTU / h, from Equation 5.4)

q_v = heat lost to the ventilation air (BTU / h)

The heat balance is solved for q_v for various outside conditions (e.g., a range that might be encountered), assuming the inside conditions will remain constant. Once q_v is known, Q_m can be calculated using equation 5.11:

$$q_v = Q_m \times \Delta h_s \qquad \text{Eq. 5.11}$$

where: q_v = heat lost to the ventilation air (BTU / h)

Q_m = mass airflow rate (lb dry air / h)

Δh_s = change in <u>sensible</u> heat content of the air (BTU / lb dry air)

Knowing Q_m, the ventilation rate for temperature control (Q or more accurately $Q_{temperature}$) can be calculated by using equation 5.9:

$$Q_m = \frac{Q_{temperature} \times 60}{V} \qquad \text{Eq. 5.9}$$

Ventilating for Moisture Control

The ventilation rate for moisture assumes moisture of the air can be controlled with ventilation only. This rate is found by performing a "moisture balance" where the sources of moisture (people, animals, cooking, water evaporation, etc.) are exactly equal to the moisture losses (ventilation moisture loss). The moisture balance equation is:

$$W_a + W_e = W_v \qquad \text{Eq. 5.12}$$

where: W_a = moisture production from animals, people, processes (lb H_2O / h)
W_e = evaporated moisture (lb H_2O / h, assumed zero for many applications)
W_v = ventilation moisture removal rate (lb H_2O / h)

Note the use of W in equation 5.10. The capital W refers to a rate of water vapor addition or removal (lb H_2O / h), whereas a lowercase w refers to the absolute humidity (lb H_2O / lb dry air).

The moisture balance is solved for q_v for various outside conditions (e.g., a range that might be encountered), assuming the inside conditions will remain constant. Once W_v is known, Q_m can be calculated using equation 5.13:

$$W_v = Q_m \times \Delta w \qquad\qquad \text{Eq. 5.13}$$

where: W_v = ventilation moisture removal rate (lb H_2O / h)
Q_m = mass airflow rate (lb dry air / h)
Δw = change in absolute humidity of the air (lb H_2O / lb dry air)

Knowing Q_m, the ventilation rate for temperature control (Q, or more accurately $Q_{moisture}$) can be calculated by using equation 5.9:

$$Q_m = \frac{Q_{moisture} \times 60}{V} \qquad\qquad \text{Eq. 5.9}$$

Choosing a Ventilation Rate
Choose the largest of the three ventilation rates ($Q_{minimum}$, $Q_{temperature}$, $Q_{moisture}$) calculated above—this is designated as Q_{actual}. Note some results when Q_{actual} is different from the three possible ventilation rates:

- If $Q_{actual} > Q_{actual}$ then more air is being moved then is necessary for air quality. Generally, this is not a problem as additional airflow improves air quality.
- If $Q_{actual} > Q_{moisture}$ then the moisture in the building will drop from the specified levels (generally an acceptable outcome).
- If $Q_{actual} > Q_{temperature}$ then supplemental heat must be added to the building to avoid a drop in temperature from the specified levels. To determine the supplemental heat rate, perform the heat balance again, this time using $Q_{m\ actual}$ (calculated from Q_{actual}). The only unknown in the heat balance equation is q_{sr}, which you can now calculate.

5.4. Drying

Drying is an important industrial and agricultural process. There are many books on drying that discuss all the situations that may occur. Suffice it to say that a complete discussion of drying would be much larger than this entire book. Thus, the situation of grain drying in a deep bed of grain is a simple way to illustrate drying.

Consider the grain bin filled with wet corn, as pictured in Figure 5.8, where air is passed through the grain. Two items of interest are: (1) the drying rate, from which the time it takes to dry the corn to a certain moisture content can be determined, and (2) the rate of energy use. Psychrometrics can be used to analyze this situation, but some assumptions are required:

- Air leaves the grain in equilibrium with the wettest grain. For corn above 20% moisture content, this means the air leaves the grain saturated, or at a RH of 100%.
- Incoming air conditions are constant over the drying period.
- No heat is lost to, or gained from, the surroundings.
- Latent heat of vaporization of moisture in grain equals that of free water.

These assumptions are reasonably good up to a point. Above an air temperature 120°F, the equilibrium assumption is not necessarily good; other theories must be used to predict drying at high temperatures. If grain depth is relatively thin, air will not leave the grain in equilibrium. Therefore, increasing temperatures and smaller depths will both reduce drying efficiency, and will limit the accuracy of simple psychrometric analyses.

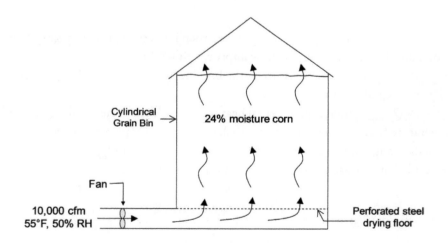

Figure 5.8: Drying Corn in a Grain Bin with Unheated Air

5.4.1 Drying rate

As the air passes through the mass of wet grain, moisture evaporates from the corn kernels and transfers to the air. This process is evaporative cooling. On a psychrometric chart, the process follows the wet-bulb line. In our illustration here (very wet corn), it will follow the wet-bulb line all the way to the saturation line. Thus, the air exiting the grain bin will be at 100% relative humidity.

Drying rate, or the rate at which moisture is removed, can be determined by:

$$DR = (Q_m) \times (\Delta w) = \left(\frac{Q \times 60}{V} \right) \times (\Delta w) \qquad\qquad \text{Eq. 5.14}$$

where: DR = drying rate (lb H_2O / h)
   Q_m = mass airflow rate (lb dry air / h)
   Δw = change in absolute humidity (lb H_2O / lb dry air)
   Q = airflow rate (ft^3 / min or cfm)
   V = specific volume (ft^3 / lb dry air)
   60 = conversion factor (60 min = 1 h)

Example 5.8

Consider the grain bin pictured in Figure 5.8. Air at 55°F dry-bulb and 54% relative humidity (state A in Figure 5.7) is blown into the bin at a rate of 10,000 cfm. Because of the evaporative cooling that occurs with drying, the air leaves the grain bin at 100% relative humidity. At what rate is moisture being removed from the corn?

From our earlier discussion and Figure 5.7, the psychrometric properties of the incoming and exiting air (states A and B, respectively) are known:

PROPERTY	STATE A	STATE B
Dry-bulb temperature, T_{DB} (°F)	55	46
Wet-bulb temperature, T_{WB} (°F)	46	46
Absolute humidity, w (lb H_2O/lb dry air)	0.0046	0.0066
Relative Humidity, RH (%)	54	100
Specific Volume, V (ft^3/lb dry air)	13.1	12.8
Enthalpy, h (BTU/lb dry air)	18.2	18.2

Now apply equation 5.10:

$$DR = (Q_m) \times (\Delta w) = \left(\frac{Q \times 60}{V} \right) \times (\Delta w)$$

$$DR = \frac{(10,000)(60)}{13.1} \times (0.0066 - 0.0046) = 91.6 \approx \underline{\mathbf{92 \; lb \; H_2O / h}}$$

Why was V_A used in example 5.4-5? There were multiple V's to choose from. Fans are almost always mounted ahead of heaters because their motors require cool air. Therefore, the airflow rate is based on outside air conditions, that is, on the conditions of the fan inlet. The mass airflow rate (lb dry air/h) does not change even if the volume flow rate (ft³/min) changes due to changes in temperature.

Example 5.9

Consider the grain bin pictured in Figure 5.9. Air at 55°F dry-bulb and 54% relative humidity (state A in Figure 5.7) is blown into the bin at a rate of 10,000 cfm and also heated 30°F by a liquid propane (LP) heater (state C in Figure 5.7). (Note that burning LP adds a negligible amount of moisture to the air.) At what rate is moisture being removed from the corn?

From our earlier discussion and Figure 5.7, the psychrometric properties of the air entering the fan (state A), entering the grain (state C), and exiting the grain (state D) are known:

PROPERTY	STATE A	STATE C	STATE D
Dry-bulb temperature, T_{DB} (°F)	55	85	60
Wet-bulb temperature, T_{WB} (°F)	46	60	60
Absolute humidity, w (lb H_2O/lb dry air)	0.0046	0.0046	0.0111
Relative Humidity, RH (%)	54	18	100
Specific Volume, V (ft³/lb dry air)	13.1	13.7	13.3
Enthalpy, h (BTU/lb dry air)	18.2	25.8	25.8

Now apply equation 5.10:

$$DR = (Q_m) \times (\Delta w) = \left(\frac{Q \times 60}{V} \right) \times (\Delta w)$$

$$DR = \frac{(10,000)(60)}{13.1} \times (0.0111 - 0.0046) = 297.7 \approx \underline{\mathbf{298 \; lb \; H_2O \, / \, h}}$$

By adding some heat, the drying rate tripled! The mass airflow rate remains the same, but the change in absolute humidity (Δw) is much greater which increased the drying rate.

5.4.2. Drying energy use

The amount of energy required for drying is an important consideration in determining cost. It can be described by:

$$E_h = (Q_m) \times (\Delta h) = \left(\frac{Q \times 60}{V} \right) \times (\Delta h)$$

Eq. 5.15

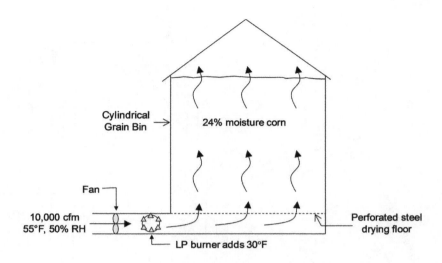

Figure 5.9: Drying Corn in a Grain Bin with Heated Air

where: E_h = heating energy (BTU / h)
$\quad$ Q_m = mass airflow rate (lb dry air / h)
$\quad$ Δh = change in enthalpy (BTU / lb dry air)
$\quad$ Q $\;$ = airflow rate (ft^3 / min or cfm)
$\quad$ V $\;$ = specific volume (ft^3 / lb dry air)
$\quad$ 60 = conversion factor (60 min = 1 h)

Example 5.10
How much liquid propane (LP) is required to heat the air in the previous example (Figure 5.9)?

$\quad$ The psychrometric properties of the outside air (state A in Figure 5.7) are known and the air after it has been heated (state C). Applying equation 5.11:

$$E_h = (Q_m) \times (\Delta h) = \left(\frac{Q \times 60}{V} \right) \times (\Delta h)$$

$$E_h = \frac{(10,000)(60)}{13.1} \times (25.8 - 18.2) = 348,092 \approx \underline{\mathbf{348,000\ BTU / h}}$$

Knowing that one gallon of propane contains approximately 85,000 BTU and assuming that a propane burner is 85% efficient:

$$E_h = \frac{348,092\ BTU}{h} \times \frac{gal}{85,000\ BTU} \times \frac{1}{0.85} = 4.818 \approx \underline{\mathbf{4.8\ gal\ LP / h}}$$

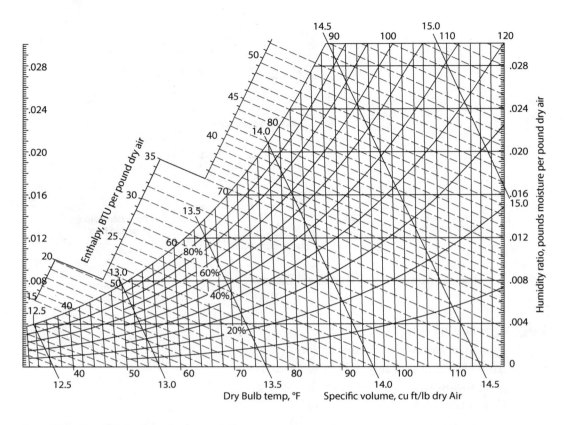

Figure 5.10: Normal Temperature Psychrometric Chart

EXERCISES

1. What is the R-value of a wall of a house made up of the materials listed below? State the units of R-value. Make a cross-sectional sketch of the wall. Starting from the outside, the materials are:
    - Wood siding, lapped
    - Insulating board (extruded polystyrene) 1.75 inches thick
    - Plywood 0.63 inches thick
    - Fiberglass 5.50 inches thick, $R = 3.25$/inch
    - Vapor barrier, $R = 0.00$
    - Sheet rock (gypsum) 0.63 inches thick

2. What is the R-value of the ceiling of an insulated shop building made up of the materials listed below? State the units of R-value. Make a cross-sectional sketch of the wall. Starting from the inside, the materials are:
    - Plywood, 0.5 inches thick
    - Vapor barrier, $R = 0.00$

- Glass wool insulation, 8.5 inches thick, $R = 4.5$/inch
  Note: An unventilated attic is above the ceiling. Air in the attic is at "inside" conditions. Choose the R-values of surface conditions carefully.

3. Consider a student apartment in Ames on a cold winter day as described here. What is the total rate of heat loss from the apartment (in BTU/h and kW)?
   - The apartment is 30.0 ft long by 24.0 ft wide with 8.0 ft ceilings.
   - One of the walls (30.0 ft × 8.0 ft), the floor, and the ceiling are common with adjacent apartments.
   - Two walls (one 30.0 ft × 8.0 ft, the other 24.0 ft × 8.0 ft) face the outside.
   - One wall (24.0 ft × 8.0 ft) faces an inside hallway.
   - Common wall $R = 14.0$; floor and ceiling $R = 20.5$; outside wall (30.0 ft × 8.0 ft) $R = 22.5$; outside wall (24.0 ft × 8.0 ft) $R = 18.5$; wall facing hallway (24.0 ft × 8.0 ft): $R = 13.0$
   - Temperatures: outside: 0.0°F; inside: 68°F; adjacent apartments: 68°F; inside hallway: 55°F

4. A house in Ames has an overall heat loss factor, $(A/R)_{total}$, of 275 BTU/hr·°F. The inside temperature of the house is kept at an average temperature of 68.0°F. The furnace in the house uses natural gas.
   a. What is the difference in heat loss (BTU/hr and kW) when the average outside temperature is 40.0°F and 15.0°F?
   b. How much extra will it cost to heat the house for a month (30 days) at an average outside temperature of 15.0°F compared to 40.0°F? Natural gas is charged in Ames according to the following schedule:
   - Non-gas costs: $0.18225/therm (1 therm = 100,000 BTU)
   - Gas costs: $0.474140/therm
   - Service charge: $0.42735/day (regardless of energy use)
   - Cost management credit: –$0.10072/day (regardless of energy use)
   - Local option tax: 1.00% on all of the above

5. Complete the following table using a psychrometric chart.

	UNITS	(A)	(B)	(C)	(D)	(E)
$T_{dry\text{-}bulb}$		68	35	80	75	
$T_{wet\text{-}bulb}$		58				80
$T_{dew\ point}$				65		
Relative Humidity (RH)			40			90
Absolute Humidity (w)					0.0072	
Specific Volume (V)						
Enthalpy (h)						

6. Air at 86°F db and 20% RH is drawn through an evaporative cooler. The air leaves the cooler totally saturated with water vapor. What is the exiting air dry-bulb temperature (F)? Draw a sketch of a psychrometric chart that demonstrates the process.

7. Air at 40°F db and 38°F wb is sensibly heated to 70°F db. What is the relative humidity (%) of the air at 70°F db? Draw a sketch of a psychrometric chart that demonstrates the process.

8. The Butterfly Conservatory at the ISU Reiman Gardens is maintained at 80°F and 80% RH. Outside air at 45°F and 50% RH is brought in to maintain air quality. The air must be heated and humidified.
   a. Draw a sketch of a psychrometric chart that identifies the outside and inside air conditions.
   b. How much sensible heat (BTU/lb of dry air) must be added to the incoming air?
   c. How much latent heat (BTU/lb of dry air) is added to the incoming air?
   d. How much water vapor (lbs H_2O / lb of dry air) is added to the incoming air?

9. Air at 75°F db and 35% RH is being moved at a rate of 12,500 cfm. What is the mass airflow rate (lbs da per hour)?

10. Air at 86°F db and 20% RH passes through an evaporative cooler at a rate of 10,500 cfm. The air leaves the cooler totally saturated with water vapor. What rate (gallons H_2O/h) must be supplied to the evaporative cooler? (Assume: 1 gal = 8.34 lbs; the air specific volume is determined at 86°F and 20% RH).

11. Air flowing at a rate of 85 cfm (at 40°F db and 38°F wb) is sensibly heated to 70°F db. How much heat is required (BTU/h)?

12. A building is being ventilated to maintain the inside air temperature. The building has an overall heat loss factor of 194 BTU/(h·°F). Inside the building, people and equipment generate heat at a rate of 15,700 BTU/h. The desired inside conditions are 75°F db and 60°F wb. The outside conditions are 45°F db and 38°F wb. The ventilation fan exhausts air from the building (fan inlet is at the inside conditions). What ventilation rate (in cfm) is needed to maintain an inside air temperature?

13. A building is being ventilated to maintain the moisture content of the inside air. There is a manufacturing process inside the building that generates 5.25 lbs of water vapor per hour. The desired inside conditions are 75°F db and 60°F wb. The outside conditions are 45°F db and 38°F wb. The ventilation fan exhausts air from the building (fan inlet is at the inside conditions). What ventilation rate (in cfm) is needed to remove the generated water vapor?

Figure and Table Sources

1. Tbl. 5.1: Kathy Walker, MWPS-1 Structures and Environment Handbook. Copyright © 1987 by Midwest Plan Service (MWPS).
2. Fig. 5.1: Kathy Walker, MWPS-1 Structures and Environment Handbook. Copyright © 1987 by Midwest Plan Service (MWPS).
3. Fig. 5.10: Kathy Walker, MWPS-1 Structures and Environment Handbook. Copyright © 1987 by Midwest Plan Service (MWPS).

6

DATA ANALYSIS

OBJECTIVES

When you complete your study of this chapter, you will be able to:

1. Describe the differences between sample and population
2. Describe data types and levels
3. Define and calculate mean, median, mode, and standard deviation of a given data set
4. Generate graphic data representation to meet needs
5. Describe Chebyshev's rule and use it to solve data distribution problems
6. Use z-score method to solve problems for normally distributed data
7. Use linear interpolation to estimate missing values for a data set
8. Use linear regression and least squares fitting for a data set

6.1 Data Description and Presentation

A technologist often needs to process and organize data, and to make predictions based on available data on potential trends. Hence, it is of great interest for a technologist to have some basic understanding about data analysis.

Data analysis is built around statistics, a branch of mathematics that deals with decision making involving uncertainty. Uncertainty is inherent in all data gathered through experiments or measurements. Statistics establishes rules that will help a technologist to analyze numerical (or even non-numerical) data derived from surveys and experiments, to draw

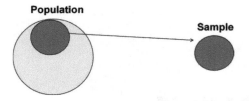

Figure 6.1: Population vs. Sample

conclusions despite built-in uncertainty, and to make predictions about trends.

Statistics can be categorized into *descriptive statistics*, which is designed to summarize and describe important features of a set of data without attempting to infer conclusions that go beyond the data; and *inferential statistics,* which allows one to utilize statistical rules to make generalizations beyond the scope of the available data, and hence make predictions.

To understand the distinction between descriptive and inferential statistics, one must understand the concept of population and sample.

By definition, a population includes all members of a certain group, or all events that fit a particular description. For example, all residents of a certain state make up the population of the state. Usually, population contains a large number of members or events, but not necessarily so. The key to make a population is that it includes all members or events without exception.

When populations become large, it may not be practical to work with all members. Instead, a more manageable subset of a certain population can be selected, to represent the key features of the population. This subset is defined as a sample of the population.

The correlation between a population and a sample is illustrated in Figure 6.1.

A measure of a characteristic of a population is called a parameter. Typical parameters include mean and median, to be discussed later. A descriptive measure of a sample of the population is called a statistic. For example, if we determine the mean age of the residents of the state of Iowa, that mean value would be a parameter; however, if we draw a sample of Iowa residents (e.g., the residents of the city of Ames), then the mean age of residents of Ames would be a statistic.

Inferential statistics utilizes statistical rules and tools to make generalizations about a population by studying a sample of the population. We make inferences about a parameter of a population from a statistic acquired from a sample of the population. Since the size of a sample can be controlled, this will make the task of estimating a parameter much easier. One example is polls. A small number of people are polled for a certain opinion to obtain a statistic, and that statistic is used to predict the opinion of the general public, a parameter.

Certainly how a sample is selected from a population is critically important. An inappropriately drawn sample can yield a bad statistic, which does not provide a good representation of the parameter. It is of great importance to design surveys and experiments using scientific methods (i.e., statistical design) so that good statistics can be obtained.

6.1.1 Types and Levels of Data

The first thing one needs to understand is types and levels of statistical data.

When dealing with statistical data, two types can be distinguished: qualitative data and quantitative data. We should be careful that not all numerical data are quantitative. The criterion that one can use to identify quantitative data is whether or not arithmetic operations between data entries can produce meaningful results. For example, jersey numbers of players on a football team are numerical, but arithmetic operations between them do not yield meaningful results, and therefore, they are not quantitative data.

Quantitative data can be further categorized into discrete data and continuous data. Discrete data are results of a count; they are exact numbers and have infinite significant figures. Continuous data, on the other hand, are results of a measurement, and they have limited significant figures.

When dealing with data it is also important to understand the concept of levels of measurement, which translate into levels of data as well. Commonly, four levels of measurement (i.e., data) are used:

Nominal: The nominal type differentiates between data entries based only on qualitative classifications, such as the names or categories they belong to; they are not ranked, and hence cannot be sorted into a meaningful order. Non-numerical data are nominal data. Some numerical data are nominal data, too. This occurs when numbers are used as labels, not as numerical values.

Ordinal: The ordinal type allows for ranked order, hence the data can be sorted. However, there are no set differences between data entries. An example of ordinal data is class rank (freshman, sophomore, junior, senior), or military rank. Another example of ordinal data is IQ scores. IQ scores are ranked for comparison purposes, however, there is no absolute zero, and a 10-point difference may carry different meanings at different points of the scale. Ordinal data are typically qualitative data.

Interval: Here we enter the domain of quantitative data. The interval type allows for the degree of difference between data points to be set, but the ratio between them is not meaningful, and a zero is arbitrarily set. A good example of this type is a temperature scale. A zero is arbitrarily selected at a certain point, and the ratio between data points is not meaningful (since 70°F cannot be said to be "twice as hot" as 35 °F!).

Ratio: The ratio type takes its name from the fact that the data are typically obtained through measurements done by estimating the ratio between a magnitude of a continuous quantity and a unit magnitude of the same kind. The ratio type has a meaningful zero value, which means the lack of the quality. Most measurement in the physical sciences and engineering is done on ratio scales. Examples include mass, length, duration, plane angle, energy, and electric charge. Ratios are allowed because having a non-arbitrary zero point makes it meaningful to say, for example, that one object has "twice the length" of another (= is "twice as long"). It should be pointed out that the ratio type is not limited to continuous data. Discrete data can also be a ratio. For example, the amount of money is a ratio; zero means no money (lack of the quality), and twenty dollars are twice as much as ten.

6.1.2 Quantitative Data Descriptors

To present or describe data quantitatively, we often use a concept called frequency distribution. A frequency distribution is a systematic collection of data illustrating how many times a certain value occurs. As shown in later sections, frequency distribution can be graphically represented as data curves, bar chart, pie chart, histogram, etc.

To generate a frequency distribution, one needs to first *classify* the data. That is, to organize data into different classes based on certain quantitative criteria. Two things must be considered when classifying a given data set: The number of classes, into which the data are to be organized, and the range of each class. The following guidelines are commonly used when constructing a frequency distribution out of a given data set.

1. Classes should be selected that cover the entire available data set.
2. The number of classes, n, should be properly determined. Usually, it is a good practice to have an n value that is between 6 and 15.
3. Each data point should belong to one, and only one class.
4. It is preferable to have the classes all have the same range.

As later sections will show, a frequency distribution is very useful for predicting trends, because it provides a picture of how often certain values are expected to appear.

Four quantitative data descriptors are often used to describe the properties of a given data set. They are: mean, median, mode, and standard deviation. Among them, mean, median, and mode measure the central tendency of a data set, and standard deviation measures the variation of a data set.

6.1.2.1 Measures of Central Tendency

The arithmetic mean, or average (often simply called mean), of a given data set, is defined as the sum of all values in a data set divided by n, the total number of data points in the data set. Suppose a data set has n data points in it, denoted as $\{x_1, x_2, x_2, x_3, x_4, \dots x_i, \dots x_n\}$, where x_i is the ith entry in the data set. Then the mean is defined as:

$$mean = \frac{\sum_i x_i}{n}$$

Eq. 6.1

Where n is the total number of data entries in a set.

The mean is a common measure of central tendency. It has several advantages: it is familiar to most people and its meaning is easy to understand; it takes into account every data point; it is always unique; and it can be utilized to make inferential predictions, as we will discuss later. However, the mean is not without its problems. Any outlier or gross error can have major impact on the value of the mean. As a popular joke shows, when Bill Gates walks into a bar, the mean net worth of the people in the bar suddenly jumps to billions of dollars! Certainly, in this case the mean is not a good representation of the prevailing net worth of the people in the bar!

To avoid this difficulty, another measure can be introduced to describe the "center" of a data set. It is called the median. The median is defined as the value of the middle item of the data set when the entire data set is sorted to go ascendingly or descendingly. For example, the median of a data set of five numbers, {1, 3, 5, 7, 101} is 5, while its mean is 23.7, which is heavily influenced by the outlier value, 101. If there is an even number of items, there isn't a specific middle item. In this case, the median is the average of the two middle items. For example, for a data set of {1, 4, 6, 8, 10, 19, 22, 100}, the median is the average of the 4th and 5th items, and it is equal to (8 + 10)/2 = 9.

The mean and median of a data set often do not coincide. Both are measures of central tendency, but in different ways. The median divides the data set into two halves, and one is above it, while the other is below it. The mean may be thought of as the center of gravity of the data set.

The median is also always in existence, and unique. It is not affected by extreme outlier values. When exclusion of the lowest and highest values in a data set significantly alters the mean, the median should be considered to provide a better measure of central tendency of the data set. When economic data are assembled, usually it is the median household income, not the mean household income that is used to provide a measure of average family income, precisely because of this reason.

In addition to the mean and the median, there is another center of a set of data, called the mode. It is simply the value that occurs with the highest frequency. For example, in a data set of 8, {1 2 3 4 3 2 3 3}, the number 3 is the mode, because it appears more times than any of the other numbers in the same set.

One thing to keep in mind is that when comparing parameters of different data sets, the same parameters are to be used. It is only fair to compare the mean of set *A* to the mean of set *B*, not the mean of one set to the median of the other!

Example 6.1: Below is the recorded length of phone calls (in min) made from a dorm during one night. Please calculate the mean, median, mode of the typical phone call time.

1	7	4	1
2	4	3	48
3	5	3	6

First, we rank the data: 1, 1, 2, 3, 3, 3, 4, 4, 5, 6, 7, 48. Once the data are sorted, we can immediately determine the median and the mode:

For the median, there are 12 entries, hence the median is the average between the 6th and 7th entries:

$$\text{Median} = (3 + 4)/2 = 3.5 \text{ min}$$

For the mode, the most frequently occurring value is 3 mins, which appears 3 times.

$$\text{Mode} = 3 \text{ mins}$$

For the mean:

$$mean = \frac{\sum_i X_i}{N} = \frac{87}{12} = 7.25\,min$$

6.1.2.2 Measures of Variation

As we mentioned earlier, data obtained through experiments or measurements have inherent uncertainty built in. A measure to indicate the degree of dispersion in a data set, that is, how much the data points are spread out or clustered together, is the variation. It is easy to see that two data sets can have the exact same means, but vastly different dispersion patterns.

It is reasonable to define the variation by how much each number in the data set deviates from the mean. To account for both negative and positive deviations, a square is taken for each of the deviations. Add all the squares together, and divide the result by the total number of data points in the data set, and we will get a parameter, defined as the variance of the data set:

$$\text{var} = \sum_{i=1,N} \frac{1}{N}(x_i - \bar{x})^2$$

Eq. 6.2

where N is the total number of data points in the data set
x_i is the value of the ith data point
$\bar{x}$ is the mean

The square root of the variance is defined as the standard deviation (s.t.d).

$$s.t.d = \sqrt{\sum_{i=1}^{N} \frac{1}{N}(x_i - \bar{x})^2}$$

Eq. 6.3

Conventionally, the standard deviation for a population is denoted as σ (i.e., a parameter), and the standard deviation calculated from a sample of the population is denoted as s (i.e., a statistic). Often times, we use the standard deviation of a sample (s) to estimate its counterpart for the entire population (σ). It has been determined that for small samples ($n<30$), equation 6.3 underestimates the σ for the population. Instead, the following equation gives a better estimation:

$$s.t.d = \sqrt{\sum_{i=1}^{N} \frac{1}{N-1}(x_i - \bar{x})^2}$$

Eq. 6.4

Hence, for small samples ($n<30$), equation 6.4 should be used to calculate its standard deviation (and variance).

Example 6.2: You are conducting quality control over manufactured metal parts, which are designed to weigh 1.20 lb. You measured 20 parts, and below is the data you collected:

1	2	3	4	5	6	7	8	9	10	11	12	13	14	15	16	17	18	19	20
1.22	1.21	1.23	1.25	1.18	1.19	1.18	1.20	1.21	1.23	1.22	1.16	1.18	1.19	1.23	1.22	1.21	1.26	1.14	1.12

What is the mean of this sample and what is the standard deviation and variance?

Here we have $n = 20 < 30$, hence equation 6.4 should be used instead of 6.3.

$$\bar{w} = \frac{1}{20}\sum_{i=1}^{20} w_i = 1.20 \text{ lbs}$$

$$s.t.d = \sum_{i=1,N} \sqrt{\frac{1}{N-1}(w_i - w)^2} = 0.035 \text{ lbs}$$

$$var = \sum_{i=1,N} \frac{1}{N-1}(w_i - w)^2 = 0.0012 \text{ lbs}$$

6.1.3 Graphic Data Presentation

Graphic data presentation is straightforward and visual, as it can quickly convey information in a data set in a vivid fashion. It is a useful tool for a technologist to master. The most commonly used graphic data representations include pie charts, bar charts, line charts, and histograms.

6.1.3.1 Pie Chart and Bar Chart

A pie chart (or a circle chart) is a circular statistical graphic, which is divided into sectors to illustrate numerical proportion. In a pie chart, the arc length of each sector (and consequently its central angle and area), is proportional to the quantity it represents. The pie chart gets its name for its resemblance to a pie which has been sliced. A typical pie chart is shown in Figure 6.3.

An obvious flaw exhibited by pie charts is that they cannot show more than a few values without separating the visual encoding (the "slices") from the data they represent (typically percentages). When slices become too small, pie charts have to rely on colors, textures or

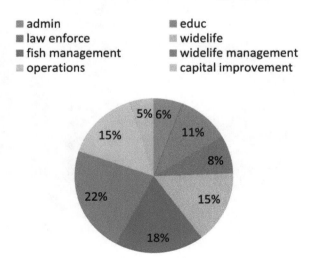

Ohio Division of wild life budget for 2001

- admin
- law enforce
- fish management
- operations
- educ
- widelife
- widelife management
- capital improvement

Figure 6.3: Pie Chart

arrows for the reader to understand them. This makes them unsuitable for use with larger amounts of data. Pie charts also take up a larger amount of space on the page compared to the more flexible bar charts, which do not need to have separate legends, and can display other values such as averages or targets at the same time.

Statisticians generally regard pie charts as a poor method of displaying information, and they are uncommon in scientific literature. One reason is that it is more difficult for comparisons to be made between the size of items in a chart when area is used instead of length, and when different items are shown as different shapes.

A bar chart or bar graph is a chart with rectangular bars with lengths proportional to the values that they represent. The bars can be plotted vertically or horizontally. A vertical bar chart is sometimes called a column bar chart.

A bar graph is a chart that uses either horizontal or vertical bars to show comparisons among categories. One axis of the chart shows the specific categories being compared, and the other axis represents a discrete value. Some bar graphs present bars clustered in groups of more than one (grouped bar graphs), and others show the bars divided into subparts to show cumulative effect (stacked bar graphs).

Figure 6.4 shows a bar chart showing the same data as shown by the pie chart in Figure 6.3.

Compared the pie chart, the bar chart has the advantage of being able to show the mean and the median, as well. Also, the bar chart can be used to show negative (i.e., decreasing) and positive (i.e., increasing) values at the same time, while pie charts can only be used to illustrate positive values.

Generally, bar charts are more useful than pie charts in graphic data representation.

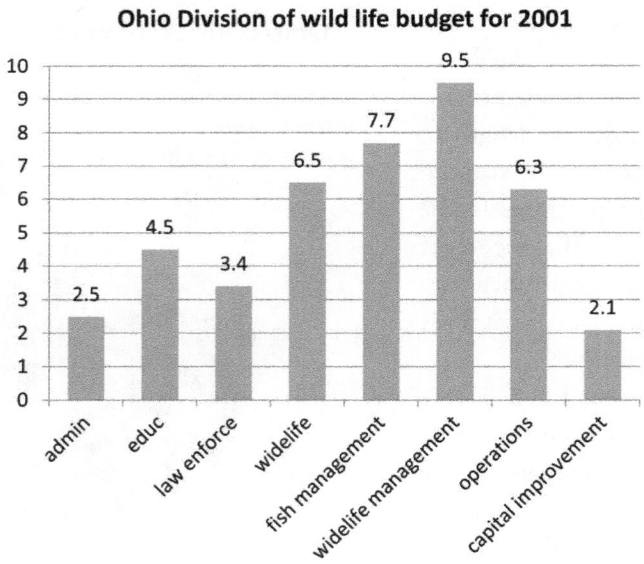

Figure 6.4: Bar Chart

6.1.3.2 Line Chart

A line chart is a type of chart which displays information as a series of data points connected by straight line segments. In a line chart, the data points are ordered or sorted (typically by their x-axis values), and joined by line segments. The biggest advantage of a line chart is that it can be used to visualize a trend, most often a trend in data over a duration of time (a time series). An example of a line chart is shown in figure 6.5.

6.1.3.3 Histogram

A histogram is tied with the frequency distribution we discussed earlier. It illustrates the probability distribution of a variable. To construct a histogram, the first step is to "bin" the range of values—that is, divide the entire range of values into a series of small intervals—and then count how many values fall into each interval. A rectangle is drawn with height proportional to the count, and width equal to the bin size. A histogram may also be normalized, displaying relative frequencies. It then shows the proportion of cases that fall into each of several categories, with the sum of the heights equaling 1. The bins are usually specified as consecutive, non-overlapping intervals of a variable. The bins (intervals) must be adjacent, and usually of equal size. The rectangles of a histogram are drawn so that they touch each other when the original variable is continuous.

Figure 6.6 shows an example of a histogram. In Figure 6.6a, a bar chart is used to display the weight of the 24 starters of the New England Patriots football team of the 2002 season. From the bar chart it is hard to tell which weight bracket (called class in statistics) has the most players. However, if a histogram is created, as shown figure 6.6b, this information would be readily available (the class of 190 to 210 lbs has the most players at 8).

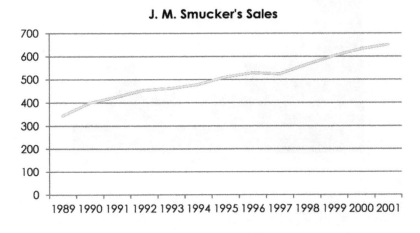

Figure 6.5: Line Chart: J.M. Smucker's Sales 1989–2001, Showing an Increasing Trend

A general rule to select the proper number of classes to construct a histogram is as follows:

$$2^k \geq n \qquad\qquad\qquad \text{Eq. 6.5}$$

Where k is the number of classes, and n is the number of total data points
In the above example, $n = 24$, hence, k should be equal to or larger than 5.

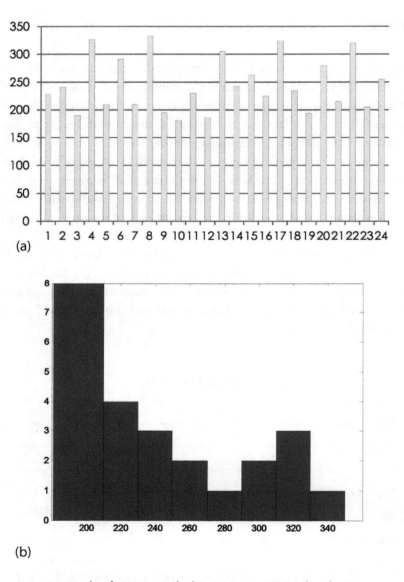

(a)

(b)

Figure 6.6: Weights of 2002 New England Patriots Starters (a). Bar Chart (b). Histogram

6.1.4 Data Distribution

It is common that a technologist needs to deal with random variables. A random variable is a variable whose value is subject to variations due to chance. A random variable can take on a set of possible different values. Random errors are inherent in all experimental measurements. Random variables are classified according to the values that the variables can assume. Discrete random variables can only assume a finite set of values. The flipping of a coin yields a classic discrete random variable, as it can only have two possible outcomes (or values).

In contrast to discrete random variables, a continuous random variable can assume values on a continuous scale.

Histograms, as we discussed in 6.1.3.3, can be used to determine the probability of a value falling into a given classification. Histograms, as we discussed before, are discrete. However, as we narrow down the range of each class, a histogram can evolve into a continuous curve, which is called a frequency distribution curve. When this happens, the probability associated with any interval is related to the area under the curve, which is bound by the interval boundaries.

6.1.5 Normal Distribution

Among many continuous distributions used in statistics, the normal distribution is by far the most useful.

The normal distribution, also called Gaussian distribution (named after the great German mathematician Carl Friedrich Gauss, 1777–1855), is a theoretical frequency distribution for a specific type of data set. Its graphical representation is a bell-shaped curve that extends to infinity at both sides, as shown in figure 6.7.

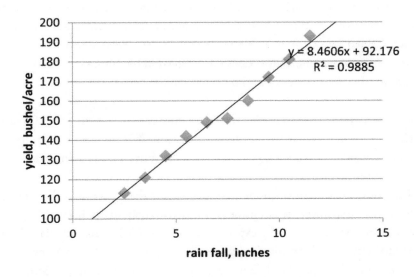

Figure 6.7: A Linear Correlation Established by Regression Modeling Between Corn Yield and Rainfall

The usefulness of the normal distribution comes from the fact that physical quantities that are expected to be the sum of many independent processes (such as experimental errors) often have a distribution very close to the normal distribution. Therefore, it is often used in both the natural and social sciences for real-valued random variables whose distribution is unknown.

Normal distribution, or the bell curve, can be specified by two parameters: The population mean (μ), which is at the center of the distribution, and the population standard deviation (σ), which describes the amount of variability or dispersion of the data. It should be noted that normally distributed data has a unique property; its median is equal to the mean. This will become very useful for making predictions as we will see later.

Mathematically, the normal distribution is represented by:

$$f(x) = \frac{1}{\sqrt{2\pi\sigma^2}} e^{-\frac{(x-\mu)^2}{2\sigma^2}},$$

Eq. 6.6

As stated earlier, the area between an interval under a frequency distribution curve gives the probability of a random variable assuming a value that falls inside this interval. From equation 6.5 we have:

$$P(x_1 < x < x_2) = \int_{x_1}^{x_2} f(x)dx$$

Eq. 6.7

Where P is the probability of the random variable x, assuming a value that falls between x_1 and x_2.

How do we understand the normal distribution? A simple explanation goes like this: Suppose you are measuring one variable repeatedly, and the value you are getting will be clustered around the true value of the variable (mean, μ), and the probability that you will get a measured value of x that falls between x_1 and x_2 can be calculated using equation 6.7.

Two normally distributed variables can have the same mean, but very different standard deviations. Standard deviation is commonly used to measure confidence in statistical conclusions. Margin of error is determined by calculating the expected standard deviation in the results, if the same measure were to be conducted multiple times. The reported margin of error is typically about twice the standard deviation—the radius of a 95 percent confidence interval.

Example 6.3: An investor has to choose between two stocks. Over the past 20 years, Stock A has had an average return of 10% , with a standard deviation of 20 percentage points (pp) and Stock B, over the same period, has had average returns of 12%, but a higher standard deviation of 30 pp. How do we interpret this data?

On the basis of risk and return, an investor may decide that Stock A is the safer choice, because Stock B's additional two percentage points of return is not worth the additional 10 pp standard deviation (greater risk or uncertainty of the expected return). Stock B is likely to fall short of the initial investment (but also to exceed the initial investment) more often than Stock A under the same circumstances, and is estimated to return only 2% more on average. In this example, Stock A is expected to earn about 10% , plus or minus 20 pp (a range of 30% to −10%), about 2/3 (68.2%) of the future years.

In finance, s.t.d. measures volatility of the investment.

6.2 Predicting Trends

Inferential statistics, as we mentioned before, allows us to utilize statistical rules to generalize results obtained from a sample to predict what can be expected for the population from which the sample is drawn. The simplest prediction one can make is about the probability of a variable assumes a certain value, or assumes a certain value that falls within a range. We will investigate how to make predictions like this.

6.2.1 Chebyshev's Rule

Chebyshev's rule allows us to make predictions regarding the probability of a variable to assume a value that falls between an upper and lower boundary.

Chebyshev's Rule:

Suppose you have measured a statistic (x) from a sample (containing a number of observations) extracted from a population, and you have determined the mean ($\overline{x}$) and standard deviation (s) of the sample. Chebyshev's rule says that, for the entire population, at least $(1 - 1/k^2)\%$ observations will yield a value x that falls between of $\overline{x} \pm ks$ for the parameter x you want to measure.

The usefulness of Cherbyshev's rule can be better explained by an example.

Example 6.4: A bus station wants to measure on average, how long a passenger needs to wait at the station to get on a bus. It conducted research that says on average, the wait is 5.0 minutes with a s.t.d. of 1.5 minutes. Now, using Chebyshev's rule, determine what percentage passengers will be waiting between 2.5 and 7.5 minutes?

First, determine the k

$$\overline{X} = 5.0, s = 1.5,$$
$$X_{min} = 2.5, X_{max} = 7.5$$
$$X_{max} - \overline{X} = 2.5 = \frac{2.5}{1.5}s \rightarrow k = \frac{2.5}{1.5} = 1.67$$
$$\overline{X} - X_{min} = 2.5 \rightarrow confirms\, k = 1.67$$
$$1 - \frac{1}{k^2} = 1 - 0.359 = 0.641 = 64.1\%$$

Conclusion

At least 64.1% passengers will be waiting between 2.5 and 7.5 minutes.

For Chebyshev's rule to be applicable, we need to know the mean and the standard deviation of a sample drawn from the population. Also two conditions need to be met:

1. The lower and upper bound need to be symmetric around the mean.

2. k value needs to be larger than 1.

Also, the probability (i.e., percentage) obtained by using Cherbyshev's rule is a lower limit. The actual probability could be larger than this lower limit.

Chebyshev's rule is powerful because it puts no requirement on the distribution of the data. As long as we can define a mean and calculate a standard deviation, we can use Chebyshev's rule. Chebyshev's rule allows us to estimate at least what percentage data fall in a given range, defined by a lower bound and an upper bound around the mean.

The process to use Cherbyshev's rule is as follows:
Step 1. Determine whether you should and can use Chebyshev's rule.
a. When you do not know what the data distribution is, you may use Chebyshev's rule.
b. Check the two conditions for Chebyshev's rule.

1. The lower bound and the upper bound must be symmetric around the mean;
2. k-value ≥ 1; k = (mean – lower bound)/std = (upper bound – mean)/std
Step 2. Use Chebyshev's rule

$$\%_{lower\text{-}upper} \geq (1 - 1/k^2) \times 100\% \qquad \text{Eq. 6.8}$$

Step 3. Explain the meaning of the %.
The percentage (%) you get by using Chebyshev's rule will tell you what minimum percentage of data fall in between the lower bound and the upper bound. It establishes a floor for the percentage. It does not give the most accurate estimation.

Example 6.5: A farmer is packing 10 lb bags of potatoes to be shipped. He packed 10,000 packs, with an average weight of 10.6 lb, and a std of 0.8 lb. Estimate at least what percentage of the bags will fall between 9.5 lb and 11.7 lb.

You have no information on the data distribution, hence you may use Chebyshev's rule.

Mean = 10.6 lb, std = 0.8 lb
Lower bound = 9.5 lb, hence k_{lower} = (10.6 – 9.5)/0.8 = 1.375 > 1
Upper bound = 11.7, hence k_{upper} = (11.7 – 10.6)/0.8 = 1.375 > 1

$$k_{lower} = k_{upper} > 1$$

Both conditions for Chebyshev's rule are satisfied!

$$\%_{9.5-11.7} \geq (1 - 1/k^2) \times 100\% = 47.1\%$$

Therefore, at least about 47.1% bags will fall between 9.5 lb and 11.7 lb.

Note: Chebyshev's rule establishes a floor for the percentage. It does not give the most accurate estimation.

6.2.2 Z-score Method

If we know that the data we are analyzing follow normal distribution, a more accurate prediction about the probability of a variable to assume a value that falls in a certain range can be made. The method is called z-score method.

To use z-score method, we need to know that the data follow normal distribution, with a mean of μ and a standard deviation of σ. Z-score method states that the probability of a variable to take a value of $x = \mu \pm z\sigma$ is determined by:

$$\% = erf\left(\frac{z}{\sqrt{2}}\right)$$
Eq. 6.9

where $erf(x) = \frac{2}{\sqrt{\pi}} \int_0^x e^{-t^2}\, dt$, it is called the error function

For normal distribution, we know that the mean is also the median, which means that 50% of all data are below it, and another 50% are above it.

The steps for using z-score method are as follows:

Step 1: Check if the data distribution is a normal distribution, and find your mean and std.

Step 2: Find your boundaries and z-score associated with each boundary.

There are five possible scenarios:

a. You want to find the range from $-\infty$ to x, $x \leq$ mean, $z = $ (mean $-x$)/std
b. You want to find the range from x to $+\infty$, $x \geq$ mean, $z = (x -$ mean)/std

$$\text{In both cases, } \% = 50\% - \frac{1}{2}\, erf\left(\frac{z}{\sqrt{2}}\right) \times 100\%$$

c. You want to find the range between x_{lower} and x_{upper}, where $x_{lower} <$ mean, $x_{upper} >$ mean
  In this case, you will have two z score, z_{lower} and z_{upper} $z_{lower} = $ (mean $- x_{lower}$)/std;

$$z_{upper} = (x_{upper} - \text{mean})/\text{std}; \%_{lower\text{-}upper} = \frac{1}{2} erf\left(\frac{z_{lower}}{\sqrt{2}}\right) \times 100\% + \frac{1}{2} erf\left(\frac{z_{upper}}{\sqrt{2}}\right) \times 100\%$$

d. You want to find the range from $-\infty$ to x, $x >$ mean, $z = (x -$ mean)/std
e. You want to find the range from x to $+\infty$, $x \leq$ mean, $z = $ (mean $-x$)/std

$$\text{In both cases, } \% = 50\% + \frac{1}{2} erf\left(\frac{z}{\sqrt{2}}\right) \times 100\%$$

Step 3: Calculate $erf\left(\frac{z}{\sqrt{2}}\right)$

The error function $erf(x)$ is not easy to calculate, hence usually an error function table is used to find the value for a given x for the $erf(x)$. One such error function table is shown in table 1.

Table 1. Error function values between $x = 0$ and $x = 3.0$

For any x value that is not listed in the table, linear interpolation can be used to calculate the value of $erf(x)$.

Table 6.1: The error function

x	erf (x)
0	0
0.05	0.056372
0.10	0.112463
0.15	0.167996
0.20	0.222703
0.25	0.276326
0.30	0.328627
0.35	0.379382
0.40	0.428392
0.45	0.475482
0.50	0.520500
0.55	0.563323
0.60	0.603856
0.65	0.642029
0.70	0.677801
0.75	0.711155
0.80	0.742101
0.85	0.770668
0.90	0.796908
0.95	0.820891
1.0	0.842701
1.1	0.880205
1.2	0.910314
1.3	0.934008
1.4	0.952285
1.5	0.966105
1.6	0.976348
1.7	0.983790
1.8	0.989091
1.9	0.992790
2.0	0.995322
2.1	0.997021
2.2	0.998137
2.3	0.998857
2.4	0.999311
2.5	0.999593
2.6	0.999764
2.7	0.999866
2.8	0.999925
2.9	0.999959
3.0	0.999978

In linear interpolation, we have two pairs of data:

(x_1, y_1), (x_2, y_2), where y is a function of x. Here, this function is the erf function, and $x_1 < x_2$.

Now, for a new x sitting in between x_1 and x_2, we need to find its y value.

The equation to use is:

$$\frac{y - y_1}{x - x_1} = \frac{y_2 - y_1}{x_2 - x_1} \qquad \text{Eq. 6.10}$$

Here are the steps:

Step 1: Find the pair (x_1, x_2) for your x.

Step 2: Find the pair (y_1, y_2) for your (x_1, x_2)

⇨ Step 3: Substitute x, x_1, x_2, y_1, y_2 into the equation to find y.

Example 6.6: Use linear interpolation to calculate $erf(0.282)$.

Step 1: We are looking for a pair that has our x value, 0.282, in between the pair.

The pair obviously are $x_1 = 0.25$, $x_2 = 0.30$

Step 2: Find the pair y_1, y_2 for x_1, x_2
From the table, we have:
$$y_1 = erf(x_1) = 0.2763; y_2 = erf(x_2) = 0.3286$$

Step 3: calculate y for $x = 0.282$, substitute numbers into Eq.10

$$\frac{erf(0.282) - 0.2763}{0.032} = \frac{0.3286 - 0.2763}{0.05}$$

⇨ $y = erf(0.282) = 0.3098$

Now, let's look at an example on how to use z-score method to make predictions.

Example 6.7. Fix-it Copiers advertises a mean time of 100 minutes for office calls with s.t.d of 25 minutes. Suppose the time follows normal distribution. What percentage of calls are completed between 90 and 125 minutes? Less than 125 minutes? Less than 75 minutes?

Solution

Step 1: Data follow normal distribution confirmed for all three cases.

Case 1: This is scenario c. We have a x_{lower} = 90 min, and x_{upper} = 125 min
$Z_{lower} = (100 - 90)/25 = 0.4$; $z_{upper} = (125-100)/25 = 1$;

For scenario c, we have:

$$\%_{lower\text{-}upper} = \tfrac{1}{2}\, erf(z_{lower}/\sqrt{2}) \times 100\% + \tfrac{1}{2}\, erf(z_{upper}/\sqrt{2}) \times 100\%$$

$$z_{lower}/\sqrt{2} = 0.282;\; z_{upper}/\sqrt{2} = 0.707$$

$$\%_{90-125} = (\tfrac{1}{2}\, erf(0.282) + \tfrac{1}{2}\, erf(0.707)) \times 100\%$$

To find $erf(0.282)$, we use linear interpolation:
$erf(0.25) = 0.2763$; $erf(0.30) = 0.3286$

$$\frac{Erf(0.282) - erf(0.25)}{(0.282 - 0.25)} = \frac{erf(0.30) - erf(0.25)}{(0.30 - 0.25)}$$

$$\frac{erf(0.282) - 0.2763}{0.032} = \frac{0.3286 - 0.2763}{0.05}$$

$\Rightarrow$ $erf(0.282) = 0.3098$

Using the same principle, we have $erf(0.707) = 0.683$

Therefore, from the above Eq. 1, we have:
$\%_{90-125} = (0.155 + 0.341) \times 100\% = 49.6\%$, 49.6% calls are completed between 90 and 125 mins.

Case 2: This is scenario d. $z = (125 - 100)/25 = 1$, $z/\sqrt{2} = 0.707$
For scenario d, we have
$\%_{<125} = 50\% + \tfrac{1}{2}\, erf(z/\sqrt{2}) \times 100\% = 50\% + 34.1\% = 84.1\%$, 84.1% calls are completed within 125 mins.

Case 3: This is scenario a. $z = (100 - 75)/25 = 1$, $z/\sqrt{2} = 0.707$

For scenario a, we have

$\%_{<125}$ = 50% – ½ $erf(z/\sqrt{2})$ × 100% = 50% – 34.1% = 15.9%, 15.9% calls are completed within 75 mins.

6.3 Linear Regression and Least-Square Fitting

There are many occasions that a forecast or prediction of a certain event is very valuable. This is difficult to do in most practical applications because of the large number of variables that may influence the analysis process. Regression analysis is a study of the relationships among variables. If the situation results in a relationship among three or more variables, it is called multiple regression. The simplest case is when relationship between two variables (one independent and one dependent) can be established as a linear function, and that can be done by linear regression.

6.3.1 Linear Regression

Linear regression establishes a linear function that can be used to correlate a dependent variable (i.e., y) to an independent variable (i.e., x), as $y = ax + b$, where a and b are constants that need to be found. Once a and b are determined, a predicted value of y can be obtained for any value of x.

The first step is to collect the data. Suppose a data set consists of n points have been acquired, (x_i, y_i), $i = 1...n$.

In regression modeling, we assume a function $y = f(x, \mathbf{b})$ can be found that describes the relationship between x and y, where $\mathbf{b}$ is a group of parameters that relate x to y.

To find this group of parameters, $\mathbf{b}$, a method called least square fitting can be used. In least square fitting, the sum of residuals, S, is minimized. S is defined as:

$$S = \sum_{i=1,\,n} r_i^2, \text{ where } r_i = y_i - f(x_i, \mathbf{b})$$

The fundamentals of the least square method was first developed by Gauss in 1795, and later independently developed by Legendre, a French mathematician, in 1805.

The simplest case of regression modeling is linear regression, where a linear function is used to relate x to y.

$$let\ y = b_0 + b_1 x_1 + b_2 x_2 + ... + b_m x_m \rightarrow y_i\ \text{measured value for}\ y$$

$$r = \sum_i (y - y_i)^2$$

finding $(b_0, b_1, b_2, ... b_m)$ that minimizes r, it has to satisfy:

$$\frac{\partial r}{\partial b_0} = 0;$$

$$\frac{\partial r}{\partial b_1} = 0;$$

...

$$\frac{\partial r}{\partial b_m} = 0;$$

Eq. 6.11

Solve the resulting algebraic equations, and $(b_0, b_1....b_m)$ can then be found.

Let's take a look at an example of how least square method works for linear regression.

Example 6.8: An agricultural experiment station collected data to show correlation between annual rainfall (measured in inches) and yield of corn per acre (measured in bushel), and the data is shown in table 1. Based on this data, estimate what the yield will be if rainfall is 12.5 inches.

2.5	3.5	4.5	5.5	6.5	7.5	8.5	9.5	10.5	11.5
113	121	132	142	149	151	160	172	181	193

Assume $y = b_0 + b_1 x$

$$r = \sum_{i=1}^{10} (b_0 + b_1 x_i - y_i)^2$$

$$= (b_0 + b_1 \times 2.5 - 113)^2 + (b_0 + b_1 \times 3.5 - 121)^2 + ...$$

$$+ (b_0 + b_1 \times 11.5 - 193)^2$$

$$\frac{\partial r}{\partial b_0} = 2(b_0 + 2.5b_1 - 113) + 2(b_0 + 3.5b_1 - 121) + ...$$

$$+ 2(b_0 + 11.5b_1 - 193) = 0$$

$$\frac{\partial r}{\partial b_1} = 2 \times 2.5 \times (b_0 + b_1 \times 2.5 - 113) + 2 \times 3.5 \times (b_0 + b_1 \times 3.5 - 121) + ...$$

$$+ 2 \times 11.5 \times (b_0 + 11.5b_1 - 193) = 0$$

solve for b_0 *and* b_1

$$b_0 = 92.176;\ b_1 = 8.4606$$

$$y = 92.176 + 8.4606x \rightarrow \text{when}\ x = 12.5,\ y = 198$$

Hence, if the rainfall is 12.5 in, a yield of 198 bushel may be expected.

6.3.2 Coefficient of Correlation

The linear regression modeling as discussed above is certainly useful. It allows us to establish models that can make predictions out of existing data. Once the linear function is found, it is certainly also important to evaluate how well it actually fits with the existing data.

This evaluation is performed by calculating a parameter called coefficient of correlation (r), or its square, R^2.

To calculate R^2, we first calculate a sum of squares for the existing measured data:

$$SS_{tot} = \sum_{i=1}^{n}(y_i - \overline{y})^2 \qquad\qquad \text{Eq. 6.12}$$

Here, $\overline{y} = \dfrac{1}{n}\sum_{i} y_i$ is the mean of the existing y's.

The sum of squares is a measure of the deviation of each data point from the mean; it measures the dispersion of the data around the mean.

We then calculate the sum of squares for the measured vs. predicted data.

$$SS_{err} = \sum_{i=1}^{n}(y_i - f(x_i, \mathbf{b}))^2 \qquad\qquad \text{Eq. 6.13}$$

SS_{err} measures the differences between the measured data and the calculated value, using the linear regression model. One may expect that if the fitting is good, then this SS_{err} value would be small, because there should not be much discrepancy between the measured and the predicted values. But this value is dependent on the unit and actual value of y. For large y values, the SS_{err} could be large, even for a good fit. Hence, it is not truly a good, objective measure of how good the fit is.

Combining equations 6.12 and 6.13, the coefficient of correlation, r, is defined as:

$$R^2 \equiv 1 - \frac{SS_{err}}{SS_{tot}}$$
$$r = \sqrt{1 - \frac{SS_{err}}{SS_{tot}}} \qquad\qquad \text{Eq. 6.14}$$

Often times, R^2 is directly used to evaluate how good a fit is. R^2 is called coefficient of determination.

R^2, or r, measure how good the fit is. When $R^2=1$, it is a perfect fit, and there is no difference between the measured value and the calculated value using the regression model. When $R^2 = 0$, the linear regression model does not fit the data well, and no reliable prediction can be made using existing data. Generally, the closer R^2 is to 1, the better the fit.

Now let's revisit the rainfall vs. yield model we obtained in the previous example. With this linear equation obtained, we can find:

Apparently, a linear correlation describes the correlation between rainfall and yield really well, with a $R^2 = 0.9885$!

It should be noted that it is wrong to interpret a high R^2 value as implying a cause-effect relationship between the independent and dependent variables, or x's and y's. It only tells you how good the fit is!

EXERCISES

1. A newly graduated college student has a monthly budget as follows:

   Student loan payment: $300
   Mortgage payment: $1100
   Car payment: $250
   Utilities; $300
   Other: $500
   Create a pie chart and a bar chart to illustrate his monthly financial situation.

2. Here is a grade table for a calculus class. Determine the mean, median, variance, and standard deviation of the data.
   56 69 68 26 95 48 78 89 95 84 48 78 79 76 65 98 74 75 65 90 62 84

3. A mechanic shop claims a mean of a 34-minutewait time for an oil change, with a standard deviation of 7.0 minutes.
   a. Assuming no knowledge on the type of the distribution of the data, what percentage of customers will be waiting between 24 minutes and 44 minutes?
   b. Assuming the wait time distribution follows a normal distribution, how many customers will be waiting for more than 45 minutes?
   c. What percentage of customers will be waiting between 25 and 35 minutes?

4. The mean number of gallons of gasoline pumped per customer at a Shell's gas station is 10.5 gallons with a s.t.d. of 2 gallons. The average time spent by a customer at the station is 6.5 minutes, with a s.t.d. of 2 minutes.
   a. What proportion (percentage) of the customers spend between 3.30 and 9.70 minutes at the station?
   Now let's assume that the distribution is normal distribution, and we can have a more accurate statistical prediction.
   b. Let's recalculate what proportion (percentage) of the customers spend between 3.30 and 9.70 minutes at the station.

c. It is found that SUV owners will pump 12.5 gallons or more gasoline, and Prius owners will only pump less than 6.5 gallons of gasoline. According to this data, please estimate what proportions of cars are Prius, and what proportion are SUVs?

5. A food manufacturer makes a product that has a mean weight of 2.40 lbs, with a standard deviation of 0.20 lbs. Quality control tests require each product to be within a ±0.30 lbs range of the mean weight to pass.

a. Assuming no knowledge on the type of the distribution of the data, at the most, what percentage of products will be failing the test?

b. Assuming the weight distribution follows a normal distribution, how many products will weigh more than 2.75 lbs?

c. What percentage of products will weigh between 2.15 and 2.55 lbs?

Figure Source

1.   Fig. 6.6: Source: https://commons.wikimedia.org/wiki/File:Gaussian_curve.svg.

7
FUNDAMENTALS OF ECONOMIC DECISION MAKING

OBJECTIVES

When you complete your study of this chapter, you should be able to:

1. Understand the concepts of simple and compound interest;
2. Convert between present value, future sums, and periodic cash flows;
3. Construct a loan amortization table;
4. Determine the Return on Investment (ROI) and Payback Period (PBP) for an investment or expenditure;
5. Compare economic alternatives using methods of Present Worth Analysis (PWS) and Annual Cash Flow Analysis (ACFA); and
6. Calculate and compare the present worth of economic alternatives with different life spans.

7.1 The Time Value of Money

The time value of money (TVM) enters into most business and personal financial decisions made today. If a company has one million dollars to invest, they must compare investment options against the baseline value that this money would be worth over time. For instance, if they invest this money into developing a new product or buying equipment that will only return 3% per year, this may be a bad decision relative to investing the money elsewhere and earning 5% interest.

TVM concepts extend further than just financial investments. For example, engineers and technologists make decisions about equipment purchases: is a machine that costs more but lasts longer a better purchase than a cheaper machine that has a shorter life? In personal finance, does Bank A offer a better mortgage than Bank B even though there are different interest rates? TVM principles help answer these types of questions.

The concept of *equivalency* is used in analyzing the value of money over time. Money or cash flow at one period of time can be converted to an equivalent amount at another period of time, taking into account interest rates. The future value of present money or the present value of future money can thus be determined.

"Interest" is money paid regularly at a particular rate for the use of money lent, or for delaying the repayment of a debt. It is often expressed as a percentage (e.g., 5%) or in calculations, a decimal percentage (e.g., 0.05). Interest rates have an infinite number of significant digits and are usually expressed with a maximum precision to the hundredths of a percent (e.g., 5.00% or 0.0500).

7.1.1 Future Value of Present Money

<u>Simple Interest</u>

Most people are familiar with the concept of simple interest if they have earned interest in a bank savings account or had to pay interest for borrowing money on a credit card. Simple interest is computed by:

$$I = (i)(n)(P)$$ Eq. 7.1

where: I = total interest earned;

  i = interest rate for specific time period (decimal %);

  n = number of time periods; and

  P = amount of money (principal or present value) for which interest is computed.

Example 7.1

How much interest would you receive at the end of a year if you invested $10,000 in a certificate of deposit at an annual interest rate of 2.0%?

$$I = (i)(n)(P)$$
$$I = (0.02)(1)(10,000) = \underline{\textbf{\$ 200.00}}$$

Thus, at the end of one year, you would have the original $10,000 in principal, plus $200 in interest, giving you $10,200. This simple interest calculation demonstrates the concept of the time value of money.

Remember that the interest rate (i) is an <u>exact</u> number, not a measured number. As such, it has an infinite number of significant figures. When doing TVM calculations, carry along as many digits as possible in your calculator, and limit the amount of rounding you do, as it may have a significant effect on your results. Also note most monetary results are, at most, expressed to the nearest cent without regard to the number of significant figures in a calculation.

Compound Interest

Interest is usually compounded. For instance, you may purchase a certificate of deposit (CD) that compounds interest quarterly. This means that every three months, the interest that is earned is added to the principal. Thus, the interest earned during the second three months is computed based on the original principal plus the interest accrued during the first three-month period. Common compounding periods are annually, quarterly, monthly, and daily. The interest rate i is defined as the interest rate per compounding period n.

The method of adding interest to the principal and then calculating future interest on the combined amount is called compounding.

The future value of compounded money (F) can be computed using the following equation. It is easily derived from equation 7.1.

$$F = P(1 + i)^n \qquad\qquad\qquad \text{Eq. 7.2}$$

where: F = future value ($);
$\qquad$ P = present value ($);
$\qquad$ i = interest for the compounding period (decimal percent); and
$\qquad$ n = number of compounding periods.

Example 7.2

How much interest would be received at the end of 5 years if $1,000 were invested with an annual interest rate of 7%?

If interest is compounded annually, then there are five compounding periods (n=5). Using Equation 7.2, the future value can be computed as:

$$F = P(1 + i)^n = \$1,000(1 + 0.07)^5$$
$$F = \underline{\mathbf{\$ 1,402.55}}$$

Nominal and effective interest rates

The interest rate (i) should always be defined as the interest rate per compounding period n. However, interest rate is often given as the annual nominal interest rate ($i_{nominal}$) without consideration of the compounding period. The word "nominal" is defined as "something being such in name only, or not the real value." If the compounding period is less than one year, an effective annual interest rate can be calculated by:

$$i_{effective} = \left(1 + \frac{i_{nominal}}{m} \right)^m - 1 \qquad\qquad\qquad \text{Eq. 7.3}$$

where: $i_{effective}$ = the effective annual interest rate (decimal percent)
$\qquad$ $i_{nominal}$ = the nominal annual interest rate (decimal percent)
$\qquad$ m = the number of compounding periods within a year

Example 7.3

Consider the previous compound interest example, except now assume daily compounding. The nominal interest rate ($i_{nominal}$) is 7%. What is the interest rate per compounding period? What is the future value after five years? What is the effective annual interest rate?

The interest rate per compounding period (i) is:

$$i = \frac{0.07}{yr} \times \frac{yr}{365\,days} = 0.000192 = 0.0192\% \text{ per day}$$

The effective interest rate ($i_{effective}$) is:

$$i_{effective} = (1 + \frac{i_{nominal}}{m})^m - 1 = \left(1 + \frac{0.07}{365}\right)^{(365)} - 1 = 0.0725 = \underline{\textbf{7.25\%}}$$

The future value (F) after five years is:

$$F = P(1+i)^n = (\$1,000)(1+0.0725)^5 = \underline{\textbf{\$ 1,419.02}}$$

Note that you could also calculate the future value this way:

$$F = P(1+i)^n = (\$1,000)\left(1 + \frac{0.07}{365}\right)^{(365)(5)} = \underline{\textbf{\$ 1,419.02}}$$

Thus, at the end of 5 years, you would have an additional $16.47 (= \$ 1,419.02 from this example minus \$ 1,402.55 from the previous example) if interest is compounded daily vs. annually.

When money is compounded at more frequent intervals than one year, the effective annual interest rate is higher than the "nominal" annual interest rate. You cannot calculate the time value of money only knowing the nominal rate—the compounding period must also be known. If the interest rate (i) corresponds to a compounding period of less than one year, the effective annual interest rate can be computed by:

$$i_{effective} = (1+i)^m - 1 \qquad \text{Eq. 7.4}$$

where: $i_{effective}$ = effective annual interest rate (decimal percent);
      i = interest rate for the compounding period (decimal percent)

          = $\dfrac{i_{nominal}}{m}$; and

     m = number of compounding periods in a year.

Example 7.4

A credit card company charges 1.5% interest monthly on outstanding balances. What is the effective annual interest rate $(i_{effective})$?

From equation 7.4:

$$i_{effective} = (1 + i)^m - 1 = (1 + 0.015)^{12} - 1 = 0.1956 = \underline{\textbf{19.6\%}}$$

In this example, you can see why credit card companies might be aggressive in "giving out" their credit cards; they can receive a high rate of return on their "investment" into their card holders.

Sometimes, you'll hear the interest rate referred to as an "annual percentage rate" or APR. This terminology is commonly used when talking about loans. The concept is the same as the effective annual interest rate, although APR sometimes includes the effect of other fees that might be associated with a loan.

Continuous Compounding

Sometimes, interest is compounded continuously, rather than annually, monthly, or daily. If this is the case, the future value (F) or present value (P) of an investment is computed by:

$$F = P(e)^{rn}$$

Eq. 7.5

$$P = F(e)^{-rn}$$

Eq. 7.6

where: F = future value of present money ($)
P = present value of future money ($)
n = number of years
r = interest rate that is compounded continuously

The mathematical constant "e" is the base of the natural logarithm. It is occasionally called Euler's number after the Swiss mathematician Leonhard Euler. It is an important number in mathematics, similar in importance to the number pi (π). Most scientific calculators are programmed with the value of "e" to the 20th decimal place, where $e \approx 2.71828\ 18284\ 59045\ 23536$.

Example 7.5

A bank is selling certificates that will pay $5,000 at the end of 10 years, but pays nothing before that. If interest is compounded continuously at 6%, at what price is the bank selling the certificates?

In this problem, the future value of the sum of money (F) is $5,000. The present value (P) is unknown. Applying Equation 7.6:

$$P = F(e)^{-rn}$$

$$P = (\$5,000)(e)^{-(0.06)(10)} = \underline{\underline{\$\,2{,}744.06}}$$

The bank, in order to make a profit on this transaction, must invest the $2,744.06 in some venture that yields more than 6% compounded continuously.

7.1.2 Cash Flow Diagrams

Cash flow refers to the amount of cash being received and spent by an organization, business, or individual during a defined period of time, sometimes tied to a specific project. Often, it helps to have a visualization of such situations. This is done through cash flow diagrams. Consider this graph:

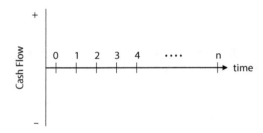

This is the basis of a cash flow diagram. The x-axis is time—days, months, quarters or years—with units corresponding to the compounding period. Usually, the y-axis is omitted, as in this example:

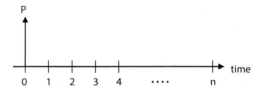

The arrow in the figure above represents a sum of money, P, at time zero (a present value). The length of the arrow represents the amount. If the arrow is in the positive direction or pointing upwards, it is a positive cash flow or revenue, that is, it is money received or money possessed. If the arrow is in the negative direction or pointing downward, it is a negative cash flow or expense, that is, money that invested or spent.

In many cash flow situations, different amounts of money are received and paid at different points in time. This can be visualized in a cash flow diagram. For example, if you had $20 now, paid $15 at month one, received $30 at month two and then paid $20 at month four, the cash flow diagram would look like this:

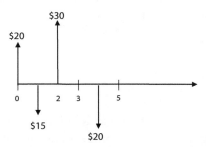

You might be tempted to say that your net cash flow is (20) + (30) − (15) − (20) = $15. This wrongly ignores the time value of money. The $20 you have at time zero is worth more than $20 sometime in the future because of the interest it could earn. The same could be said for the other amounts.

Note that it is appropriate to include the interest rate as part of any cash flow diagram, as in this example:

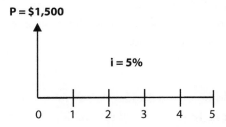

Since cash flow at any particular time is additive, cash flow diagrams can be "re-written" in different ways. Consider the following cash flow diagram:

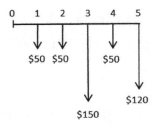

This could be "rewritten" as the following:

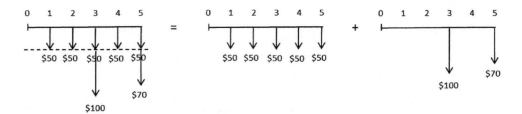

As you'll see later, determining the value of a series of equal cash flows at another time is less cumbersome than determining the value of a number of unequal cash flows.

7.1.3 Present Value of Future Money

There are many instances where you are trying to compare financial options by comparing a future sum (F) to its equivalent present worth (P). Re-arranging equation 7.2 to solve for the present value of future sums of money results in:

$$P = F(1 + i)^{-n}$$ Eq. 7.7

where: P = present value ($)
        F = future value ($)
        i = interest for the compounding period (decimal percent)
        n = number of compounding periods

Example 7.6

How much money should be invested today to pay for your newborn child's college tuition? The experts estimate that in 18 years, it will take $200,000 to pay for a 4-year degree. Assume an annual effective interest rate of 6%.

Using equation 7.7:
$$P = F(1 + i)^{-n} = (\$\,200{,}000)(1 + 0.06)^{-18} = \underline{\mathbf{\$\,70{,}068.76}}$$

Example 7.7

Consider the previous example. What if you could obtain an 8% rate of return (i.e., $i = 8\%$). How much money should be invested today to pay for your newborn child's college tuition with the new interest rate?

Using equation 7.7:
$$P = F(1 + i)^{-n} = (\$\,200{,}000)(1 + 0.08)^{-18} = \underline{\mathbf{\$\,50{,}049.81}}$$

By finding a two percentage point better rate of return (interest rate), you've "saved" over $20,000!

7.1.4 Present or Future Value of Uniform Cash Flow

Another type of problem involves computing either the present or future worth of an annual (or monthly or daily) cash flow. For instance, you may be interested in computing the future value of 36 monthly rental payments on your apartment. The cash flow diagram below shows a series of annual or uniform cash flow amounts, each with the value of "A." "A" occurs at the end of the period; there <u>is no</u> cash flow at time zero and there <u>is</u> cash flow at the final time.

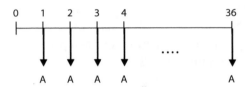

This series of uniform cash flow (A) can be converted to a present value (P at $n = 0$) or a future value (F at $n = 36$).

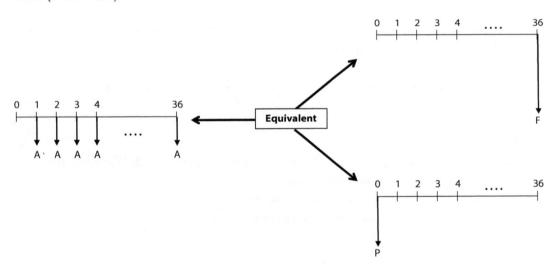

The following equations provide a way to compute the present or future worth of a uniform cash flow, or the uniform cash flow for a desired present or future sum of money. These types of cash flows have names associated with them.

$$A = F\left[\frac{i}{(1+i)^n - 1}\right] \quad \text{(Sinking Fund)} \qquad \text{Eq. 7.8}$$

$$F = A\left[\frac{(1+i)^n - 1}{i}\right] \quad \text{(Series Compound)} \qquad \text{Eq. 7.9}$$

$$A = P\left[\frac{i(1+i)^n}{(1+i)^n - 1}\right] \quad \text{(Capital Recovery)} \qquad\qquad \text{Eq. 7.10}$$

$$P = A\left[\frac{(1+i)^n - 1}{i(1+i)^n}\right] \quad \text{(Series Present Worth)} \qquad\qquad \text{Eq. 7.11}$$

where: A = end-of-period amount in a uniform series for n periods ($)
F = future value ($)
P = present value ($)
i = interest for the compounding period (decimal percent)
n = number of compounding periods

Example 7.8

How much should be saved annually to have $200,000 available to pay for a child's college tuition in 18 years? Assume a 6.00% annual interest rate.

In this case, compute the annual uniform investment or cash flow (A) required for a future value (F) of $200,000. This is called a Sinking Fund (Equation 7.8):

$$A = F\left[\frac{i}{(1+i)^n - 1}\right] = (\$200,000)\left[\frac{0.06}{(1+0.06)^{18} - 1}\right] = \underline{\textbf{\$ 6,471.31}}$$

Example 7.9

How much should be saved monthly to have $200,000 available to pay for child's college tuition in 18 years? Assume 6% annual rate of return compounded monthly.

This example is similar to the previous one. However, since the interest is compounded monthly, the annual nominal interest rate must be converted to the interest rate for the compounding period (one month).

$$i = \frac{0.06}{12} = 0.005 = 0.5\%$$

Now, use equation 7.8 with $n = (18)(12) = 216$:

$$A = F\left[\frac{i}{(1+i)^n - 1}\right] = (\$200,000)\left[\frac{0.005}{(1+0.005)^{216} - 1}\right] = \underline{\textbf{\$ 516.32}}$$

Example 7.10

A home mortgage is $100,000 for 30 years at 6% nominal annual interest. What are the monthly payments?

In this example, compute the uniform monthly payment (A) based on a present value (P) of the loan. Since A is to be computed on a monthly basis, the annual nominal interest rate must be converted to the interest rate for the compounding period (one month).

$$i = \frac{0.06}{12} = 0.005 = 0.5\%$$

Now, apply equation 7.10 (Capital Recovery) with $n = (30)(12) = 360$:

$$A = P\left[\frac{i(1+i)^n}{(1+i)^n - 1}\right] = (\$100,000)\left[\frac{(0.005)(1+0.005)^{360}}{(1+0.005)^{360} - 1}\right] = \underline{\mathbf{\$\,599.55}}$$

By paying \$599.55 each month for 360 months, a total of \$215,838 (\$599.55 × 360) is paid for a \$100,000 house loan.

Example 7.11

What is the future value (F) of that same monthly house payment if invested at 6% annual interest for 30 years?

In this example, the monthly investment ($A = \$599.55$) and monthly interest rate ($i = 0.5\%$) is known, and the future value (F) of this monthly investment in unknown. Thus, Equation 7.9 (Series Compound) is used:

$$F = A\left[\frac{(1+i)^n - 1}{i}\right] = (599.55)\left[\frac{(1+0.005)^{360} - 1}{0.005}\right] = \underline{\mathbf{\$\,602,256.99}}$$

Example 7.12

Your current credit card balance is \$3,088. The minimum payment required is 2% of the balance (\$61.76), and the nominal annual interest rate is 19%. By paying \$61.76 each month, how long would it take to pay off the balance?

In this case, the current value of the debt ($P=\$3,088$) is known and the monthly payment (A) is unknown. First, calculate the monthly interest rate.

$$i = \frac{0.19}{12} = 0.015833 = 1.5833\%$$

$$A = P\left[\frac{i(1+i)^n}{(1+i)^n - 1}\right] \rightarrow (\$61.76) = (\$3,088)\left[\frac{(0.015833)(1.05833)^n}{(1.05833)^n - 1}\right]$$

This last equation must be solved for n. There are several ways to do this. Financial calculators are sometimes programmed to do it. There are various mathematical techniques that can be employed.

The "goal seek" function in a Microsoft Excel spreadsheet will give you an exact result. Or, trial and error (especially easy in a spreadsheet) can get an answer that's reasonably close.

By trial and error: $n = 100 = $ **8 years and 4 months**.

7.1.5 Present and Future Value of Gradients

There are many situations in life and technology and engineering that require estimating the current or future value of a uniform gradient. An example is the maintenance cost of a car or a piece of equipment. You would expect that the maintenance cost would be low early in the life of the car or equipment, and it would increase with age. If this increase in the maintenance cost increases in a uniform, linear fashion, the cost can be described by a uniform gradient.

A uniform gradient has two components. The first component is the underlying annual cost (A), as described in the previous section. The second component is the annual increase in maintenance cost, beginning with zero in the first year, and increasing in a linear fashion. The yearly increase in the maintenance cost is said to be the uniform gradient (G). This is shown in the cash flow diagram below.

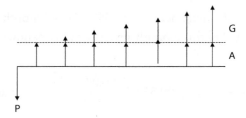

In order to compute the present value of the maintenance cost, the present value of the recurring annual cost (A) and the gradient (G) must both be computed. The present value of a gradient can be computed by:

$$P = \frac{G}{i}\left[\frac{(1+i)^n - 1}{i} - n\right]\left[\frac{1}{(1+i)^n}\right]$$

Eq. 7.13

The gradient G can also be converted into an annual recurring amount A by:

$$A = G\left[\frac{1}{i} - \frac{n}{(1+i)^n - 1}\right]$$

Eq. 7.14

where: G = uniform gradient increment ($/time)
A = Annual recurring amount ($)
P = present value ($)
i = interest for the compounding period (decimal percent)
n = number of compounding periods

Example 7.13

How much should be set aside today to pay for the expected maintenance cost of a car for the first 5 years? Assume costs occur at end of each year and the annual interest rate is 5%. The total annual maintenance cost is shown in Table 7.1 below.

   The total maintenance is broken up into a uniform annual cost (A) of $120 per year and a uniform gradient increase (G) of $30 per year.

   The goal is to compute the present value (P) of both the uniform annual cost (A) and the uniform gradient cost (G).

$$P_1 = A\left[\frac{(1+i)^n - 1}{i(1+i)^n}\right] = (\$120)\left[\frac{(1.05)^5 - 1}{(0.05)(1.05)^5}\right] = \$519.54$$

$$P_2 = \frac{G}{i}\left[\frac{(1+i)^n - 1}{i} - n\right]\left[\frac{1}{(1+i)^n}\right] = \frac{(\$30)}{(0.05)}\left[\frac{(1.05)^5 - 1}{(0.05)} - 5\right]\left[\frac{1}{(1.05)^5}\right] = \$247.11$$

$$P = P_1 + P_2 = \$519.54 + \$247.11 = \underline{\mathbf{\$766.65}}$$

Table 7.1. Annual Maintenance Costs for Example 7.13

YEAR	TOTAL MAINTENANCE COST	UNIFORM PART (A) OF ANNUAL MAINTENANCE COST	UNIFORM GRADIENT PART OF MAINTENANCE COST
1	$120	$120	$0
2	$150	$120	$30
3	$180	$120	$60
4	$210	$120	$90
5	$240	$120	$120

7.1.6 Shorthand Notation

You may have noticed that writing the TVM formulas can be a little tedious. There is a shorthand notation that is used. Here is an example:

$$A = F\left[\frac{i}{(1+i)^n - 1}\right] = F\left(\frac{A}{F}\right)_{i,n}$$

where: $\left(\dfrac{A}{F}\right)_{i,n} = \left[\dfrac{i}{(1+i)^n - 1}\right]$

   Notice that the shorthand notation (A/F) is written so that, just like in the unit factor method, the "Fs" cancel. The notation for each of the equations is listed in the next section.

7.1.7 TVM Summary

The follow table summarizes the relationships between sums of money at different times and compounding periods, incorporating the concept of the time value of money.

Table 7.2. Summary of TVM Equations and Terms

UNKNOWN	KNOWN	SHORT-HAND NOTATION	FORMULA
F	P	$F = P\left(\dfrac{F}{P}\right)_{i,n}$	$F = P(1+i)^n$
F	A	$F = A\left(\dfrac{F}{A}\right)_{i,n}$	$F = A\left[\dfrac{(1+i)^n - 1}{i}\right]$
A	F	$A = F\left(\dfrac{A}{F}\right)_{i,n}$	$A = F\left[\dfrac{i}{(1+i)^n - 1}\right]$
A	P	$A = P\left(\dfrac{A}{P}\right)_{i,n}$	$A = P\left[\dfrac{i(1+i)^n}{(1+i)^n - 1}\right]$
P	F	$P = F\left(\dfrac{P}{F}\right)_{i,n}$	$P = F\left[\dfrac{1}{(1+i)^n}\right] = F(1+i)^{-n}$
P	A	$P = A\left(\dfrac{P}{A}\right)_{i,n}$	$P = A\left[\dfrac{(1+i)^n - 1}{i(1+i)^n}\right]$
P	G	$P = G\left(\dfrac{P}{G}\right)_{i,n}$	$P = \dfrac{G}{i}\left[\dfrac{(1+i)^n - 1}{i} - n\right]\left[\dfrac{1}{(1+i)^n}\right]$
A	G	$A = G\left(\dfrac{A}{G}\right)_{i,n}$	$A = G\left[\dfrac{1}{i} - \dfrac{n}{(1+i)^n - 1}\right]$
$i_{effective} = \left(1 + \dfrac{i_{nominal}}{m}\right)^m - 1$			$i_{effective} = (1+i)^m - 1$

where: P = present value ($)
       F = future value
       A = series of consecutive and equal end-of-period amounts of money ($)
       G = uniform gradient increment ($/time)
       i = interest rate per compounding period (decimal percent)
       $i_{effective}$ = effective annual interest rate (decimal percent)

$i_{nominal}$ = nominal interest rate with m periods (decimal percent)

m = number of compounding periods within the nominal interest period

n = number of compounding period

7.2 Loan Amortization

In the previous sections, a number of examples were given converting a present value to a series of regular amounts (e.g, eq. 7.11, converting P to A). Common examples of this are a car loan or a home mortgage.

Most such loans are "amortizing" loans where the principal is paid down over the life of the loan (i.e., amortized) according to a schedule, typically through regular payments. A portion of each regular payment goes to paying the interest accrued during the compounding period. The remainder reduces the amount of principal to be repaid. At the end of the schedule, the amount of principal to be repaid is zero and loan repayment is satisfied.

The amount of interest accrued during a compounding period is the interest rate times the remaining loan balance at the beginning of the period. The amount paid to reduce the principal is the difference between the payment and the interest accrued.

The schedule of payments, and the corresponding amounts of interest and principal paid is called an amortization table.

Example 7.14

You are purchasing a vehicle and take out a loan for $20,000 for 48 months at a monthly interest rate of 0.25% (equivalent to an effective annual rate of 3.00%). Determine the monthly payment and construct the amortization table.

Using equation 7.11, the monthly payment can be calculated:

$$A = P\left[\frac{i(1+i)^n}{(1+i)^n - 1}\right] = (\$20,000)\left[\frac{(0.0025)(1+0.0025)^{48}}{(1+0.0025)^{48} - 1}\right] = \$442.69$$

The monthly payment is $442.69. The beginning of the amortization table is:

Table 7.3. Beginning of the Amortization Table for Example 7.14

MONTH	PAYMENT	INTEREST PAID	PRINCIPAL PAID	REMAINING BALANCE
0	n/a	n/a	n/a	$ 20,000.00
1	$ 442.69			
2	$ 442.69			
3	$ 442.69			
etc.		Continue for each intervening month.		
46	$ 442.69			
47	$ 442.69			
48	$ 442.69			

The first payment is made at the end of "month zero," that is no payment is made until a month after the loan is received. At the beginning of Month 1 (the end of Month 0), a payment of $442.69 is made. The interest and principal paid for the previous month's use of the borrowed money is:

Interest Paid = (Interest rate)(Previous Remaining Balance)
        = (0.0025)(20,000.00) = $50.00
Principal Paid = [Payment] – [Interest Paid]
        = $ 442.69 – $50.00 = $ 392.69
Remaining Balance = [Previous Remaining Balance] – [Principal Paid]
        = $ 20,000.00 – $ 392.69 = $ 19,607.31

Thus the amortization table now looks like:

Table 7.4. Amortization Calculations for Month 1 in Example 7.14.

MONTH	PAYMENT	INTEREST PAID	PRINCIPAL PAID	REMAINING BALANCE
0	n/a	n/a	n/a	$ 20,000.00
1	$ 442.69	$ 50.00	$ 392.69	$ 19,607.31
2	$ 442.69			
3	$ 442.69			
etc.		Continue for each intervening month.		
46	$ 442.69			
47	$ 442.69			
48	$ 442.69			

Continue to Month 2. The interest and principal paid for the previous month is:

Interest Paid = (Interest rate)(Previous Remaining Balance)
        = (0.0025)(19,607.31) = $ 49.02
Principal Paid = [Payment] – [Interest Paid]
        = $ 442.69 – $ 49.02 = $ 393.67
Remaining Balance = [Previous Remaining Balance] – [Principal Paid]
        = $ 19,607.31 – $ 393.67 = $ 19,213.65

The amortization table now looks like:

Table 7.5. Amortization Calculations For Month 2 in Example 7.14.

MONTH	PAYMENT	INTEREST PAID	PRINCIPAL PAID	REMAINING BALANCE
0	n/a	n/a	n/a	$ 20,000.00
1	$ 442.69	$ 50.00	$ 392.69	$ 19,607.31
2	$ 442.69	$ 49.02	$ 393.67	$ 19,213.65
3	$ 442.69			
etc.		Continue for each intervening month.		
46	$ 442.69			
47	$ 442.69			
48	$ 442.69			

Continuing this process for the remaining months of the 48-month loan gives the complete amortization table. Due to the length of the table, Months 4 through 45 were omitted.

Table 7.6. Completed Amortization Table For Example 7.14.

MONTH	PAYMENT	INTEREST PAID	PRINCIPAL PAID	REMAINING BALANCE
0	n/a	n/a	n/a	$ 20,000.00
1	$ 442.69	$ 50.00	$ 392.69	$ 19,607.31
2	$ 442.69	$ 49.02	$ 393.67	$ 19,213.65
3	$ 442.69	$48.03	$ 394.65	$ 18,818.99
etc.		Continue for each intervening month.		
46	$ 442.69	$ 3.30	$ 439.38	$ 1,321.45
47	$ 442.69	$ 2.21	$ 440.48	$ 882.06
48	$ 442.69	$ 1.10	$ 441.58	$ 0.00

At the end of the 48 payments, the Remaining Balance is $ 0.00 and the loan is repaid. The total amount of interest paid (the sum of the values in the 3rd column) is $1,248.95. The total amount of principal paid (the sum of the values in the 4th column) is $20,000.00, which is exactly equal to the amount borrowed. The amount of principal paid plus the amount of interest paid is exactly equal to total amount paid of $21,248.95 (the sum of the values in the 2nd column or 48 × $442.60).

In an amortized loan, the payment is the same for each of the payment periods. The remaining balance decreases with each payment period as payments are applied. The amount of interest paid decreases with each succeeding payment period. This is because the remaining balance is decreasing, and thus the amount of interest accrued or owed decreases. The amount of principal paid increases each with each payment period because the corresponding amount of interest decreases while the payment remains the same.

With an amortization table, you can determine the "payoff" amount or the amount necessary to repay the loan in full at any point in time (if the terms of the loan agreement allow the loan to be paid off early).

An amortization table can be easily constructed in a spreadsheet. There are also numerous websites that will construct an amortization table for you, although there are occasionally those that do so incorrectly.

7.3 Evaluating an Expenditure or Investment

With any expenditure, this question should be asked: Is it worth it? There are many factors that affect the answer to this question. Often times, these factors are not financial in nature. For example, solely in terms of the cost of providing transportation, why buy a car that is visually appealing versus one that is not? However, considering the financial implications of any expenditure, it is the prudent thing to do.

Many such situations involve an initial expenditure or investment which results in some additional revenue or cost reduction over time. There are many ways to evaluate the "worth" of an expenditure or investment. Two that are commonly used by technologists and engineers are Payback Period (PBP) and Return on Investment (ROI). These two measures give an idea of the value of an expenditure or investment, either in terms of time (PBP) or interest rate (ROI).

7.3.1 Payback Period

Payback Period (PBP) is simply the length of time it takes for the benefits of an expenditure or investment to equal the cost. Often, PBPs of months or years are used to evaluate the value of an expenditure. There is no single standard for what is an acceptable PBP, as it varies from industry to industry, and situation to situation. After the initial expenditure or investment is recouped, any benefit accrued is "pure profit."

A typical situation might be that an expenditure is being considered to build a machine that results in ongoing annual revenue, or an expenditure may result in monthly cost savings. How long would it take to recoup the initial expenditure, (i.e., what is the payback period?).

A simple payback period can be defined as:

$$Simple\ PBP = \frac{Initial\ Expenditure}{Periodic\ Benefit}$$
Eq. 7.16

where: $Simple\ PBP$ = simple payback period (time period, e.g., years)
$Initial\ Expenditure$ = amount expended or invested (\$) at t=0
$Periodic\ Benefit$ = benefit realized on a periodic basis (\$/time period)

Simple PBP is a good way to get a rough estimate of the value of an expenditure. One might think of it as a good "back of an envelope" calculation. However, simple PBP ignores the TVM. For small expenditures, the potential error may not be great. For larger expenditures, the TVM must be considered. In this case, PBP is determined by:

$$PBP = n$$

Eq. 7.17

with

$$P = A \left[\frac{(1+i)^n - 1}{i(1+i)^n} \right]$$

Eq. 7.11

where: PBP = payback period (number of compounding periods);
P = present value ($) of the initial expenditure or investment;
A = the periodic benefit ($/compounding period); and
n = the number of compounding periods so that $P = A$.

Example 7.15

A company is considering an upgrade to the insulation in a factory building. The initial cost of the upgrade is $45,000. The company estimates that it results in a net annual savings of $9,500 in energy costs. Assume an annual effective interest rate of 7.50%. What is the payback period for this potential expenditure?

The two types of PBP can be calculated.

$$Simple\ PBP = \frac{Initial\ Expenditure}{Periodic\ Benefit} = \frac{\$45{,}000}{\$9{,}500\,/\,yr} = \underline{\textbf{4.7 years}}$$

$$PBP = n \text{ where } P = A \left[\frac{(1+i)^n - 1}{i(1+i)^n} \right]$$

$$45{,}000 = 9{,}500 \left[\frac{(1.075)^n - 1}{(0.075)(1.075)^n} \right]$$

Note that it is not trivial to solve directly for n (# of compounding periods) in this equation. This can be solved using a mathematical numerical method, trial and error, or most easily, using the "goal seek" function in Microsoft Excel or a similar spreadsheet.

Using this method in Excel gives the following result:

$$PBP = n = \underline{\textbf{6.1 years}}$$

In this case, simple PBP underestimated the amount of time necessary to recoup the investment because it ignored the time value of money. After the PBP (6.1 years), the initial expenditure has been recouped and any benefit in subsequent years is profit without expense.

7.3.2 Return on Investment

Expenditures or investments can also be evaluated in terms of an interest rate or Return on Investment (ROI) they create. If an expenditure results in a future benefit, the TVM formula can be used to determine the resultant interest rate.

$$ROI = \frac{(Benefit - Expenditure)}{Expenditure} \times 100\%$$

Eq. 7.18

where: ROI = Return on Investment (%) for the compounding period
$Benefit$ = the benefit ($) during the compounding period
$Expenditure$ = the equivalent expenditure ($) during the compounding period

ROI is usually expressed on an annual basis, (i.e., as an annual effective interest rate). Note that an expenditure is usually equivalent to a present value (P) at $t = 0$. Its value must be converted to an amount for the compounding period. Thus, the TVM must be considered.

Just like PBP, there is no single standard for an acceptable level of ROI, as it varies from industry to industry, and situation to situation. What is an acceptable ROI for one situation may not be acceptable for another.

Example 7.16

A company is considering an upgrade to the insulation in a factory building. The initial cost of the upgrade is $45,000. The company estimates that it results in a net annual savings of $9,500 in energy costs for 10 years, after which the insulation has zero value and must be replaced. What is the Return on Investment (ROI) for this potential expenditure?

In this case, equation 7.10 or 7.11 applies. Using equation 7.11:

$$P = A\left[\frac{(1+i)^n - 1}{i(1+i)^n}\right]$$

where: P = the initial investment ($) = $45,000
A = the net annual savings ($) = $ 9,500
n = the number of compounding periods (years) benefits are accrued = 10
i = the ROI or effective annual interest rate (decimal percent)

$$45,000 = 9,500\left[\frac{(1+i)^{10} - 1}{i(1+i)^{10}}\right]$$

Now, solve for i. As with the previous PBP calculations, this is tedious to solve algebraically. Using "goal seek" in Microsoft Excel yields the following result:

$$i = ROI = 0.1654 = \underline{\mathbf{16.54\%}}$$

7.4. Comparing Economic Alternatives

Consider this work-related situation. You are charged with purchasing a new piece of equipment. You are considering two options. Vendor A can sell you the equipment for $50,000, with a useful life of four years, no salvage value at the end of its useful life, and an annual maintenance cost of $5,000. Vendor B can provide you with a similar piece of equipment for $70,000 that will do the same job—it will last six years, and have no salvage value at the end of its useful life, with an estimated $4,000 per year maintenance cost. Which vendor should you choose?

Engineers and technologists are often faced with making economic decisions such as this and just as often, the most economical decision is not obvious. By considering each alternative in light of the time value of money, the best choice can be made.

7.4.1 Present Worth Analysis (PWA)

One method to make the decision between economic alternatives is to compute the present worth of each alternative, and then select the alternative that has the highest present worth (or lowest present cost). This is called Present Worth Analysis (PWA). This technique allows you compare two or more series of cash flows by converting them into their present value equivalents.

Example 7.17
Story County (Iowa) wants to build an aqueduct to bring water from the upper part of the state. There are two alternatives, each equally satisfactory:

- **Alternative 1:** The system can be built at a reduced size now for $300 million and be enlarged 25 years later for an additional $350 million.
- **Alternative 2:** The system can be built at full size now for $400 million.

Assuming an effective annual interest rate of 6%, which alternative is cheaper?

First, compute the present worth of the costs associated with Alternative 1—an initial investment of $300 million, plus a future cost of $350 million in 25 years.

$$
\begin{aligned}
PW_1 &= (\$300 \text{ million}) + (\$350 \text{ million})(P/F, 6\%, 25 \text{ years}) \\
&= (\$300 \text{ million}) + (\$350 \text{ million})(1.06)^{-25} \\
&= \$300{,}000{,}000 + \$81{,}548{,}521 \\
&= \$381{,}548{,}521, \text{ or about } \underline{\mathbf{\$\ 381.6\ million}}
\end{aligned}
$$

Now, compare this to the present worth of the costs for Alternative 2. In this case, the present worth of Alternative 2 is simply the $400 million investment today.

$$
PW_2 = \underline{\mathbf{\$\ 400\ million}}
$$

Since PW_1 is less than PW_2, Alternative 1 should be chosen. (Convincing the public to pay for either alternative is a whole other matter!)

Present Worth Analysis with Different Life Spans

In present worth analysis, the useful life of each alternative must be identical. Often, alternatives have different useful lives. Thus, the least common multiple analysis period must be used for PWA comparisons when the useful life is different for each alternative.

Example 7.18

You are trying to purchase a new piece of equipment for a factory that manufactures plastic cowlings for construction equipment. You have two options.

- Vendor A can sell you the equipment for $50,000, with a useful life of four years, no salvage value at the end of its useful life, and an annual maintenance cost of $5,000.
- Vendor B can provide you with a similar piece of equipment that will do the same job—it will last six years, have no salvage value at the end of its useful life, and cost $70,000, with an estimated $4,000 per year maintenance cost.

Assume an effective annual interest rate of 7%. Which vendor would you choose?

First, it might be easier to visualize this situation with cash flow diagrams:

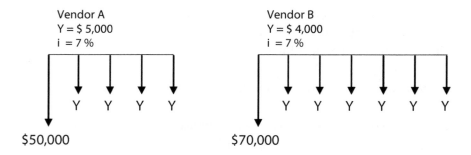

Now, find a common multiple life span. In this case, the lowest common multiple of four and six years is 12 years. The cash flow diagrams now look like this:

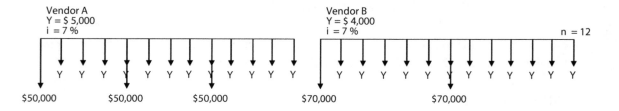

Note that there is a recurring expense to buy the equipment. Will the equipment actually cost the same in four or six years? Probably not, but we will not actually be buying equipment then. This method is just for comparison purposes.

Determine the present worth for Vendor A (PW_A). There are four components: (1) $50,000 at time zero, (2) $50,000 at year four, (3) $50,000 at year eight, and (4) a uniform cash flow of $5,000 for 12 years.

$$PW_A = P_1 + P_2 + P_3 + P_4$$

$P_1 = \$50,000$
$P_2 = (\$50,000)(P/F)_{i=7\%,\ n=4} = (50,000)(1.07)^{-4} = \$38,144.76$
$P_3 = (\$50,000)(P/F)_{i=7\%,\ n=8} = (50,000)(1.07)^{-8} = \$29,100.46$

$P_4 = (\$5,000)(P/A)_{i=7\%,\ n=12} = (5,000)\left[\dfrac{(1.07)^{12}-1}{(0.07)(1.07)^{12}}\right] = \$39,713.43$

$PW_A = \$156,958.65$

Now, determine the present worth for Vendor B (PW_B). There are three components: (1) $70,000 at time zero, (2) $70,000 at year six, and (3) a uniform cash flow of $4,000 for 12 years.

$$PW_B = P_1 + P_2 + P_3$$

$P_1 = \$70,000$
$P_2 = (\$70,000)(P/F)_{i=7\%,\ n=6} = (70,000)(1.07)^{-6} = \$46,643,95$

$P_3 = (\$4,000)(P/A)_{i=7\%,\ n=12} = (4,000)\left[\dfrac{(1.07)^{12}-1}{(0.07)(1.07)^{12}}\right] = \$31,770.75$

$PW_B = \$148,414.70$

Since $PW_B < PW_A$ (Vendor B's equipment costs less than Vendor A's), you should **choose Vendor B's equipment**, all other things being equal.

Example 7.19
A grain producer wants to purchase and install a grain elevator (i.e., a bucket elevator). There are two alternatives listed below, and both will serve the desired purpose. Use present worth analysis to determine which grain elevator is most economical. Assume an effective annual interest rate of 10%.

Table 7.7. Alternatives in Example 7.19.

	ELEVATOR 1	ELEVATOR 2
Installation and first cost, $	$45,000	$54,000
Service life	10 years	15 years
Annual operating cost, $	$2,700	$3,000
Salvage Value, $	$3,000	$4,500

Since the useful life is different for each elevator, we need to find the least common multiple, which is 30 years. Elevator #1 will have to be installed and replaced 3 times during 30 years due to the 10-year useful life.

The cash flow associated with elevator #1 (over 30 years) is shown below.

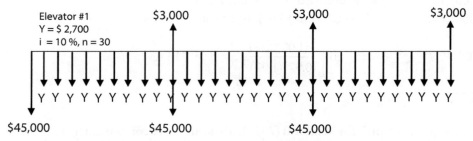

Here are the components to the present worth of Elevator #1: (1) $45,000 at time zero, (2) $42,000 at 10 years, (3) $42,000 at 20 years, (4) $3,000 at 30 years, and (5) a uniform cash flow of $2,700 for 30 years.

Note that at 10 and 20 years, the cash flow is $45,000 – $3,000 = $42,000.

$$PW_1 = P_1 + P_2 + P_3 + P_4 + P_5$$
$$P_1 = \$45,000$$
$$P_2 = (\$42,000)(P/F)_{i=10\%, n=10} = (42,000)(1.10)^{-10} = \$16,192.82$$
$$P_3 = (\$42,000)(P/F)_{i=10\%, n=20} = (42,000)(1.10)^{-20} = \$6,243.03$$
$$P_4 = (-\$3,000)(P/F)_{i=10\%, n=30} = (-3,000)(1.10)^{-30} = -\$171.93$$

$$P_5 = (\$2,700)(P/A)_{i=10\%, n=30} = (2,700)\left[\frac{(1.10)^{30}-1}{(0.10)(1.10)^{30}}\right] = \$25,452.67$$
$$PW_A = \$91,716.59$$

The cash flow associated with elevator #2 (over 30 years) is shown below.

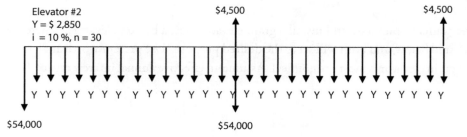

There are four components to the present worth of Elevator #2: (1) $54,000 at time zero, (2) $49,500 at 15 years, (3) $49,500 at 30 years, and (4) a uniform cash flow of $3,000 for 30 years.

$$PW_2 = P_1 + P_2 + P_3 + P_4$$

$$P_1 = \$54,000$$
$$P_2 = (\$49,500)(P/F)_{i=10\%,\, n=15} = (49,500)(1.10)^{-15} = \$\,11,849.51$$
$$P_3 = (-\$4,500)(P/F)_{i=10\%,\, n=30} = (4,500)(1.10)^{-30} = -\$\,257.89$$

$$P_4 = (\$2,850)(P/A)_{i=10\%,\, n=30} = (3,000)\left[\frac{(1.10)^{30}-1}{(0.10)(1.10)^{30}}\right] = \$\,28,280.74$$
$$PW_2 = \$\,93,872.66$$

Since $PW_1 < PW_2$ (elevator #1 costs less than elevator #2), the grain producer should **choose elevator #1**, all other things being equal.

Of course, with any decision, there are factors other than cost that might influence your decision. Perhaps the producer likes the color of elevator #2. Perhaps it has some feature he or she likes. Or perhaps the person selling it is his or her brother-in-law. Perhaps the producer doesn't want to have to replace the elevator after only 10 years. But if you were looking solely at the cost, elevator #1 would be your choice.

7.4.2 Annual Cash Flow Analysis (ACFA)

In the previous section, we examined how to compare financial alternatives by moving all the cash flow events to the present. Another way to compare alternatives is to compute the annual cost of different alternatives by representing all cash flow events as annual costs. This is called the Annual Cash Flow Analysis (ACFA) method. The advantage of this method is that it can be more easily used to compare alternatives that have different useful life spans.

This method breaks up cash flow into costs and benefits:

EUAC = the equivalent uniform annual cost
EUAB = the equivalent uniform annual benefit

The Total Annual Benefit or Total Annual Cost can be calculated:

Total Annual Benefit = EUAB − EUAC   Eq. 7.14
Total Annual Cost = EUAC − EUAB   Eq. 7.15

Example 7.20
Use Annual Cash Flow Analysis (ACFA) to determine which of the machines listed below is the best economic alternative. Each machine has an estimated life of 10 years. Assume an 8% effective annual interest rate. Given that both machines perform the desired function equally well, which machine should be chosen?

Table 7.8. Alternatives in Example 7.20.

	MACHINE 1	MACHINE 2
Initial Cost	$15,000	$25,000
Materials and labor savings per year	$14,000	$9,000
Annual operating costs	$8,000	$6,000
End of life salvage value	$1,500	$2,500

Start with machine #1 and calculate the EUAB (annual benefit) and EUAC (annual cost). The cash flow diagram for machine #1 looks like this:

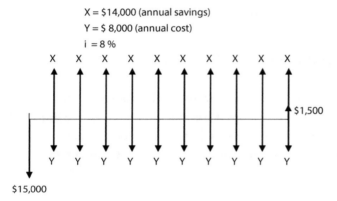

X = $14,000 (annual savings)
Y = $ 8,000 (annual cost)
i = 8%

$1,500

$15,000

Convert all the savings (revenue or upwards arrows) to an Equivalent Uniform Annual Benefit (EUAB):

$$(\text{EUAB})_1 = \$14,000 + \$1,500(\text{A/F})_{i=8\%,\ n=10}$$

$$= \$14,000 + (\$1,500)\left(\frac{0.08}{(1.08)^{10}-1}\right) = \$14,000 + \$103.54$$

$$(\text{EUAB})_1 = \$14,103.54$$

Now, convert all the costs (downwards arrows) to an Equivalent Uniform Annual Cost (EUAC):

$$(\text{EUAC})_1 = \$8,000 + \$15,000(\text{A/P})_{i=8\%,\ n=10}$$

$$= \$8,000 + (\$15,000)\left(\frac{(0.08)(1.08)^{10}}{(1.08)^{10}-1}\right) = \$8,000 + \$2,235.44$$

$$(\text{EUAC})_1 = \$10,235.44$$

$$(\text{Total Annual Benefit})_1 = (\text{EUAB})_1 - (\text{EUAC})_1 = 14,103.54 - 10,235.44$$
$$(\text{Total Annual Benefit})_1 = \underline{\mathbf{\$3,868.10}}$$

A similar cash flow diagram could be drawn for machine #2. Compute the annual benefit and cost for machine #2:

$$(EUAB)_2 = \$9,000 + \$2,500(A/F)_{i=8\%,\, n=10}$$

$$= \$9,000 + (\$2,500)\left(\frac{0.08}{(1.08)^{10} - 1}\right) = \$9,000 + \$172.57$$

$$(EUAB)_2 = \underline{\mathbf{\$9,172.57}}$$

$$(EUAC)_2 = \$6,000 + \$25,000(A/P)_{i=8\%,\, n=10}$$

$$= \$6,000 + (\$25,000)\left(\frac{(0.08)(1.08)^{10}}{(1.08)^{10} - 1}\right) = \$6,000 + \$3725.74$$

$$(EUAC)_2 = \underline{\mathbf{\$9,725.74}}$$

$$(\text{Total Annual Benefit})_2 = [(EUAB)_2 - (EUAC)_2] = 9,172.57 - 9,725.74$$
$$(\text{Total Annual Benefit})_2 = \underline{\mathbf{-\$553.16}}$$

Machine 1 has a total annual benefit of $3,868. Machine 2 has a total annual benefit of $553. Thus, Machine 1 is the best alternative, promising a positive cash flow, where Machine 2 promises a negative cash flow.

ACFA with Different Life Spans

ACFA works well when considering economic alternatives in which there are different life spans. The lowest common multiple of life spans does not have to be determined as with a Present Worth Analysis (PWA). The following example illustrates the relative ease of the ACFA method:

Example 7.21
You are trying to purchase a new piece of equipment. You have two options.

- Vendor A can sell you the equipment for $50,000, with a useful life of four years, no salvage value at the end of its useful life, and an annual maintenance cost of $5,000.
- Vendor B can provide you with a similar piece of equipment that will do the same job—it will last six years, have no salvage value at the end of its useful life, and cost $70,000, with an estimated $4,000 per year maintenance cost.

Assume an effective annual interest rate of 7%. Which vendor would you choose?

Instead of the Present Worth Analysis (PWA), ACFA will be used. Here again are the cash flow diagrams for this situation:

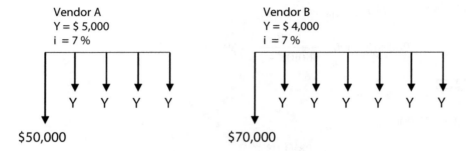

There are no "benefits" in this situation, only cost. The Equivalent Uniform Annual Cost (EUAC) for Vendor A is:

$$(EUAC)_A = \$5,000 + \$50,000(A/P)_{i=7\%,\, n=4}$$

$$= \$5,000 + (\$50,000)\left(\frac{(0.07)(1.07)^4}{(1.07)^4 - 1}\right) = \$8,000 + \$14,761.41$$

$$(EUAC)_A = \underline{\mathbf{\$19,761.41}}$$

The calculations for Vendor B:

$$(EUAC)_B = \$4,000 + \$70,000(A/P)_{i=7\%,\, n=6}$$

$$= \$4,000 + (\$70,000)\left(\frac{(0.07)(1.07)^4}{(1.07)^4 - 1}\right) = \$4,000 + \$14,685.71$$

$$(EUAC)_A = \underline{\mathbf{\$18,685.71}}$$

Since $(EUAC)_B < (EUAC)_A$ (Vendor B's equipment costs less on an annual basis than Vendor A's), you should **choose Vendor B's equipment**, all other things being equal. This is the same conclusion that we reached by using the PWA method.

Either the Present Worth Analysis (PWA) or Annual Cash Flow Analysis (ACFA) can be used to evaluate economic alternatives. While the resulting numbers will be different, the conclusion will always be the same.

EXERCISES

1. Which would you rather have (i.e., which is worth more five years in the future) if the annual effective interest rate is 3.5%:
   a. $12 000 today, or
   b. Five (5) annual payments of $3,000 beginning at the end of year one.

2. A company charges 2.1% monthly on past due accounts, (i.e., money owed to them by their customers). What is the effective annual interest rate (in %)?

3. You have a windfall of $13,789—you sold a truck you've been fixing up. You decide to deposit the money in your checking account and "let it ride," that is, you aren't going to spend any of it. Your checking account has an annual effective interest rate of 0.03%. After two years, what is the value (in $) of your windfall?

4. You have another windfall of $ 12,500—you sold a car you've been fixing up. You decide to deposit the money in your checking account and "let it ride" for 4 years, that is, you aren't going to spend any of it. Your checking account has an annual effective interest rate of 0.03%. After 4 years, what is the increase in the value ($) of your windfall?

5. You aren't satisfied with the interest rates in your checking account and decide to invest some of your money elsewhere. Your friend needs a loan to pay off his U-bill. Against your better judgment and the advice of your parents ("loaning money to friends is a good way to lose a friend"), you decide to loan your friend $2,325 at an agreed upon effective annual interest rate of 3.2%. Your friend is grateful because the interest rate you are charging is much lower than the only other source of money available (his credit card). After one year, how much does your friend owe you?

6. You are saving money to buy a laptop computer, one with "lots of horsepower" so that you can run 3D CAD software. In one year, you will need $2,500 for the purchase. How much should you save each month for 12 months, starting at the end of next month, to reach your goal, if the effective monthly interest rate is 3.9%?

7. You want to purchase a used car that will cost you $9,200 beyond the cash you have on hand. You can get a loan from your local bank with a nominal annual interest rate of 2.6% with a total of 24 monthly payments. What will your monthly payment be(in $)?

8. You've purchased your first home. The property taxes on it are $3,500 per year. The mortgage stipulates that the owner must pay 1/12 of the annual taxes each month to the bank so that the taxes can be paid on April 1. Your first payment is at the end of April and the last payment is at the end of March of the following year. Assume that the cost of money is 6.5% nominal annual interest, compounded monthly.
   a. Draw the cash flow diagram for one year.
   b. What is the effective annual interest rate (in %)?

9. Determine how much profit (in $) the mortgage company makes each year on the owner's tax money. Profit in this case is the difference in the sum of the amount you pay and the amount paid in property taxes.

10. Joan Student is projecting that she will owe a total of $18,750 in student loans when she graduates. The loans have an annual nominal interest rate of 6.5%, compounded monthly. The entire amount must be repaid within 10 years and she will make the minimum monthly payments (120 payments).
   a. Draw the cash flow diagram that describes this situation.
   b. What is the effective annual interest rate (in %)?
   c. Determine what her minimum monthly payment will be.

11. A firm purchased some equipment at a price of $150,000. The equipment resulted in an annual net savings of $6,000 per year during the 10 years it was used. At the end of 10 years, the equipment was sold for $110,000. Draw a cash flow diagram that depicts the situation. Assuming an annual effective interest rate of 6.5%, what was the equivalent cost to the company of this transaction on the purchase date?

12. Two machines are being considered to do a certain task in a manufacturing plant. Machine A costs $240,000 new and $26,000 to operate and maintain each year. Machine B costs $320,000 new and $12,000 to operate and maintain each year. The machines are identical in all other aspects and will have no salvage value after eight (8) years. Assume an annual effective interest rate of 7.0%. Determine (by the equivalent uniform annual cost method) which alternative is least expensive.

13. Two workstations are being considered by your company. Workstation 1 costs $12,000 new and $1,300 to operate and maintain each year. Workstation 2 costs $15,000 new and $600 to operate and maintain each year. Assume both will be worthless after six years and that the interest rate is 5.25%. Determine by the Annual Cash Flow Analysis (ACFA) method which alternative is the better buy.

14. You wish to retire at age 62 and at the end of each month thereafter, for 23 years (276 months), to receive $4,000. Assume that you begin making monthly payments into an account at age 24. You continue these payments until age 62. If the annual nominal interest rate is constant at 6.0%, how much must you deposit monthly between the ages of 24 and 62 (468 months)?

15. You have been assigned the task of estimating the annual cost of operating and maintaining a new assembly line in your manufacturing plant. Your calculations indicate that during the first four years, the cost will be $400,000 per year; the next five years will cost $520,000 per year; and the following six years will cost $600,000 per year. If the interest rate is constant at 6% over the next 15 years, what will be the equivalent uniform annual cost of operation and maintenance? (Hint: convert the sums mentioned above to a single "A" value over the 15 years.)

16. Acme Manufacturing has estimated that the purchase of a robotic workstation costing $150,000 will reduce the firm's manufacturing expenses by $12,500 per month during a two-year period. If the workstation has a zero salvage value in two years, what is the firm's expected annual rate of return on investment (ROI)? (Return on Investment or ROI is the equivalent interest rate that must be earned on the investment to produce the same income as the proposed project.)

Hints: You should answer this question: What is the interest rate for which $150,000 today is equivalent to $12,500 per month for two years? Note that this is not an easy thing to calculate exactly, as you will learn if you set this up correctly. Try using "goal seek" in Excel or solve by trial and error.

Printed in the USA
CPSIA information can be obtained
at www.ICGtesting.com
LVHW082035230924
791921LV00014B/40

9 781516 522163